GOAL GETTERS

GOAL GETTERS

COACHING YOUR KIDS ALONG THE COVENANT PATH

LEANN HUNT AND NICHOLE ECK

Covenant Communications, Inc.

Cover image *Magical Summer Landscape* © Grivina. Courtesy of iStockphoto.com
Interior Graphics and Goals with Kids Branding © Jack Hunt

Cover design copyright © 2020 by Covenant Communications, Inc.

Published by Covenant Communications, Inc.
American Fork, Utah

Copyright © 2020 by LeAnn Hunt and Nichole Eck
All rights reserved. No part of this book may be reproduced in any format or in any medium without the written permission of the publisher, Covenant Communications, Inc., P.O. Box 416, American Fork, UT 84003. This work is not an official publication of The Church of Jesus Christ of Latter-day Saints. The views expressed within this work are the sole responsibility of the author and do not necessarily reflect the position of The Church of Jesus Christ of Latter-day Saints, Covenant Communications, Inc., or any other entity.

Printed in the United States of America
First Printing: February 2020

27 26 25 24 23 22 21 20   10 9 8 7 6 5 4 3 2 1

978-1-52441-269-2

To Daryl, Richard, Nichole, Jeremy, Elena, Jackson, Morgan, and Julia
Without you, there would be no stories.
Without the stories, there would be no life lessons learned.
Without the life lessons learned, there would be no book.
Thank you all. I will always love you.

To James, Sage, Claire, and Lydia
Thank you for being my clinical material and letting me be yours.

TABLE OF CONTENTS

Part I...1

Chapter 1
    Engage..1

Chapter 2
    The Goal Loop..11

Chapter 3
    Role 1: The Goal Setter...21

Chapter 4
    Role 2: The Goal Coach..43

Chapter 5
    Role 3: The Engaged Parent...65

Part II..95

Chapter 6
    Principle 1: Expectations..97
    How knowing where our goals come from helps us choose better goals

Chapter 7
    Principle 2: Tuners..111
    How accepting and using our strengths and weaknesses makes us better goal setters

Chapter 8
    Principle 3: Motivation...123
    How we can support clean motivation in our kids

Chapter 9
> Principle 4: Outcomes..141
>
> *How we can pursue goals even though outcomes aren't guaranteed*

Chapter 10
> Principle 5: Improvement...149
>
> *How failing frequently with small goal loops fuels progress*

Chapter 11
> Principle 6: Emotions..167
>
> *How calming emotions and thoughts keeps goals and goal conversations on track*

Chapter 12
> Principle 7: Becoming...179
>
> *How engaging in goals helps us become what we are striving for*

Chapter 13
> Traction and a Lifetime of Goals..195

CHAPTER 1
ENGAGE

IMAGINE YOU'VE BEEN GIVEN CONTROL of a small country. Complete and magical control. You are the steward, the president, the emperor, and social media manager, all rolled into one. If you wave your hand and say the word, every factory in the country will start making hamburgers. You decide what goods are shipped where, how many churches are built, which exercise machines the gyms carry, which behaviors are illegal, what all the newspapers are talking about, and anything else you can think of. Decisions you make are accepted without question.

Can you imagine how that would feel? How amazing it would be to see things you decreed put into effect to aid the citizens without complaint or red tape? How tiring it might be to master all the moving parts of a functioning country? How overwhelming it might feel to single-handedly make decisions for all the citizens underneath you?

This fantastical situation has some strong parallels to parenting. Specifically, parenting a newborn, when a parent's ultimate control is most obvious.

Now, this control is somewhat of an illusion, as the citizens will do as they please. Babies cry when they want, poop when they feel like it, and get ill without our consent. Even as mythical rulers, we can't control how our subjects act; we can only control how we react and form the environment around them. As parents, we decide what our kids wear, what and when they eat, when they go to bed, who they spend time with, and so much more.

We don't have to imagine how that experience feels because we already know. It's amazing because of how much we can help our children to grow and learn. It's tiring because of sleepless nights and constant supervision. It's intimidating because of how much we love our children and want good things for them in an uncertain future.

We are, in a sense, the all-powerful rulers over the little countries we have birthed. At least temporarily.

It doesn't take long to learn that we are actually only stewards. Our decision-making powers are nearly absolute in the first year or so, but from then on, as our children learn to speak and think and voice opinions, we must slowly transfer power over every aspect of their lives to them. This, theoretically, should take about eighteen years, and every little piece of power we hand over can be a struggle. A struggle for them to receive it and a struggle for us to give it.

How does a good steward share or transfer power? How do we know when to let go of which things? How do we handle the messes, the relapses, and the emotional rollercoaster of a developing monarch? When is their failure a sign of learning, and when is it a sign that we've given too much responsibility too soon? How do we keep our relationships from getting unbearably complicated?

As temporary stewards, we can clearly see the beginning and the end points. We can see how much our brand-new countries need us for everything when they're born, and we can imagine watching our purely independent countries with pride in the far future, but the path in between is paved with doubt.

This doubt is amplified by the fact that we've got to simultaneously run our own country. We've got our own taxes and laundry and friends and meal plans and careers and hobbies to worry about. Maybe we've even got three or four other little countries we are stewarding over at the same time. Sometimes it's hard to know how to allocate our limited resources and attention.

Raising children with the character, capacity, resilience, and self-reliance to run their own lives is a lofty goal, to be sure. One which leads every parent to ask some version of the following question:

How Can I Know I'm a Good Enough Parent?

In some real respect, the hard truth is that you can't. There's not some blood test a doctor can run. There's not a brain or a heart scan. There's not some math equation you can plug all the minutes of your day into. Even if a certified psychologist and parenting expert followed you around twenty-four hours a day, they wouldn't be able to tell you one way or another that you're a good enough parent in any way that would stick. They'd probably be able to give you lots of great tips and point out some of your strengths, but there's nothing they could say to cure you of this basic insecurity that plagues all parents.

Many parents judge their parenting based on how their kids turn out, but even this doesn't tell you everything you need to know. Even if your kid checks all the boxes, even if your kid says please and thank you and plays soccer and gets into the right college and is dating somebody great, that's not enough to prove that you're doing enough as a parent.

That might sound disheartening, but it's only true because the converse is true. If your kid doesn't check all the boxes, is addicted to drugs, flunks out of high school, or has panic attacks trying to ask someone on a date, that's not enough to prove that you aren't doing enough as a parent. It goes both ways.

This might sound unintuitive, but here's an example for you to consider: is Heavenly Father a good enough parent to His children?

Of course He is.

But some of His children chose the wrong side in the War in Heaven and lost their salvation. He was a perfect parent, yet some of His children made terrible choices.

Good parenting matters, but it doesn't guarantee outcomes. We can hold both of these truths in our heads at the same time and realize that agency is so important that no amount of parenting can overcome it.

Engaging on the Covenant Path

Here's an idea of hope to consider: engaging is enough. What does it look like to engage with our kids along the covenant path?

In Lehi's vision of the tree of life he beholds a "strait and narrow path" (1 Nephi 8:20). The word *strait* means narrow, so the scriptures emphasize the nature of the path by repeating the word. It's really a "narrow and narrow path." Strait also sounds like the word straight, which means without a bend. Strait (narrow) sounds like straight (without bending), so we tend to imagine the covenant path as a narrow, unbending path like a sidewalk going from birth to death. Sometimes we even draw it that way on the whiteboard when we explain it to our kids or our classes. We draw a straight line and mark the covenants they will make along the path. For many kids, those covenants will be made by the time they are in their twenties, but with an average life span of eighty years, what are the other sixty years for?

Imagine the strait and narrow covenant path laid out on mortal terrain. It would look something like the illustration. This is what each mortal life ends up looking like. This is the map of someone on the covenant path aiming toward Christ as the target the entire time. This is someone being faithful. This is someone who understands that a lot of unexpected things are going to happen on the gospel path but is resilient and keeps acting with faith on whatever little stretch of road he or she is currently on. These people keep repenting. They keep taking little steps of faith, one at a time, all the way to the end. They are going to learn a lot and build their spiritual muscles.

We've all been on a hike before—a narrow path can lead us through all sorts of meadows, hills, switchbacks, caves, mountains, cliffs, grass, gardens, variety, beauty, and struggle. After hiking a real trail like this, we'd be tan and buff. After a month of hiking the covenant path like this, our spirit develops that way too— whatever a spirit's version of tan and buff is, it will be noticeable.

Our path starts exactly where we are right now and enters unpredictable circumstances. President Russell M. Nelson said, "The joy we feel has little to do with the circumstances of our lives and everything to do with the focus of our lives."[1] The joy of walking the covenant path does not depend on the mortal terrain it's laid on but on the focus and direction we hold in our minds and our hearts as we live.

The nature of the path is that we can traverse quicksand, mountains, meadows, and forest fires all in the same day. Of course, every mortal landscape will be completely different. We're going to find bees, skunks, and sinkholes in the lushest of meadows as well as magnificent scenes in the stickiest of swamps. And the whole time we traverse this unpredictable winding path, we can be firmly on the covenant path.

The following is Elder Dieter F. Uchtdorf's description of the winding, mortal nature of the covenant path:

> The restored gospel is, in a sense, a renewal of the call to adventure we accepted so long ago. The Savior invites us, each day, to set aside our comforts and securities and join Him on the journey of discipleship.
>
> There are many bends in this road. There are hills, valleys, and detours. There may even be metaphorical spiders, trolls, and even a dragon or two. But if you stay on the path and trust in God, you will eventually find the way to your glorious destiny and back to your heavenly home.[2]

---

1 "Joy and Spiritual Survival," *Ensign* or *Liahona*, Nov. 2016.
2 "Your Great Adventure," *Ensign* or *Liahona*, Nov. 2019.

When we understand the unpredictable nature of the gospel path, even with its promises, we can better navigate our way through our lives. We can quit trying to guess or guarantee outcomes, and we can pay close attention to what's happening right in front of us right now and engage with that instead.

What Does It Mean to Engage?

To engage can mean to pay attention. An engaging performance is one that has kept our attention. When we engage with our goals, our lives, and our kids, we pay attention to what's going on with them.

To engage can mean to participate or become involved in something. When someone engages in service, that means he or she is doing it. He or she isn't sitting on the sidelines. When we engage with our goals, our lives, and our kids, we don't sit on the sidelines. We jump in and do things with them.

To engage can mean to move into position so things start working, like a gear. When two gears engage, that means that they line up or fit together in a way that lets the machinery work. When we engage with our goals, our lives, and our kids, we adjust our behaviors and expectations to help the machinery of our homes work better.

When we're children we imagine that as long as we stay on the strait and narrow path, doing what's right, that everything is going to work out for us. It's like a simple math equation. Our lives will be predictable, only good things will happen, and we will always be happy. It doesn't take long, obviously, to realize that's not the case. Dealing with the unpredictability of the path requires engagement. We pay attention to what's happening right now on this moment's segment of the path, we participate, take action, and do something about it, and we move ourselves into a position that helps things start working better.

Is It Working?

While you sit and read this book, your life is functioning all around you. A lot of positive decisions you made and patterns you created in the past are still serving your life well now.

There are always some things in our parenting that need fine-tuning. We know these things better than anyone. We often find parenting frustrating and believe that if we were somehow doing it right, we wouldn't be having these problems. But what if we reframe that? What if we realize that there is no such thing as flawless parenting?

Our little country's needs and abilities are constantly changing, so the balance of power will always be changing too. What if that makes us always feel a little off-balance? What if that's the way it's supposed to feel? What if having a protest in the middle of our country's capital is actually a sign of a functioning government starting the process of change? What if mistakes are merely messages letting us know about the reality of certain circumstances? What if running a country is always a little hard and awkward, even when we're in control? What if that's just how parenting is supposed to go? What if our lives are working the way they're supposed to right now?

That doesn't mean we don't need to change. It just means we don't need to be motivated to change by guilt, shame, or a lack of confidence. We can engage with our changing countries and lives with self-compassion and a knowledge of our strengths that are constantly working (often behind the scenes) to make our lives work.

Goals with Kids

This book, *Goal Getters*, lays out a goal-setting model called Goals with Kids. The principles and model in this book are useful as a whole or as individual tools. They don't suggest a parenting model that will replace everything we are doing right now. Our parenting doesn't need some huge overhaul.

The purpose of Goals with Kids and *Goal Getters* is to help parents learn how to talk to their kids about goals. What's the difference between Goals with Kids and *Goal Getters*?

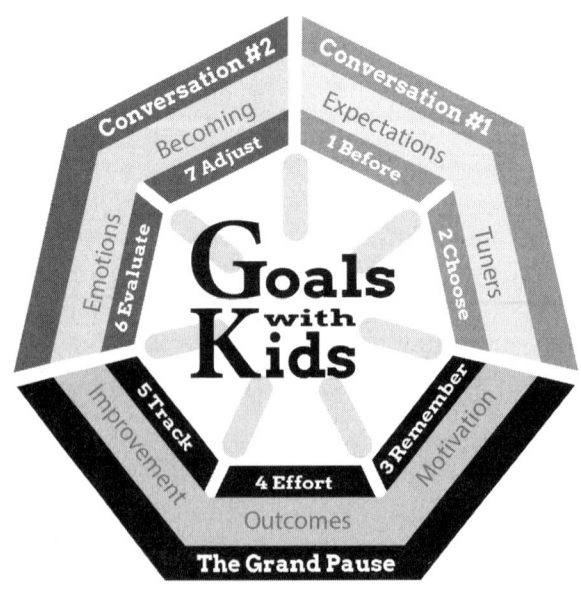

The Goals with Kids model is a way of looking at home-centered goal setting. It consists of the principles, roles, conversations, and goal steps that are represented in the Goals with Kids graphic. LeAnn and Nichole created the model in Nichole's basement, and it was later developed by LeAnn's team to help parents learn how to talk to their kids about their goals. Don't worry about the graphic for now. The pieces are intuitive to goal setting and the graphic will become a simple visual reminder of what you read in *Goal Getters*.

Goals with Kids is also a workshop and online course taught by LeAnn in her business, Life Changing Principles. Throughout the book, the Goals with Kids model will be used as the basis of learning how to talk to your kids about goals. Goals with Kids workshops will also be mentioned because the workshops were like laboratories for learning how to teach parents about home-centered goal setting.

If you are interested in taking a workshop, you can learn more about Goals with Kids workshops at lifechangingprinciples.com/goalgetters.

LeAnn and Nichole wrote *Goal Getters*, the book you are holding in your hand, to share the Goals with Kids model more widely.

Goal Getters

Parents seem to want some of the same things. For new parents with infants, it seems the thing we want most is sleep. When our kids grow but are still little, the thing we want most is to know how to get our kids to behave. When the kids get older, the thing we want most is for kids to take initiative, to do something of their own free will and choice, to act without being asked. We want our kids to go out there and get some goals.

Most parents don't care which goals their kids have. They just want them to have some. That's a parent's dream. Kids with goals.

The authors believe there is something in *Goal Getters* for every parent, and they hope that you will pick out the suggestions you need while keeping in mind the strengths you already have. As you read and feel inspired to try new things in your parenting, remember that engaging is enough, even when engaging feels a little uncomfortable. Also remember that every parent and family is unique and some things will not apply. This book will help you make space to practice engaging with goals—both your own and your kids'.

Positive Psychology

Goal Getters is based on positive psychology research. About twenty years ago, the president of the American Psychology Association challenged researchers to shift from studying what's wrong with humans to finding out what's right. Since then, there's been an explosion of research on how to thrive and flourish on topics like these:

- Self-compassion (how to stop beating ourselves up)
- Strengths (how to use what we are good at to approach our lives)
- Self-efficacy (how to build our faith in ourselves)
- Stages of change (what influences readiness to change)
- Self-determination (why we all need agency, competence, and relationships to stay motivated)
- Well-being (what helps us flourish)
- Coaching mechanisms (how we can coach others)

This research supports the practices, patterns, and core purpose of this book: to help you help your kids learn how to engage with goals. Whether they succeed or fail at a specific goal is less important than them learning the goals process. Looping through goals helps people learn how to experiment with their lives and builds character, capacity, resilience, and self-reliance—all things modern research shows will help children develop into adults who can manage modern life with less likelihood of encountering disabling depression and anxiety.

The 2020 children and youth development initiative of The Church of Jesus Christ of Latter-day Saints has these same purposes in mind. The May 8, 2018, letter announcing the Children and Youth initiative reads, in part, "This new approach is intended to help all girls and boys, young women and young men discover their eternal identity, build character and resilience, develop life skills and fulfill their divine roles as daughters and sons of God."[3]

The initiative is all home-centered, Church-supported. It is also quite comprehensive with its home-centered learning, service, activities, and personal development. To help develop children and youth, the First Presidency is challenging families to spend some time in the scriptures, spend some time outside, spend some time helping someone out, and spend some time working on goals. Those four challenges are intentionally designed to help children and youth develop and become more resilient in their lives spiritually, socially, physically, and intellectually.

Hope

Goal Getters was born of LeAnn's love of teaching, especially the twelve years she served as Stake Institute instructor in Gilbert, Arizona. When her stake

---

3 "Church Announces Plan for Worldwide Initiative for Children and Youth," Official Statement given May 8, 2018; https://newsroom.churchofjesuschrist.org/article/new-program-children-youth.

president called her, he said, "These women come into class with heavy loads. Do not add to their burdens. They need to leave class lighter than when they entered. They need hope." Those words had a huge impact and guided her as she taught and created curriculums over the next twelve years.

Although she no longer holds that calling, she and Nichole have taken the same message to heart with *Goal Getters*. There is a lot of information in this book, but it's not meant to be overwhelming. It's meant to lighten the burdens of every reader, not add to them. It's far too easy to come away from a book, article, or conversation about parenting feeling discouraged. Sometimes being reminded about the complexity and struggles of parenting is hard. This book is meant to leave you feeling capable and hopeful.

Let's learn how to use the power of engaging with goals to teach our little countries to run themselves.

CHAPTER 2
THE GOAL LOOP

The Goal Loop Engine

THE FIRST LATTER-DAY SAINT PIONEERS to cross the Plains had the job of mapping the route for others who would follow them. The available maps at the time had several routes west, but they were incomplete and sometimes inaccurate. The pioneers wanted their map to include water stops, tough terrain, timber, grasslands for animals, and distances to landmarks. At the end of each day, the travelers would disagree about how far they'd come, which made it difficult to create an accurate map.

William Clayton decided to measure the daily distance. He measured the circumference of a wagon wheel, marked a spoke on the wheel, and counted the number of times it went around. Three hundred sixty turns of the wagon wheel were a mile. He counted 4,070 turns on the first day, a distance of 11.3 miles.

On the one hand, counting that many revolutions each day was a tedious, boring task. But on the other hand, they knew how far they'd come. Every single revolution of the wagon wheel got them that much closer to their destination. Every single turn of the wheel was progress. They eventually created a wooden gear mechanism called the Mormon Odometer to track the wheel turns for them.

When we progress toward goals, we can also get lost or underestimate how far along we are in the terrain of the goal. In Goals with Kids, we use goal loops to manage the terrain of a goal. Goal loops follow the same principles as the pioneers' wagon wheels. Each turn of a goal loop gets us closer to our goal. We'll see variations of the image below again in this book because goal loops are very visual, but don't get too tangled up in the details right now. Just remember that goal loops are ongoing and repetitive in nature. They roll around over and over in our lives like a wagon wheel, taking us places we want to go.

7 Stages of a Goal

A goal loop is a natural sequence of seven basic steps:
1. Before a goal
2. Choose a goal
3. Remember a goal
4. Put effort into a goal
5. Track a goal
6. Evaluate a goal
7. Adjust a goal

We can see the seven steps reflected in the graphic. The wheel turns around from step one, before a goal, to step seven, adjust a goal, then starts right back again at the beginning. The end of each loop naturally leads into the beginning of the next one.

If we notice the shades in the graphic, the steps are grouped into three conversation stages, which are the heart of how we coach our kids through goals. In its very simplest form, a goal loop is a conversation with our kids about a goal, followed by a space for independent work on the goal, then another conversation about the goal where we use three evaluating questions.

The first little conversation is to brainstorm and choose a goal. Then there's a space where our kids are left to remember, put in some effort, and track their goal (or not, as the case may be). Finally, there's another little conversation to evaluate what happened and choose how to end the goal loop by trying the goal again, adjusting the goal, or choosing a completely different goal. That's it.

These goal conversations happen in a safe space where nobody gets in trouble and everyone is calm. Well, parents are calm, because that's the only thing we get to control. In a later chapter, we'll discuss these conversations in detail and present a short, simple format we can follow so everyone will know what to expect. These conversations aren't intimidating or lecturing. They're brief and casual.

This constantly turning loop of goal steps and goal conversations is like an engine that drives us forward in our lives and gives us momentum. Goal loops help us engage with our kids and their goals. This loop of engaging with and talking about our goals is the foundation of real growth. It builds individual resources, makes the outcomes we shoot for more likely, and teaches us something new every step of the way.

Starting Goal Conversations with Simple Questions

Goal conversations and goal loops start with simple questions. To best illustrate this, we are going to skip to step six near the end of the goal loop and think about how we evaluate goals we've just worked on, especially the goals our kids set. We tend to overemphasize the importance of whether we succeed or fail at a goal. We feel a surge of happiness when we finish a goal and a surge of disappointment when we fail at it. But there's more that can be taken from a goal than just those two little spikes of emotion.

Imagine a soccer coach sitting down after a game to talk with the team. Now imagine his entire spiel was saying "Congratulations!" if the team had won and saying "Sorry!" if the team had lost. No talk of strategies or tactics. No talk of brilliant plays that saved the day or errors that cost the game. No talk of how hard the kids were working on the field. No words of positive or negative encouragement about future games. No guidance toward the rest of the season. Just "Congratulations!" or "Better luck next time!" and a slap on the back.

Anyone who's seen an inspirational sports movie knows there's more to it than that. We don't just want to talk about if we won or lost the game; we want to talk about how we played. We don't just want to talk about if we succeeded at or failed at the goal; we want to talk about the process. So how do we talk to our kids about goals?

By using three simple questions.

The Three Questions for Evaluating Goals

1. What went well and why?
2. What didn't go well?
3. What did you learn?

Before we use these questions with our kids, let's run through them with a goal of your own in mind. In fact, let's make this exercise even simpler and use something you are doing right now this minute: reading this book. Pause for a second and ask the three questions.

The question, "What went well with your reading so far and why?" might have answers like these:
- The soccer analogy gave me a new way to think about parenting because I was open to new ideas.
- I finally got ten minutes to myself to read because I made the effort to put my kids down for a nap on time.
- I've learned something about goals because I started reading this book.

The question, "What didn't go well?" might have answers like these:
- The TV is on too loud and it's distracting me.
- I still don't know how to get my kids to make their own goals.
- I'm feeling discouraged about my parenting skills right now.

The question, "What did you learn?" might have answers like these:
- I enjoy reading self-help books.
- It's normal to feel overwhelmed sometimes with more than one country in the house.
- Reading while my kids watch TV in the same room is distracting.

Asking these questions about a goal gives you information about your experience of moving toward it. They help you pay attention to how you are playing the game. The more you learn about your own special playing styles, strengths, and weaknesses, the more prepared you will be for the next game in the season.

Now that you've got a feel for the three evaluating questions, let's look at them a little more in depth.

What Went Well and Why?

This question is used by Martin Seligman, the father of positive psychology. Our brains are predisposed to focus on the negative, but asking this question creates a positive bias as our brains start searching for the good news in the experience, for anything that went well.

When you answer the second part of the question, "Why did that go well for you this time?" you begin to see causes behind results that might have seemed random or out of your control before. You realize that good things can happen in your life because you were brave or prepared well or asked for help.

Answering "What went well and why?" builds your self-efficacy, or your belief in your own ability to influence the results of a situation. You begin to believe that you are up to the tasks in front of you because your brain has found evidence of that in the past.

What Didn't Go Well?

Of course, we can't just skip over things that didn't go well in the name of positive thinking. The second question is a chance to study the full truth of the situation. It's a chance to claim failure without identifying with it.

LeAnn was in graduate school when she first heard the phrase "my bad" from a teacher. She asked her about it later, and she explained that it was a way to say, "See that failure? That failure over there across the room? That's mine. I own it. It's my mistake. My bad. But it's not me."

LeAnn has been a "my bad" fan ever since. She likes that she can own something that didn't go well and take responsibility for it while maintaining some distance from it and not internalizing it or labeling it as a part of who she is.

Asking what didn't go well is also a way to notice outside obstacles that got in the way of a particular goal. Sometimes the obstacle to accomplishing a goal is outside of our control or something we did not plan for or take into consideration. Other times it's within our control. Asking what didn't go well helps us notice both how other things or people get in our way and also how we get in our own way.

This question doesn't have a "Why?" attached to it like the first question does because our brains are so predisposed to think negatively. Long-term, it's better to work from a position of strength than from a position of weakness. Try not to add to the answers your brain naturally gives you to this question. You don't have to know why something went wrong to find a solution.

What Did You Learn?

This last evaluating question helps us glean knowledge from the successes and even from the worst failures and outcomes. Did things work out the way you thought they would? What surprised you? Even the most prepared and confident goal setters will find the unexpected all around them if they pay attention and learn from what they see.

Learning new things about how the world around us works gives us new information to use in the future. It helps us understand the lay of the figurative land around us, like the pioneers mapping new territory. They had a good guess of what was ahead of them, but until they actually traveled there, they didn't know for certain. They were almost guaranteed to find something they might have missed if they hadn't been looking.

Like William Clayton, we can also benefit from being cartographers, or mapmakers, of our own lives and tracking how far we've come. When asking ourselves what we've learned, we can try making a record of it to refer back to later, either by telling someone what we've learned or by writing it down, like a map.

This is a great question to ask in all aspects of our lives—after church, after a school day, after a family event. It helps kids to actually learn from their experiences.

Elder David A. Bednar also taught the importance of asking what we've learned from our experiences: "Each of us should look for the lessons and warnings found in the simple events of everyday life. As we seek for a mind and heart open to receive heavenly direction by the power of the Holy Ghost, then some of the greatest instructions that we can receive and many of the most powerful warnings that can safeguard us will originate in our own ordinary experiences. Powerful parables are contained in both the scriptures and in our daily lives."[4]

Making a habit of asking this question will teach us to be curious and open-minded about our experiences. Even if the lessons we learn seem small or insignificant, they will add up over time, building our strengths and the capacity we have both to see and to change the world around us.

Questions in the Seven Steps of a Goal Loop

The other steps in a goal loop use simple questions like the three we've already explored as a way to engage with our kids and their goals. Let's look at some of the simple questions that will help us push a goal loop forward with our kids.

Before a goal starts with asking our kids the question, "What do you want in your future?" The future could be years away, like going on a mission or to college. It could also be tomorrow, like being ready to give a report in school. The Church's youth website has a great interest inventory that helps youth brainstorm spiritual, social, physical, and intellectual goals. It asks what they are interested in, what they want to explore, what skills they will need for the future, what life events they need to prepare for, and what roles they currently have. The idea is to be open, creative, and generative.

Choosing a goal focuses first on the question, "Which goal do you want to choose?" The brainstorming list from the previous step is used as a springboard here. In Goals with Kids, a goal is simply something you want that you are willing to put effort toward. It doesn't need to be lofty, long-term, hard, or impressive to be a worthy goal, so we don't let preconceptions limit our view.

The next question we ask our kids in this step is "Can you be in charge of this goal?" It's not going to work well for our kids to set a goal for a sister to stop calling names.

Asking "How can we make this goal more manageable?" narrows the goal down so we can see progress during the next goal conversation. It's the difference

---

[4] "Watchful unto Prayer Continually," *Ensign* or *Liahona*, Nov. 2019.

between having a goal to learn the piano versus having a goal to practice scales and arpeggios three times this week.

The last questions in the choose a goal step are "Do you need a reminder?" and "Do you need a way to track this goal?" These questions help us prep our kids for the next three steps, which they complete on their own. Then we schedule our next goal conversation and send them on their way.

Remembering, putting effort into, and tracking a goal are steps that happen outside of a goal conversation, so there are no questions for parents to ask here. We call this stage The Grand Pause. At this point, our kids are in charge of everything, and we—the parents—operate in a mode we call radio silence.

Radio silence is a military term where you are not allowed to transmit any communications. Sometimes it's because you don't want the enemy to intercept any communications. Sometimes it's because you are trying to listen for a distress signal or other faint communication. Submarines have a version of this called silent running where they glide slowly through the water trying to make no noise at all. Even the crew is encouraged to rest and refrain from talking or making any unnecessary sound. That's what happens in this phase. Parents go about their day talking with their kids about everything but the goal. They watch and listen and refrain from reminding, poking, prodding, or even hinting. No looks either. Radio silence.

Evaluating a goal uses the three evaluating questions we went over in detail earlier.
1. What went well and why?
2. What didn't go well?
3. What did you learn?

These questions help us talk about the experience in a way that is simple, clear, nonjudgmental, and truthful.

Adjusting a goal is where we close the goal loop. This starts with the question, "Do you want to work on this goal some more?" Sometimes the answer is no, which is okay. If our kids don't want to work on this goal anymore, they can say goodbye to it and record the lessons they learned.

If the answer is yes, then ask the follow-up question, "Do you want to do the same goal again or change it in some way?" Kids sometimes want to repeat a goal because they enjoyed it, were good at it, or want to practice more. Other times they make adjustments like making the goal smaller or adding a reminder to it and choosing it again. The essential thing here, whether they're choosing the same goal or letting it go, is to end the current goal and close the loop.

Completing a Goal vs. Completing a Goal Loop

That was a quick summary, but hopefully we're beginning to understand the momentum, energy, and progress that completing goal loops can provide. Turning this wheel over and over, even with very small goals, can help fight paralysis and feeling overwhelmed. Every single goal loop we complete with our kids is progress in their life and progress in our relationship with them.

Don't get confused here: there's a big difference between completing a goal and completing a goal loop. They are both powerful, but they have different benefits.

Completing a goal is what most people are familiar with. It's finishing the thing we set out to do. It's success. Maybe we lost those five pounds, or we beat that race time, or we asked that girl out on a date. It feels good to accomplish things. It builds confidence. It builds skills. It moves us forward in our lives.

Completing a goal loop means we have a real conversation about whatever just happened with the goal at hand. Maybe it's success, maybe it's failure. Probably it's a little bit of both. Maybe we only lost three pounds, or we had our slowest race time yet, or we asked that girl out, but she gave us a confusing answer. Whatever the result, we get to talk about what went well and what didn't go well and what we learned. We get to practice understanding ourselves, understanding the world around us, and paying attention to details.

We already know what it feels like to complete a goal. Let's explore what it feels like to complete a goal loop. To start, let's look at some of the things we are already doing through the lens of a goal loop.

Recognize Our Current Actions as Goals

Goal loops and their questions don't apply only to the traditional, formal, written-on-a-3x5-card goals we all think of first. We are already accomplishing goals in our lives right now, big and small, even if we don't think of them that way. Goals are things we want in our future that we are willing to put effort toward.

Here's a thought experiment to try. Think of some things you've done in the last twenty-four hours. They don't have to be positive or even productive at all. They can be going to the grocery store, watching a movie, or putting your kids to bed. Now choose one of those items and start asking the evaluation questions. What went well with putting your kids to bed and why? What didn't go well this time? What did you learn while putting your kids to bed tonight? You've just completed a goal loop!

We are doing goals already in our everyday lives. We just don't call them that. We can learn from what we are already doing by asking questions and reflecting on our current efforts without scheduling any extra activities, setting new goals, or putting forth extra effort. Completing small goal loops like this creates momentum. The things we learn from the questions can propel us into trying things a new way or tweaking our efforts.

Once we understand goal loops, we can introduce them to our kids. When LeAnn's kids were little, a violinist in their ward offered to teach the kids violin lessons. The teacher set up a great way to get kids interested in playing. To begin, Daryl and LeAnn rented a violin and together took a couple of lessons from her. They wanted to learn along with their kids and needed to know enough to help their young kids practice. Each week they would come home and practice, first with the bow by itself, and then with the violin. The kids were intrigued and wanted to play with the new instruments. Daryl told them they could but that the teacher said no one was allowed to touch a violin or bow until they had a lesson first. The kids couldn't wait to start lessons and get their hands on their own violin.

Similarly, we can entice our kids to try out goal loops by doing it ourselves first. Choose things you are already doing in your life and run them through goal loops. Make your goal work visible by posting it on the fridge. There are a variety of simple Goals with Kids charts to choose from at lifechangingprinciples.com/goalgetters. Print one of the charts and put it on the fridge. As we add checkmarks, star stickers, or notes to our charts, our kids may become interested in what we are doing. Use this as an opportunity to tell them about goals and invite them to try it out too.

CHAPTER 3
ROLE #1: THE GOAL SETTER

The Roles

IN A GOAL LOOP, THERE are two roles that can be filled: the goal setter and the coach. The goal setter chooses goals and puts effort toward them. The coach uses conversations and questions to guide the goal setter through a goal loop.

It's possible to play both of these roles ourselves in a single goal loop once we understand them both. This sort of self-coaching is not the focus of this book, but some of the experiments in it will hone our self-coaching skills naturally.

As parents helping our kids set goals, we will adopt the coaching role while our kids adopt the goal-setter role. Chapters 4 and 5 will focus on how to occupy the coaching role as a parent, but let's start by learning about the role of the goal setter.

Understanding the goal setter's perspective in each of the seven steps will allow us to better help and understand our kids as they set goals. It will also improve our self-coaching skills should we want to add more goal loops to our own lives. These steps are a natural progression in typical goal setting, and taking a closer look will help us understand how goals really work.

Step 1: Before a Goal

Before we start evaluating, working on, or even choosing a goal, we need to brainstorm some ideas to choose from.

There are an infinite number of goals we could brainstorm, but most of them won't be interesting to us. For example, there are nearly 7,000 languages spoken on earth, but most people aren't interested in learning to converse in more than the language they already speak. Our possible goals will be unique to us and our values. Remember, goals are things we want for the future that we are willing to put effort toward. We get to decide. What do we want for our futures?

Some people seem to be born knowing the answer to this question. They pursue what they find interesting with little regard or regret for the options they are ignoring. They are satisfied with their choices.

Other people, the authors included, agonize over this question. What do we really want? What's worth our limited time and effort? Don't people often mistakenly conflate what they want with what's actually good for them? What if we start out wanting something but change our minds later? The stress of brainstorming goals for our futures can cause us to list safe goals, impressive goals, or goals we feel like we *should* be doing instead of goals we *want* to be doing. There's often this pressure to get it right. Why waste time chasing the wrong goal, right?

Wrong. Chasing the wrong goal in a goal loop is a brilliant idea.

Elder Jeffrey R. Holland's son Matthew shared a story about coming to a fork in the road while returning from a trip with his dad. He and his dad didn't know which path would take them home, but after sincere prayer, both felt impressed to choose the path on the right. However, after only a few hundred yards, the path came to a dead end. It was clearly the wrong road, so they turned around and chose the other path. The surest way to get them on the right path, with an assurance that it was the right path, was for them to know without a doubt that the other path was the wrong one. The wrong road detour taught them more, faster than the right road would have.[5]

When we finish a goal loop pursuing a wrong goal, we can gain a similar assurance. There is knowledge and guidance waiting for us at the end of goal loops that we can't possibly predict at their beginning.

Nichole once spent an entire afternoon learning to make a ratatouille recipe because she thought it would be delicious. Twenty minutes of cutting vegetables and an hour of arranging vegetable slices in a spiral pattern turned out a mediocre, mushy dish that fell far short of her expectations. Evaluating that goal loop, she decided that she didn't want to make time for meals that took so long to cook. Did she regret the time she spent that afternoon? No, because it wasn't all a waste. She learned something she couldn't have imagined beforehand. She learned something she didn't want to do.

---

5   See Matthew Holland, "Wrong Roads and Revelation," *New Era*, July 2005.

An afternoon cooking a recipe might be a small example, but here's a more consequential example from her college years. While pursuing an English degree, she was encouraged to acquire some other "hard skills" to make her more employable. Since her older brother is a brilliant computer programmer, she took an introductory computer programming class, thinking the skill might run in the family.

It did not.

She spent an entire semester painfully slogging through rules and code and error messages. And failed the class anyway. She had to retake the class twice more in future semesters to finally get that A she really wanted for her transcripts, then she swore off computer programming forever. Not with bitterness or regret, mind you. Without taking the class, she never would have learned (among other things) that she doesn't want to be a computer programmer.

Nichole had to try the goal to figure out it wasn't for her. Then she could let it go and try something else. Realizing we can change our minds about what we want for our future whenever we want helps us become masters of our goals rather than servants to them. We don't have to fear choosing the wrong goal, because starting a goal loop isn't a massive commitment. We can follow it until it leads us somewhere we want to go, until we learn something, or until we realize it's not the path for us.

Brainstorm goals in a variety of different areas. The Church consistently uses these four categories to spark ideas for planning activities and setting goals:

1. Spiritual
2. Social
3. Physical
4. Intellectual

These categories mirror Luke 2:52, which summarizes Jesus Christ's formative years before His ministry: "And Jesus increased in wisdom and stature, and in favour with God and man."

1. Increasing in wisdom = setting intellectual goals
2. Increasing in stature = setting physical goals
3. Increasing in favor with God = setting spiritual goals
4. Increasing in favor with man = setting social goals

Having a wide array of skills and experiences in a variety of areas will help us be more self-sufficient and able to manage our lives. Sometimes we put too much focus on one of the four categories because we want to improve a weakness or feel more comfortable working with our strengths. Sometimes the circumstances or seasons of our lives mean we need to prioritize one category over the others for a while. But, like Christ, we can use goals to increase in wisdom, stature, favor with God, and favor with man.

With all that in mind, it's time to get some ideas down on paper. Anything from building a treehouse in your backyard to planning a birthday party for your kid next week. It's not important to get our brainstorming lists perfect. Not now and not ever. This is not a bucket list with everything we'll ever do. Our lists will never be comprehensive and will always be changing because we are always changing. That's okay. The important thing is to get some ideas down and let the goal loop process sort it all out.

Step 2: Choose a Goal

Now that we have a list of options, we can choose a goal. Remember, it doesn't have to be the right goal—whatever that means—just a goal we're interested in moving toward. Throw a dart if you have to.

As an example in this chapter, let's imagine choosing to build a treehouse in our backyard as our first goal.

We're not ready to move on to the next step just yet though. We need to clarify this goal with some questions and visualize the rest of the loop.

Clarify

A goal as big as building a treehouse is an easy-to-imagine but hard-to-implement goal. If we walked out to our backyards right this moment with "I want to build a treehouse" as our guiding star, we'd probably have no idea where to actually start. Do we pick a tree first? Figure out how much supplies will cost so we can start saving? Head right to Home Depot to buy wood? Check out a book from the library about carpentry? Before jumping right into a complicated goal, we need to clarify it first.

A good place to start when clarifying is to ask ourselves, "Why did I choose this goal?" These answers can range from "I want my kids to have a fun secret fort treehouse like I did when I was a kid" to "I want to teach my two older kids some of my carpentry skills" to "I want to build something with my own two hands that is strong and sturdy and will last."

Different purposes will change how we clarify. If our purpose is wanting our kids to have fun, maybe we'll invite them to design and decorate it. If we want to teach our kids skills, maybe we'll involve them in designing blueprints, shopping for wood at the store, and making the wood cuts themselves. If we want to build something with our own two hands, maybe we'll tackle most of this project by ourselves.

Purposes that speak deeply to the core values in our lives like family, honesty, creativity, health, or self-improvement, just to name a few, will be more motivating and help us keep a positive attitude while we are putting forth unpleasant or boring efforts to achieve our goals. More shallow answers like, "I saw my neighbor building a treehouse and it looked cool" or "I just feel like it" can be valid reasons, but they might not offer enough motivation to pull us through long or complicated goals.

Another way to clarify goals is to ask ourselves, "Am I in charge of this goal?" If we want to build a treehouse but the rules of our homeowners' association won't allow it, then there's no point in pursuing that goal. It's out of our control. We could switch our goal to petition the HOA for an exception to the treehouse rule. Writing a petition is under our control. Know what you're in charge of.

A third clarifying question to ask is, "Would this goal benefit from being more specific?" President Thomas S. Monson said, "When one deals in generalities, he will rarely have a success; but when he deals in specifics, he will rarely have a failure."[6] Big goals like building a treehouse can be overwhelming and hard to implement. Breaking them into smaller goals like calling a woodworking shop, buying the right size nails, and making the ladder are all more specific and actionable goals.

Imagine running a huge goal—like wanting to go on a mission—through a goal loop. We'd never learn anything because it would take us ten years to make it to the end! We don't want to find ourselves hopelessly trapped in a goal loop, failing to ever finish it or get feedback.

On the flip side, we can also make goals too small. If we decide to prepare for our mission by reading the Bible, running through a goal loop after every word we read would be ridiculously repetitive and time wasting (unless you were a four-year-old learning to read scripture language for the first time).

Mid-level goals like reading five chapters each week are going to be more efficient and useful for most people. It's the Goldilocks principle. Some goals are too big, some goals are too small, and some goals are just right.

---

6   "The Priesthood—A Sacred Trust," *Ensign*, May 1994.

If the outcome we want is a treehouse, the goal loops we create will all make progress toward the finished product. Each goal loop is a separate, manageable, bite-sized goal. Having lots of goal loops lets us evaluate more frequently so we get a better feel of how we are progressing toward the final goal. Different-sized goals are manageable at different times in our lives. We can have goal loops extend to the end of the day, the end of the week, reaching a specific landmark, a number of steps, or sometimes, when terrain is tricky or when we're discouraged and tired, a single wheel turn of five minutes of effort is beneficial as a goal.

Size is an important clarifying factor, but even more important is the type of goal we are setting. Traditionally people tend to set the same kinds of goals: I will (fill in the blank here) every day, or I will accomplish this great thing by this date. There's more to goals than this. Different types of goals take different types of effort and give you different kinds of results and growth. Here's a list of some of the types of goals people can set. We'll probably recognize the types that are more common than others.

For our treehouse example, some clarified goals might look like these:
- Information Gathering: Ask our neighbor about their experience building a treehouse and what they would have done differently.
- Exploration: Follow a video tutorial about making a doghouse to see if carpentry is something we enjoy.
- Experiment: Find out if working on this project as a family works better on weeknights or on Saturday mornings.
- One-timer: Pick out the type and color of wood we want to use.
- Stopping a Habit: Stop leaving our tools in the backyard overnight.
- Starting a Habit: Start double-checking our measurements before we cut so that we make fewer mistakes.
- Recurring: Work on the treehouse every Saturday morning for at least thirty minutes.
- Daily: Childproof the treehouse every day after we work on it because we haven't finished the railings yet.
- Skills: Learn how to make a to-scale blueprint of a project.
- Attitude: Take deep breaths instead of swearing when we get frustrated or make a mistake.
- Practice: Practice using the nail gun on the ground before using it up in the tree.
- Flawless Performance: Install the entire south-side railing without needing to pull any nails out.
- Awareness: Notice when we are getting too focused on finishing the project and not focused enough on involving our kids in the process.

- Problem-solving: Cut down a branch that's growing into the treehouse window.
- Remembering: Remember to return the saw we borrowed to our sister-in-law this weekend.
- Character: Be patient with our kids when we are teaching them how to measure, mark, and cut wood.
- Self-care: Take a five-minute break inside and get a drink after thirty minutes of working outside in the summer.

Depending on our purpose, some of these goals may benefit from being made even more specific. We may not have a clue how to acquire the skill of making blueprints on our own, so we might have to make a smaller goal to ask a friend, visit a woodworking supply shop for some tips, take a class, or check out a book from the library. Or maybe our goal to be more patient with our kids while teaching them to cut wood is too vague and we want to start trying specific calming techniques that would work in the middle of a conversation. We may discover that a goal that seemed simple has hidden steps we need to tackle one at a time. Remember the Goldilocks rule. We want goals that are just right. We won't always get the size right the first time, but that's one of the things we can adjust in the last step of a goal loop if we learn that our goal was too big or too ill-defined.

It's worth spending a little extra time here discussing daily goals because they are so pervasive in our culture. After all, if something is worth doing, doing it more often is better, right?

Not necessarily.

A useful way to think about daily goals is to use the economic theory of diminishing returns. This just means that the return—or value—we get from something diminishes the more of it we get. Each additional unit of something has less value than the last one.

For example, if we're dying of thirst in a desert and stumble across a water salesman, we'll pay however much he asks to get the first water bottle, and maybe the second and third bottles too. But by the time he's offering us our fiftieth water bottle, we won't be willing to pay as much for it because it's offering us less value. It's not saving our lives like the first few were. Of course, we'll need more water again soon—consistency is important—but the fiftieth bottle right now isn't saving our lives like the first few were.

This same principle can be applied to a lot of things. The first pair of shoes someone has offers more value than the fiftieth pair. The first car someone owns offers more value than the eighth car. The first friend someone can talk to has more value than the hundredth friend. The first day of scripture reading someone does in a week has more value than the sixth day. Consistent effort over time is more important than doing something all the time.

Many people naturally turn to goals like "read my scriptures every day," "pray every morning and every night," "exercise every day," or "use my language-learning app for ten minutes every day," but goals like these are a recipe for depression. Failing once often feels like a game of Chutes and Ladders where we've slid all the way back to square one and need to start building our perfect streak all over again. Focusing on doing something perfectly discounts the progress we make in our imperfection.

Let's imagine a thirteen-year-old young man named Jaden who wants to read the scriptures more. He has set a goal in his Sunday School class to read the scriptures every day for a week, and here's how that goal goes for him.

- The first week, he completely forgets his goal the moment he walks out of class.
- The second week, he puts up a sign on his bathroom mirror and remembers three times.
- The third week, he moves the sign to his pillow and puts his scriptures there too. He remembers six times.
- The fourth week, he is so mad at himself for missing his goal by only one day that he reads one time, then intentionally avoids it because it reminds him of how frustrated he is and how he feels like he'll never be good enough at reading his scriptures.
- The fifth week, he doesn't do anything.
- The sixth week, he decides to try again and puts the sign back up and sets a reminder in his phone. He remembers four times.

It would be easy for Jaden to look at his efforts as a failure. He never actually accomplished his goal of reading the scriptures every single day for a week. But over the course of just the first month of his goal, Jaden read the scriptures ten more days than before he had the goal. He shouldn't just ignore that progress because his original goal demanded perfection.

Reframing our accomplishments in this way is not a cop-out, a consolation prize, or a way to feel better about not excelling. Often it is taking a hard look after the fact at our tendency to create daily flawless performance goals when there are plenty of other kinds of goals to choose. We admire those people who have read their scriptures every day for the last ten years because they are one in a million. We can lead lives of growth and effort without aiming for this kind of perfection.

Jaden could try a more-often-than-not goal where he adds a tally mark to a list every day he read scriptures. He could experiment with different kinds of scripture reading to see how he likes them. Use measures that have more options than total success or total failure. Goals are rarely "I did this goal perfectly" or "I failed completely," but daily goals can make us forget this. There's always a middle ground.

Studying the purpose behind our goals can help us realize if they really benefit from the "daily goal" title. Did Jaden just want to know what it felt like to be a "perfect" scripture reader for a week? Did he want to practice the scripture-reading routines he will follow on his mission? Did he just want to invite more of the Spirit into his life? Did he want to prepare for a talk he's giving soon? Knowing our purpose helps us discern how best to design a goal to serve that purpose.

Visualize

Once we've clarified our goal, it's time to visualize it turning through the next four steps. This is where we imagine what the rest of the goal loop might look like to anticipate each step and prepare for any obvious problems we might run into.

Anticipating "Remember a Goal"

Sometimes the hardest part of a goal is remembering to do it at the right time or in the right place. Do we need a reminder? Whether we use a phone app, Post-it notes, or an accountability partner, now is a good time to set up any memory triggers we think we might need to set ourselves up for success.

Anticipating "Put Effort into a Goal"

Imagine in detail what putting effort into this goal will look like. Where will we be? What day and time will it be? What people or supplies will we need to have nearby? What will our hands be doing? We can imagine watching a movie of ourselves accomplishing the goal from start to finish. It's great to say we want to build a treehouse, but do we actually know what our hands need to do? Do we have a strong action word like *call, write, visit, staple, vacuum,* or *read* to direct our next action? Do we actually know what to do next?

If we don't visualize ourselves working on the goal ahead of time, we run the risk of heading out to our backyard on Saturday morning to build a treehouse and standing in our backyard asking, "Now what?" That's frustrating and demotivating, so let's think ahead to try to avoid that. If we can't confidently say "Yes!" to the question, "Do I know what to do next?" in this step, then our goal either isn't specific enough or needs to be changed to an information-gathering goal.

There are usually many different ways to see a goal through to its end, and people who can see these different pathways tend to be more resilient and hopeful. Since there isn't one "right" pathway, there isn't one "right" next action step. We believe whatever action step we choose will bring us closer to our goal.

To work on our goal, we might need physical supplies like a saw or a nail gun. We might also need other types of resources like the address of the local lumberyard or a basic knowledge of how to work a table saw. Come up with a plan to prepare or gather the necessary resources.

Coming up with a detailed plan might be necessary for some people to confidently tackle large goals like building a treehouse, but others might not need to break it down so much. If building a treehouse is something we are already confident about and experienced with, we very well might be able to simply go outside and start working. Different actions and goals are intuitive to different people. Goal loops give us feedback and help us stay engaged with a goal that is not obvious or intuitive to us. We don't need to break a big goal down into a lot of small goals unless we have good reason.

Anticipating "Track a Goal"

Goal setters benefit from tracking goals that have a lot of small or repeated steps. Tracking goals provides data we can use to learn about ourselves and to evaluate our goals later. The choose a goal step is a good time to set up some sort of tracking system for our goals if we think it would help.

Anticipating "Evaluate a Goal"

Determining end conditions for our goals before we start them will motivate us to work on them and help us evaluate them when we're done.

Nichole went on a pioneer trek with her stake as a young woman. They started in the evening, trekking and taking turns pulling the handcarts until the sun went down. And then they kept walking. They were trying to reach a campsite the leaders had picked out ahead of time, but no one in the handcart line seemed to know how far away it was. It was too dark to see any landmarks they were passing or that stood in front of them. While the walking wasn't physically very strenuous, it was frustrating and demoralizing to feel like they were going to be walking along in the dark forever.

The next day, they knew much more about when they were going to stop for lunch and breaks. Indicators like "Once we all reach that hill," "Once you find the spot where the road forks," or "Once you see the yellow flag in the clearing up ahead" made it easier to keep spirits up and keep putting effort in when the trekkers weren't worried about maintaining that same level of effort forever. Having a finish line in sight matters.

Ask the question, "What does *done* look like for this goal?" What is the finish line? Will we have made a phone call? Put in a certain number of hours of effort? Tried something a certain number of times?

Once we've thought about what *done* looks like, it's time to ask the final question—"When will I evaluate this goal?"—and set up a time to get together again with our coaches.

In a conversation with a goal setter and a goal coach, this would mean setting up a day and time to meet together again after The Grand Pause to ask the three evaluating questions. When we are coaching ourselves through a goal loop, it can still be helpful to pick a day and time to check in as if we are meeting with someone else.

For small goals, The Grand Pause might only be an hour or two. Longer goals might need a grand pause of a week or a month. In general, we find it's better to create smaller goals and grand pauses to maintain motivation and momentum.

It seems like there's a lot of questions we need to ask just to choose a goal, but it can really be quite simple when we get the hang of a basic goal loop. We don't ask every question every time. It's natural to anticipate and prepare ourselves to launch into a new goal or new efforts toward a big goal by asking questions that help us figure out what we actually want to do next. It doesn't take long for it to become automatic to know which questions to ask for which goals.

Step 3: Remember a Goal

As a goal setter in Step 3, we've just left the comfort of planning and entered the realm of execution, where we must remember, put effort into, and track our goals.

Remembering a goal can be hard because remembering usually happens at a different time and place than when we set the goal. Think of the typical

routine of young music students who forget to practice. During a weekly lesson, they are assigned to practice their instrument and leave committed to improve the new song or technique. They go home to eat dinner, the music gets set aside, and the week carries on as normal with no thought of the assignment. When it's time for the lesson again, the students pick up the books or arrive at the lesson and suddenly remember the commitment to practice. The students associate the commitment to practice with the lesson day, time, place, or materials.

You know those funny stories about people walking into a room and forgetting why they came? Well, how do they remedy the situation? They walk back into the first room and start doing whatever they were doing before. Mere moments later, they get stuck in the same place as before and ta-da! They remember. The task or goal they left the room for was associated with whatever they were doing before they left. When they go back to that place, it all comes back to them. That's brain association in action. We can create a number of different memory triggers to take advantage of the associative nature of our brains and help us remember our goals when it's useful to do so.

Use time triggers like phone reminders, calendars, or alarm clocks for goals that need to happen at a certain time or on a certain day. If we want to start cooking dinner earlier or call our friend on his birthday, we might need a time trigger.

Use place triggers, either notes or objects, for goals that are location based. If we want to be a more patient driver, a note on the steering wheel might be effective. If we want to remember to wear our safety goggles while sanding wood, leaving them on top of the sander instead of putting them away at night might be what we need.

Use routine triggers, either notes or objects, that will be noticed in the middle of an established routine. If we want to add a moment of gratitude to our lives, it might stick easiest if we do it right after our scripture study. A simple bookmark or gratitude journal stored on our scriptures could be enough to trigger us to add this new goal into our regular study routine.

Use global triggers for pervasive or long-term goals. A global trigger is a reminder of something you want to do or be all the time. One of LeAnn's global triggers is a dragonfly. Her husband, Daryl, took two of the kids on a six-mile walk to see historic Church sites in New York. During the walk, the kids decided they were too tired to go on. They'd run out of water, and the sun was sweltering. On the ground near where they sat on the side of the road lay a blue-jeweled, perfectly preserved dragonfly, dead as a doornail. It only took Dad pointing out that "if we rest here forever, we'll end up just like this dragonfly" for the kids to haul themselves back up and resume the journey. Over the years, this story and the dead dragonfly have become symbols of the importance of never giving up. Now, every time LeAnn sees a dragonfly—usually alive, thankfully—she remembers never to give up. It's surprising how many times she notices dragonflies in the skies, in pictures, or in decorations around town since she started looking for them.

Each of these triggers can be prepped by creating an if-then statement for it. For example, "If I see my safety goggles in the garage when I'm going to sand something, then I will put them on first." Thinking through these if-then statements creates an intention to implement the goal that makes it easier to execute in the moment.

Practice each reminder a couple of times to get the brain used to the new association. Do a run-through. Rehearse noticing the trigger and then actually doing the action. Go into the garage and put on the goggles, then pick up the sander. Maybe four or five times in a row. Anything we can do to connect our action to a certain time, place, routine, or object will make our reminders more effective.

Step 4: Put Effort into a Goal

Effort is what gets us results. It's where the rubber meets the road. It's where we have to push through discomfort because change and growth are on the other side.

There are many different kinds of effort, such as mental focus, creativity, physical exertion, taking action while riding an emotional wave, persisting in the face of boredom, and having courage in the face of fear. For our goal of building a treehouse, some of our effort might look like reading books about carpentry, nailing a hundred planks together, being patient with ourselves when we nail them together wrong, climbing the ladder even though we're a little scared of heights, and painting pictures on the walls with our kids once we're done.

Different types of effort can be hard for different reasons. Trying new things can make us feel vulnerable or foolish. Working on boring, repetitive tasks can seem like a waste of time. Physical exertion can be uncomfortable and exhausting. Mental and emotional effort can leave us feeling drained.

Some days, we'll be better at making an effort than on other days, and that's okay. We can acknowledge that the effort we're making is hard, but we don't stop there. We also remember all the reasons we want to do this goal and accept that we need to pay a cost to get the things we want in life, and often that cost is effort and engagement.

In general conference Terence Vinson said about Oliver Granger, who was tasked with an almost impossible task, "'and when he falls he shall rise again, for his sacrifice shall be more sacred unto me than his increase, saith the Lord' [D&C 117:12–13]. That may be true of all of us—it's not our successes but rather our sacrifice and efforts that matter to the Lord."[7] The Lord knew it was unlikely for Oliver to succeed, but he was sent anyway. The Lord was not counting on success; He was counting on effort.

Dwight D. Eisenhower said, "In preparing for battle I have always found that plans are useless, but planning is indispensable."[8] We find the same is true in preparing for goals. As we put effort into the goals we've chosen, we need to be able to roll with the punches, overcome obstacles, and persist in moving forward toward the outcome we want. Things will rarely align perfectly with the plans we made in the choose a goal step, but we will still benefit immensely from having made those plans at all.

If we find ourselves in the middle of effort that isn't turning out the way we thought it would, don't worry. Soon, we're going to be gently evaluating what we've learned and accomplished with a curious, nonjudgmental mindset.

Step 5: Track a Goal

Talking about tracking a goal often brings to mind gold stars and children's chore charts on a refrigerator. But charts and stars are not just for children; adults love them too! It's the same reason that many of us add an already complete item to our to-do lists so we can immediately cross it off. Our brains like seeing progress.

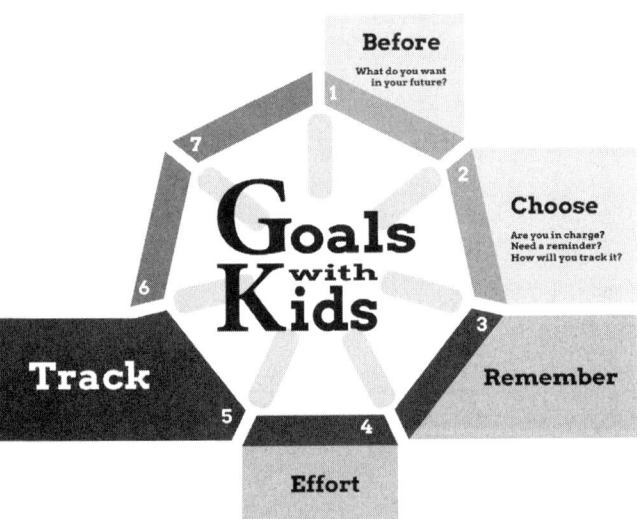

Just a note about charts. Studies about using charts and external rewards tend to show that they are not good motivators. They can kickstart a new behavior, give us data about our progress, and serve as good visual reminders for a goal we are already motivated to do, but the charts or rewards associated with them have only short-term usefulness as a motivation tool.

Kids sometimes need a little nudge to try something new or start a new routine. Kickstarting with rewards or a forced first-time try isn't a bad idea. So

---

7   "True Disciples of the Savior," *Ensign* or *Liahona*, Nov. 2019.
8   Quoted in Richard M. Nixon, *Six Crises* (Garden City, New York: Doubleday & Company, Inc., 1962), 235.

put up a star chart or let them earn some money to start a new goal. Just don't continue the chart after the first while because it devalues the activity. If we give kids a pizza for every ten books they read, some kids will lie about reading the books, and others will choose shorter books. When we make a game of learning or goals, kids will play the game rather than focus on the desired behavior.

The visual nature of charts makes them good tracking tools. Nichole once spent several months using a wall calendar and multi-colored star stickers to track her goals at the time. Rather than making daily goals, she instead tracked whatever days she happened to work on her goals and added a star. Red for every day she read her scriptures. Blue for every day she wrote for at least thirty minutes. Purple for every chapter she finished of the book she was reading. Green for the days she exercised.

She only did this for a few months, but it was exciting and motivating to look back and see a month full of stars. Of course, there were gaps all over the place. Not a single day had every color star, and not a single-colored star was on every day. But that didn't matter. She wasn't trying to be flawless. She wasn't trying to do these things every day, no matter what, rain or shine; she was just trying to do them more.

There are other options besides calendars that can help us visually track goals. Let's imagine some that would work with our treehouse goal.

- Add a marble to a jar for every half hour we work on the treehouse.
- Keep a poster on the fridge where our kids can add stickers, checkmarks, or tally marks every time they help. (Or let them make a notch on a special part of the treehouse!)
- Make a thermometer chart to track the money we're saving so we can buy the materials for our treehouse.
- Create a chart with the action steps laid out so we can check off each step along the way.

Using visually exciting or clear ways like these to track our goals can remind us that our efforts aren't going to waste, even if we might not remember all the details a month later.

However, not all tracking needs to be visual in nature. Journaling can be a useful tool to record emotions, thoughts, and situations that our fallible memories will forget. When Nichole first started homeschooling her five-year-old, she tracked her progress with an Excel spreadsheet on her computer. Each column had a question to answer or a metric to record. She rated the morning on a scale from 1–10, she recorded her daily attitude and emotions, she recorded how much school her kids finished, she recorded how screen time was used that day, she recorded any behavioral issues she or her kids were having, and—since she's a big frustration crier—she even recorded if she'd cried or not that day. Tracking so many things about her homeschooling efforts only took five to ten minutes every day, but being able to mine that data later for patterns and for strengths and weaknesses in her efforts was invaluable. It also offered a way for her husband to involve himself in their efforts, understand the problems, and offer solutions.

She only used this intensive tracking method for about six weeks before moving to a simpler method, but she still views this as a useful tool she can use if she needs it. If we're not sure what's happened with a goal we're working on, tracking different things about it in a journaling form can offer answers by increasing awareness.

In addition to visual charts and journaling, tracking a goal can also be a practical, professional tool. Some goals are so complex that we need to track them to finish them. Tracking how close we are to retirement or keeping track of other people's responses to a project they are involved in can help us stay organized and calm.

Of course, not every goal needs to be tracked. A saying commonly attributed to Albert Einstein says, "Many of the things you can count, do not count. Many of the things you cannot count, really do count." If we think our goal doesn't need to be tracked, we can skip this step.

Step 6: Evaluate a Goal

This step is where the second goal conversation with the goal coach starts up again. If we're coaching ourselves through a goal, this is a time we've set aside specifically to ponder this goal and ask the evaluating questions.

1. What went well and why?
2. What didn't go well?
3. What did you learn?
4. What can you bank?

It's vital to keep this appointment with our coaches or with ourselves, even if we didn't finish the goal. Even if we ran out of time, even if we put in zero effort, even if we completely forgot, even if we made progress but didn't finish, even if we're positive that one more hour or one more day or one more week will give us enough time to finish the goal—we can't postpone or avoid this meeting. If it didn't happen before your appointment, it didn't happen. That's okay.

It's natural to want to avoid situations that make us feel like we've disappointed someone, whether that person is ourselves or someone else. Remember that finishing the goal loop is more important than finishing the goal, and that evaluating a goal that didn't get done will usually teach us more than evaluating a goal that got finished. If we don't evaluate our efforts, we can't learn from them.

Have the meeting no matter what, see what you learn, adjust the goal, and start a new goal loop. If we forget our planned appointments, we can do them as soon as we remember. Better late than never.

As we start to look more closely at our efforts to see what worked and what didn't, we will find things that were unexpected. Things or people around us may not have acted the way we thought they would. Maybe we didn't act the way we thought we would. Maybe we made assumptions that turned out to be wrong. Maybe we made mistakes we feel we should have been able to avoid.

Avoid Negative Self-Talk

However our efforts toward our goals turned out, now is not the time for negative self-talk like berating, shaming, or guilt-tripping ourselves. This stage is about being calm and curious about whatever we witnessed happening in the previous steps, good or bad. Negative self-talk can sometimes seem to appear out of nowhere. Strategies for handling these uninvited thoughts are covered in chapter 11.

We can also sometimes spark negative self-talk with our mistaken beliefs. There are two big traps that can cause a negative self-talk spiral when we evaluate our mistakes: hindsight bias and jumping to the worst conclusion.

Hindsight bias is the tendency for people to believe that events were more predictable than they actually were before they happened. It's like saying "I knew it!" about something that you couldn't possibly have known. Essentially, it's the hidden belief that both hindsight and foresight are 20/20. This belief can often cause needless guilt over things we can't fix and couldn't have actually predicted.

For example, let's say we drive to the hardware store one night only to find that it closed an hour ago and we've wasted gasoline and time. It's an easy mistake to make, but one that many of us might beat ourselves up over. After all, 20/20 hindsight might tell you that the store hours were just a Google search away. Shouldn't we have checked before we drove over? Why didn't we think to check? How stupid of us!

We can't assume that because something happened a certain way, we should have been able to predict it or prevent it. Just because something was knowable doesn't mean that we should have known it. We're not Holmesian detectives who hyper-observantly notice and remember every clue to the mystery of life.

The human brain necessarily filters out all kinds of information that seems unimportant in the moment. Otherwise we'd be too focused on cataloguing every detail of our environment to have meaningful interactions with others. It's only natural that our filters will miss a cue or two that turn out to be important later. We can't predict the future. We're allowed to make mistakes. We're allowed to miss things that were there for us to see. It's fully human.

We knew what we knew and acted in the way we thought was best at the time. Hindsight may be 20/20, but foresight is as blurry as ever.

Jumping to the worst conclusion is another mental trap we can fall into when an obstacle or a mistake pops up in a goal. If we didn't get the treehouse done in time for our son's birthday party, that doesn't mean we're terrible parents and we never get things done on time. If we accidentally bought the wrong type of nails at the store or didn't assemble the treehouse railing correctly and now have a kid with a broken arm, that doesn't mean we are unfit to ever build anything again and we should give up on our treehouse dreams right now and sell all our tools and supplies so we never feel tempted to try again. When obstacles or mistakes present themselves, we make the smallest correction possible and don't assume more responsibility than is appropriate.

Extreme language or absolute language is one way this sort of jumping to conclusions sneaks into our negative self-talk. When we mismeasure a piece of wood, we might think bitterly to ourselves, "I never get this part right." When we can't decide what type of wood to get at the store, we might think sadly, "I always take forever to make decisions." Watching for this sort of extreme language in our thoughts and our words as we evaluate our goals helps us be more realistic about the size and implications of our mistakes.

Remember Your Purpose

What rubric should we use to evaluate our goals? Part of the answer to this question lies in the purpose we had when we chose the goal.

If our primary purpose was to teach our kids, it might not matter that the railing is a little wonky. But if our primary purpose was trying to win a treehouse-building competition or impress our father-in-law, then the wonky railing might matter a lot. The same outcome could be evaluated as either a success or a failure based on the purpose we had going into it.

Sometimes, traditional measures of success can distract us from the ones that are actually important to our personal goals and purposes. Try not to get distracted by feedback that's irrelevant.

For a decidedly non-treehouse example, if our primary purpose on Sunday mornings is to allow our kids to get themselves ready for church, having our kids show up with tangled hair and wearing mismatched shoes (or no shoes at all!) might be a perfectly acceptable outcome. But if our primary purpose is to have children dressed in their respectful Sunday best, the mismatched outfit and messy hair might signal a problem. Neither purpose is inherently better than the other, but which one we prioritize will change the way we think about and evaluate our actions and their outcomes.

What Can You Bank?

The last optional step in evaluating a goal is to bank our accomplishments and the lessons we learned. Banking something means writing it down somewhere, like on a sheet of paper we throw out at the end of the month or in our journal.

The act of writing these things down cements them in our minds. If we bank an accomplishment like, "I finished installing the whole roof today," it makes us feel more proficient. It increases our self-efficacy, our belief that we are up to whatever goal might come our way next. If we also include a personal strength that aided us in that achievement, like "I finally humbled myself and asked my neighbor for some roofing advice," our belief in ourselves and our ability to make things happen in our lives is strengthened. This is essentially the "Why?" part of the "What went well and why?" question. We can also record the lessons we learned, like "I can ask my neighbor for help, and he'll say yes." We are more likely to internalize and remember things we write down.

Some of these accomplishments and lessons learned can be put in a long-term storage place for us to refer back to later. Like the stars on Nichole's tracking calendar, these notes can comfort and motivate us long after our fallible, distracted brains have forgotten all the good work we've put in and the rewards we've reaped. We might want to have a place where we can store things we can review on a rainy day, a Vault of Strengths and Learning, if you will. We can include our small wins, strong moments, and lessons learned to remind us how strong and experienced we really are.

Step 7: Adjust a Goal

Now that we've chosen, tackled, and evaluated our goal, we have a choice to make. What's the next step? Do we want to repeat the goal, adjust the goal, or let it go?

Repeat the Goal

There are lots of reasons to repeat a goal. Maybe we want more practice. Maybe we really enjoyed it or want to learn more by doing it again. Maybe we want to really solidify a new habit. Maybe temporary circumstances outside our control threw us off before, but we think the goal will go better this time around. Maybe we didn't succeed for reasons we're not sure of and we want to try again to see if we can notice a pattern.

Whatever the reason, we don't want to get stuck on the exact same goal for too many loops. Tweaking things about our goal can teach us new things about ourselves and about how to get traction toward what we want to accomplish.

Adjust the Goal

If we liked certain aspects of the goal we set but struggled with others, we can take what we learned and make adjustments. Maybe our goal was too big. Maybe it wasn't specific enough. Maybe we need to add a reminder or a deadline. Maybe we want to try a different kind of goal in the same arena. Maybe we need to create a goal to remove a roadblock before moving forward. Maybe we need to gain a new skill or resource first.

Many goals we set are made up of microgoals, each one a small step toward the outcome we want. These microgoals don't usually take the shortest possible path to get us from Point A to Point B. They zigzag us closer to what we want by finding out what works and what doesn't, by sidestepping or overcoming obstacles we encounter, and by launching and adjusting based on where we land. Maybe our adjustment is to pick a microgoal that can act as the next step toward our larger goal.

Let the Goal Go

We don't have to finish a goal just because we started it. It's important to finish the goal loop, but we can choose not to complete the goal. Maybe we realize after the fact that we chose the goal for a shallow or silly reason. Maybe our priorities have shifted since we set the goal. Maybe we've learned that the goal is not what we thought it was. Maybe something else has caught our interest more and we'd rather pursue that instead. There are lots of good reasons to release a goal, but we don't need a reason at all. We can release a goal just because we want to.

Marie Kondo is an internet tidying sensation who teaches people worldwide how to tidy up their homes and fold their socks. She has an interesting way to discard an item we don't want anymore. We don't just toss it in the trash, feeling angry, embarrassed, disappointed, or dismissive. To release it properly, she teaches us to treat it as though it were alive and thank it for whatever service or purpose it provided us or whatever lesson it taught us.

When LeAnn and Nichole cleaned out their closets and thanked the shirts they were discarding, they learned a lot about why they buy and keep clothes. "Thank you for making me feel like a part of girls' camp seven years ago." "Thank you for reminding me I don't look good in yellow." "Thank you for being there for me when I was twenty-three pounds lighter." "Thank you for that rush of excitement when I bought you on sale." "Thank you for teaching me to never again purchase clothing that is dry-clean only." Saying goodbye and releasing things in our lives is freeing. It puts us in charge. It opens space for what we need now by removing outdated priorities, purposes, and expectations that we tend to keep around.

The same principles can be applied to goals. Just because a goal is in our mental closet doesn't mean we have to keep it. We can always tidy up. And the way we frame this tidying up matters. We can say, "I'm giving up. I quit this goal." Or we can say, "Thanks for teaching me that I really don't want to build a treehouse. Thanks for teaching me that I really just want a project to do with my kids, but I need a smaller-scale one while they're so young." Either way, we're releasing the goal. Why not choose a way of thinking that is encouraging and empowering? Discarding a goal doesn't have to be a moment of failure or defeat. It can be a moment of confidence, of taking ownership of what we want in life to make room for those things instead.

Starting Another Goal Loop

The natural progression of goal loops means it's easy to immediately start a new loop as soon as we've finished adjusting an old one. The wagon wheel just keeps rolling around and around. We don't even need to wait to start a new goal conversation to choose a new goal. As we revisit the start of the next goal loop, we can work from our old brainstorming list or start a new one.

If we're feeling overwhelmed or other things have come up in our lives that demand attention, we can take a break. We don't always have to be in the middle of a goal loop. Take a break for the weekend and start again Sunday night. Or take a longer break and start up again in a month. Goal loops will be patiently waiting for us whenever we're ready to start them rolling again.

CHAPTER 4
ROLE #2: THE GOAL COACH

Now that we understand the perspective of the goal setter, we're ready to become a goal coach. Whereas the goal setter drives the topics and actions of goal loops, the coach sets the stage for and carries out curious, open conversations to guide goal setters through goal loops.

There are many professionals who nurture personal development and well-being, such as therapists, psychologists, mentors, ministers, social workers, educators, and trainers. Goals with Kids uses a coaching model. Coaches are trained to build rapport with someone they've never met so that person feels comfortable confiding their best hopes for the future and working out a plan to get there. Coaches aren't making changes in their clients' lives; they are providing a space where the clients can focus and make changes in their own lives. Coaching is especially well suited to goal conversations because it focuses on solutions rather than problems, prioritizes the present and future over the past, and cultivates a partnership rather than an expert-client relationship.

Focus on Solutions

The human brain has an amazing capacity to filter out information that it isn't focusing on. A Harvard University study asked participants to watch a video of six people—three wearing white shirts and three wearing black shirts—passing basketballs around. Their task was to silently count how many times the people wearing white shirts passed the basketballs. In the middle of the video, a person wearing a gorilla costume walks into the center of the circle, thumps his chest, then walks out the other side. Half of the participants counting passes never even noticed the gorilla. They were so focused on one thing that their brain filtered out even highly unusual information. What we focus on can blind us to other things around us. If we choose to focus on problems, it's likely we'll miss solutions that wander into our lives, thumping their chests and hoping we'll notice them.

When we notice a problem or weakness in our lives, it's tempting to try to dissect it. We may ask ourselves when it developed, what exactly caused it, and how exactly it's negatively affecting our lives. However, the solution to a problem is often less related to the cause of the problem than we may think. Whether we developed a crippling fear of crowds from family reunions, a school play, or a county fair doesn't matter as much as coming up with strategies to tackle that fear in the present.

LeAnn attended a coaching training in Switzerland that taught this lesson with the imagery of a surfer. Coaches help clients ride the waves of their lives, taking advantage of their forward momentum. Coaches don't dive deep beneath the surface to find out what causes everything. Diving deep down stops forward motion.

Prioritize the Present and Future

An emphasis on the present is empowering. We have no control over things that happened in the past or things that will happen in the future. We can learn from the past and hope for the future, but the present is the only time of action.

Additionally, staying in the present moment and focusing on our actions keeps us grounded. If emotions of regret for the past or fear for the future overwhelm us, paying attention to the present moment and our emotions can help us weather the storm.

Focusing on the future rather than the past broadens our thoughts and sparks our creativity. Rather than being stuck with the singular reality of something that happened in the past, we can instead imagine a plethora of possible future solutions. Coaching encourages us to imagine what a solution might look like and to notice how parts of that solution already exist in our lives. Coaching helps us create a vision for our future of our own making.

Cultivate Partnership

Many helping professionals like athletic coaches, psychologists, educators, and social workers are sought out at least in part for their expert status within their field and their unique abilities to advise, train, educate, or equip their clients. This naturally creates a sort of hierarchy in the relationship, where the expert is at the top doling out information and instructions to the client below.

When discussing goals and action plans, most adults are very familiar with a hierarchical structure where decisions are made at the top and assignments are given to the bottom. This ranking model is seen in businesses, church groups, and families, but this is not how coaching works. Harvard coaching instructors teach that "coaches first look to collaborate and partner rather than showing up as experts who primarily analyze problems, give advice, prescribe solutions, recommend goals, develop strategies, teach new skills, or provide education."[9]

In a coaching relationship, the coach and the client are on the same level. Coaches may be experts in change, but clients are the experts in their own lives. In some models of coaching, coaches never put on the expert hat to give advice, explain principles or facts, or present an opinion. Other models are less strict and believe that coaches may occasionally suggest resources and offer advice and teach a client within their area of specialty, but always with the permission of the client and never with any strings attached.

In coaching, the autonomy of the client is given top priority. "We want clients to discover their own answers and to create their own possibilities, as far as possible, rather than to be given answers or direction by the coach. Client-originated visions, plans, and behaviors are the ones that stick."[10]

Coaching Requires a Safe Space

Think about the types of one-on-one conversations our kids are used to having with adults. Sometimes these conversations are pleasant chats driving home from a soccer game, but often when an adult talks with a kid, it's a formal, scheduled, critical meeting. If a kid is talking to a teacher or principal, it's often because something went wrong. If a kid is talking to a helping professional like a social worker, school counselor, therapist, or psychologist, it's often because something went wrong. If a kid is talking to a parent one-on-one, it's also often because something went wrong.

We can feel the dread of a kid going into one of these conversations just knowing that he is in trouble and wondering what's going to happen. Even one-on-one meetings with piano teachers and math tutors can cause reluctance for a kid who's not prepared.

Even if kids are not in trouble, things are often decided for them in these conversations and they feel like they have no say. They are told what's best for them, how they should behave, and even things they should want.

Part of the resistance our kids may have to attending scheduled meetings with an adult is a natural part of childhood development. But part of it has been trained into them after years of negative conversation experiences with adults acting as experts.

---

9   Margaret Moore, Bob Tschannen-Moran, and Erika Jackson, *Coaching Psychology Manual*, 2nd ed. (Philadelphia: Wolters Kluwer, 2016), 5.
10 *Coaching Psychology Manual*, 5.

We don't want goal conversations—which are conversations with coaches, not experts—to feel like one of those meetings where a kid is going to get in trouble or be told what to do. Goals with Kids conversations are a place where no one ever gets in trouble and no one gets told what to do. This is not the place for discipline. This is a supportive and secure environment for being understood.

Of course, it might take some time for our kids to trust these conversations. We shouldn't be surprised if our kids appear reluctant to participate or attend at first, imagining that these conversations will be like so many others they've experienced where they get criticized or lectured. We want to break the mold. After a few iterations of goal conversations, kids will hopefully be able to trust the process, the familiar questions, and the chill atmosphere and relax.

The most important principles necessary to create a safe space where inquisitive, open conversations can happen are honoring autonomy and maintaining an unconditional positive regard.

Autonomy is the power to make our own informed, uncoerced decisions. It's vital to early childhood development and a central part of motivation. In a safe space, people don't feel pressured to make a specific decision or feel a certain way. They can choose for themselves with no strings attached. No one wants someone to force them to do things. Coaches don't jump in and tell clients how to solve their problems; they ask questions about their clients' best hopes for the future and help them turn those desires into actionable goals.

Unconditional positive regard is the support and acceptance of a person no matter what the person does or says. It means we don't judge people for the vulnerable or emotional things they tell us. We respect their personhood and their ability to make decisions that affect their lives. Coaches practice empathy and strive to understand beliefs, emotions, and experiences without judgment.

When people feel embarrassed, shamed, mocked, scolded, or otherwise judged, they clam up. They don't feel safe sharing their thoughts and feelings.

As parents, we can't maintain safe conversation spaces all the time. There are times we need to educate, train, advise, and discipline our children. But learning how to create safe spaces is an essential tool for parents who want to learn anything real about their child's inner life.

Creating safe spaces in our families doesn't have to be limited to goal conversations. Growing up in the Hunt family, two safe conversation spaces were Check-ins and Fess-up Sessions.

When LeAnn and her husband had a houseful of teenagers, they made a tradition of doing Check-ins around once a week. A Check-in in their family is when one parent and one child go on a short walk or take a drive to a fast-food restaurant with a spending limit of one dollar (small fries or a soda were the popular orders). And then the point was for the kid to talk and the parent to listen. The parent would ask open-ended questions: "Tell me about your day." "How are things going?" "How's school?" "How are things with friends?" No problem-solving. No lecturing. Just checking in on how things are going. After a while, kids started asking them to go on Check-ins on their own. It might have been for the ninety-nine-cent hamburger, but they also knew it was a safe place for them to talk about stuff without any reaction or input from parents. They learned to trust the rules of the conversation space.

Fess-up Sessions were a much rarer safe space, occurring spontaneously when everyone was in a good mood and relationships were strong. A parent would randomly say, "Okay, Fess-up time! Tell us anything you've done wrong or against the rules and you won't get in trouble for it." They'd get all kinds of confessions from years past that they could laugh over together.

- "It was me that cut the seat belt with scissors because I wanted to know if they were strong enough."
- "It was me who carved his name into the bottom of the desk."
- "I'm the one who put gum in Jackson's hair while he was sleeping."
- "I snuck out twice through the window a year ago when you grounded me."

These Fess-up Sessions were a space for parents to learn more about their kids and their inner lives. The fact that most confessions were from years past and about smaller things made it easy to stay positive and laugh about them. These conversations never would have worked if the parents had broken the rules and punished the confessed behaviors they'd promised immunity for. They had to honor the boundary to keep the communication flowing.

Coaching conversations about goals are one type of safe space we can create. All safe spaces must respect autonomy and maintain an unconditional positive regard, but coaching spaces must also focus on solutions rather than problems, prioritize the present and future over the past, and cultivate a partnership rather than an expert-client relationship.

The Coaching Hat

Parents step into and out of different roles with their kids all the time. When our kid runs into the house with a cut on his hand from a run-in with a tree branch, we step into a nursing role. We automatically speak calmly, tell them it's going to be okay, walk them to the sink to wash it off, and put on a Band-Aid. A nurse does the same thing. We know what our kids need in certain situations.

If our kid is older, we might just tell him to not forget the antibiotic ointment and to not drip blood on the carpet while he handles it himself.

The Goals with Kids coaching hat is just another tool in our arsenal of parenting skills. We can don the occasional nurse hat, math tutor hat, rule-enforcer hat, cooking-instructor hat, or coaching hat. Many of the hats we don come to us naturally, but some can be or need to be taught. Most people have never been trained to create a safe conversation space, so it will take some study and practice.

A psychology professor was having trouble teaching his students how to better listen to clients in a therapy session. In frustration, he pulled aside the secretary of the department and briefly taught her the five attending behaviors of a good counselor (the behaviors that show you are paying attention). These behaviors were pleasant and regular eye contact, a relaxed posture leaning slightly toward the client, an occasional nod while listening, facial expressions responsive to what was being said, and verbal acknowledgements like "mmm," "uh-huh," or "tell me more." When the secretary practiced these five simple behaviors in class with a client, she seemed more like a professional therapist than students who had been studying psychology for years.

Likewise, a few simple coaching behaviors can immediately improve our performance and increase the likelihood of a successful goal conversation. When we start acting like a coach, even with very little experience, we seem like a trustworthy coach to those around us. Keeping in mind the purpose of becoming a better coach for our kids, here are nine practical steps we can practice to create a safe coaching space in our family that our kids will learn to trust.

9 Ways to Create a Coaching Space

1. Name the Conversation

Give whatever safe space you're creating a name. The Hunt family used Check-ins and Fess-Up Sessions most frequently, but you could use Goal Conversations, What-Went-Well Conversations, Kid-Talk Time, or anything else you want. Get creative.

Having a name to use allows people to talk more clearly about the patterns and expectations of the safe space. Parents or kids can easily request to start a conversation and enter into the safe space: "Hey, can we have five minutes of Kid-Talk Time right now?" Or they can ask each other if they're already in the safe space: "Wait, are we having a Goal Conversation or just planning our day tomorrow?" Using a clear name lets everyone know what hats to put on.

Some safe spaces will happen naturally without ever being named, like the sort of closeness and safety we feel when discussing something personal with a close friend. But coaching conversations we expect to have over and over about sometimes vulnerable topics can benefit from having a formal name to invoke.

2. Make the Rules

Now that we have a name, it's time to come up with some basic conditions and boundaries. Rules don't need to be laid out in a formal charter, but if some of these principles or policies are a change from our normal interactions, it will help to explain to our kids the changes we're trying to make. Then let our behavior help set the expectations. The most basic rules can be found by answering the questions *who*, *where*, and *how long*.

Who will be in this conversation? A coaching space is usually filled by one client and one coach, or one kid and one parent, because it's easier to connect with one person than with a whole room. There might be times when multiple kids can be in the same coaching space or both parents want to coach a kid together, but less is usually more. Whatever we decide, the general rule needs to be clear and agreed upon by everyone. Inviting other people into the safe space without checking with the other person first violates that safe space.

Where are these conversations going to happen? Coaching spaces can happen in lots of places—restaurants, sidewalks, bedrooms, offices, cars, garages, backyards, just to give a few ideas. When suggesting a location, consider the privacy and distraction level of the physical space.

Privacy is key to a safe space, both the assurance that our words won't be repeated or gossiped about and also the assurance that our words won't be overheard by people around us. It's entirely possible that kids would be comfortable having strangers overhear parts of their conversations at a restaurant but would be embarrassed to have their siblings overhear those same conversations at home. Agree on a level of privacy to maintain in this coaching space.

Another factor to consider is how many distractions and interruptions our location presents. When coaches or clients allow distractions and interruptions to break the flow of the safe space, it signals to the other person that the conversation isn't very important. Either person might start feeling self-conscious for taking up so much of the other person's time or feeling frustrated that their own time is being wasted, which hampers open, nonjudgmental communication.

Be respectful of the time and engagement of both parties by setting up an environment ahead of time where distractions are minimized. Turn off your phone. Meet while the other kids are at soccer practice. Put a "Do Not Disturb" sign on the spare bedroom door. If walking around the zoo is too distracting, try walking around the block. If it's hard to find a place in your home to have these conversations without getting interrupted, they might need to be had outside of the home—in a car, yard, or other location. Remember that other family members aren't the only things that can distract us.

How long are these conversations? Putting time limits on events can make people more willing to participate. For example, Nichole's kids are more willing to clean quickly when they set a timer rather than try to clean a whole room. "Let's clean the playroom" is overwhelming and hard to imagine for them, but "Let's each pick one song to listen to while we clean, then when the music is done, so are we" is much easier to grasp. They're more willing to start the job because they don't fear being trapped inside it for a long time.

Maybe we set an actual timer for fifteen minutes. Maybe we walk around the block three times and then we're done. Maybe we talk while we put away laundry together, and when the laundry is done, so are we.

Even if we haven't hit our time limit yet, it's okay to end the conversation early if the safe space is beginning to break down. Sometimes emotions get the best of us and make it hard to maintain unconditional positive regard. Don't force a coaching space if it's not happening. It's better to take a break, calm down, and try again later.

3. Build Rapport

Rapport is a relationship with someone based on empathy, mutual understanding, and good communication. It can be as simple as making a good first impression with someone and putting him or her at ease. When we have rapport with someone, both people are warm and positive, attentive to each other's actions, and "in sync." We feel a connection. Even when we're coaching our own kids, building rapport with them is a part of wearing the coaching hat.

Think about the people you talk to that you feel safe with. Not the one person you reveal your innermost secrets to, just people you can tell your stories to. If you don't have someone like that now, imagine someone you could talk to. What are those people like?

- They are generally light-hearted.
- Nothing you say surprises them.
- They accept you for who you are and don't try to get you to change.
- You can tell they really listen.
- They don't judge what you tell them.

That's what we need to be to coach people through goals—someone who will listen to their stories without reacting or judging.

Much of rapport building is the basics of good communication. Be kind and genuine; remember the things they share; have an open, positive posture and facial expression; find common interests to discuss; and pay attention to social cues.

One simple technique that can help put people at ease is called mirroring. Mirroring is where we follow our kid's cues and adjust our own behavior to match those cues more closely to make them more comfortable.

We can mirror physical actions, excitement levels, and speech patterns. If a kid is casually lounging on a couch, sitting primly on the edge would signal a big difference in character or current emotion rather than a similarity. If a kid is shy and reserved, we could be a little calmer than usual. If a youth uses more academic language than casual, we can follow suit where we feel comfortable.

Obviously, mimicking every single gesture or word or attempting to copy things like strangers' accents has a high likelihood of offending the person you are trying to build rapport with. Try to show that you have something in common with your kids without making them feel that you are imitating or mocking them.

4. *Don the Coaching Hat*

A successful lawyer arguing a case in court might don an aloof, critical, or aggressive mindset that serves their purposes at work. But if they can't switch into a softer parenting mindset at home and end up interrogating their kids about what they did every minute of the day, home relationships will suffer. Being able to switch mindsets lets us tailor our behavior and feelings in ways that best serve whatever situation or relationship we're dealing with.

Sometimes it can be hard to switch into mindsets, either because they are unfamiliar or because we are in too different of an emotional state. Taking a few deep breaths might be enough to help us adopt the calm, coaching mindset. We could also come up with a few personal keywords or phrases about how we want to show up to the conversation. Something like these:

- Calm. Curious. Nonjudgmental.
- Empathetic. Chill.
- Ask questions and really listen.
- Safe space. Calm voices.
- Talk less, listen more.

Repeating these phrases can remind us of the mindset we want to have when we talk to our kids about goals. Entering a new mindset will often naturally affect our body language, facial expressions, and verbal qualities like intonation, word choice, phrasing, pace, volume, and intensity. Paying attention to these cues can help us realize which hat we're wearing.

Wearing new hats can feel awkward and uncomfortable at first. Try this experiment at overcoming awkward. Stop now and fold your arms. Now switch them around so the other hand is poking out. Feels awkward, right? There is no one way to fold our arms, and doing it differently feels weird at first, but it doesn't take long for it not to feel strange. Same with a coaching hat. It might feel awkward at first, but try it. It'll feel natural soon. This is a good way to teach the kids you coach to try new things too.

In the Goals with Kids coaching model, it is appropriate to occasionally wear an expert hat on top of your coaching hat. As adults and coaches with experience in life and enacting change, we may wish to share a life lesson or practical skill with our client. However, we need to signal to the other person that we would like to temporarily put an expert hat on top of our coaching hat. Asking for permission first honors the client's autonomy. Here are some things we could say to gauge the other person's willingness to talk to an expert instead of a coach for a minute:
- "Can I tell you a story?"
- "Can I tell you something I've learned about change?"
- "Have you heard of hindsight bias?"
- "Are you ready to hear some advice right now?"

Offer advice and lessons extremely sparingly. Avoid prescriptive advice and words like "should." If you tell a story to teach a principle, like Christ did in His many parables, let the client pick out the principle themselves. If you can't think of a story, ask yourself how you learned the principle.

Watching for resistance in body language or words when we are wearing the expert hat can tip us off that the other person is unwilling to hear expert advice or a lesson right then. When we notice this, we respect their autonomy and keep our coaching hat on and our expert hat off. We may be more of an expert at living or enacting change, but the client is the ultimate expert in his own life.

5. *Practice Reflective Listening*

Effective coaches need to be good listeners. The basics of good communication apply in a safe space—like don't interrupt or dominate the conversation—but coaches also use other tools like reflective listening to engage even more deeply with conversations.

So what are we listening for as coaches?

We listen for content. We want to hear what is happening in our kids' lives, what they want for their futures, and what they are struggling with. We might pick up on something new they want to try that they haven't talked about before.

We listen for emotions. We might hear excitement and energy around an idea. We might hear fear or reluctance about a goal they don't feel ready to start.

We listen for action language and resistance language. We might hear what they are ready to put effort toward and what they are feeling pushed to do halfheartedly.

Once we hear content, emotions, action language, or resistance language that the other person is sharing, we can echo them back to the speaker for confirmation.

Summarizing and describing what you just heard with an intent to understand makes the other person feel heard and validated and gives the person a chance to clarify her thoughts. It can be useful in calming down a tense or emotional situation or in exploring ideas in an already calm setting. Naming a negative emotion someone is feeling can literally calm that emotion. Finding words for her own emotions and hearing someone else try to understand those emotions brings into existence goals and plans that didn't exist before except as vague notions and longings.

Reflective listening will only work if we're paying really close attention to what the other person is saying and not getting caught up in our own thoughts, emotional reactions, or memories that might be triggered by the other person's words. It takes practice. We should not be planning our own personal response to someone's words while we are listening, only seeking to understand and clarify what someone is telling us.

Here are a few ways to start sentences to practice active listening:
- "It sounds like you feel . . ."
- "It seems like . . ."
- "I hear you saying that . . ."
- "What I'm hearing is . . ."
- "So you're saying that . . ."
- "In other words . . ."
- "Let me see if I understand . . ."

Adding these phrases to our vocabularies will probably feel awkward or stilted at first, but remember it becomes natural quickly when we use them. If we're not confident in our reflection, it's fine to check them with questions like, "Did I get that right?" or "Am I understanding this correctly?"

There are a few things that get in the way of active listening. These barriers can interrupt a safe coaching space. Literally interrupting our kids or being sarcastic are two of the most obvious barriers, but here are a few more (along with dialogue tags to help us spot them):

Giving Advice
- "If I were you . . ." or "You should just . . ."

Commanding
- "Don't do that . . ."

Criticizing
- "You're too . . ." or "You always . . ."

Distracting
- "Don't worry about it; let's talk about . . ."

Placating
- "Everything will be fine . . ." or "Don't listen to her; you're beautiful and smart and . . ."

Interrogating
- "Why would you . . ."

Moralizing
- "Well, you know that the early bird gets the worm . . ."

Denying
- "That's probably not what happened . . ." or "You don't really feel that way . . ."

Comparing
- "You're not doing the goal like your sister . . ."

Phrases like these can make kids feel judged rather than validated. That's not to say that we should never use any of these strategies in our daily lives. Most parents know that distracting a toddler from a tantrum is a proven and effective technique and that offering constructive criticism to children is part of the parenting deal. But when we're wearing our coach's hat and occupying a safe space, overuse of these barriers shuts down open communication and autonomy and weakens a safe space.

6. *Notice Resistance*

A good principle to coach by is that people don't resist change, they resist being changed. Resistance from the client is often an early warning sign that the coach is—consciously or unconsciously—putting forth pressure or influence to get the client to change. Things like guilt trips, moral judgments, rewards and punishments, and advice and comparisons can increase resistance and interfere with a positive coaching space.

We are trained to notice resistance from a young age. When kids roughhouse, it's all fun and games. Until, all of a sudden, it's not. As kids, we learned to pay attention to when the laughing or screaming of the kids we were playing with changed to signal that they were not having fun anymore. Even if we didn't intend to make them sad or scared or angry, it was our responsibility to stop once we realized how our actions were being perceived. Paying attention to how someone is receiving something matters.

It's the coach's responsibility to be attentive to signs of resistance in a coaching conversation and figure out what caused it, even if it was unintentional.

Resistance can reveal itself in language like, "I don't think I can do that" and "I'm not up for that right now." Our tendency when we hear statements like these may be to cheerlead the person to a greater confidence in his abilities, but as a coach it is better to mentally note the resistance and move on.

Coaches may also notice resistance as a lack of participation or a noticeable shift in the middle of the conversation, often accompanied by closed-off or aggressive body language. If we notice our kid getting angry or defensive (that classic fight-or-flight response), we may need to pause the conversation and explore it. A simple few sentences, like "I'm going to pause the conversation because I felt a shift and I'd like to explore it" or "It seems like you're extra quiet all of a sudden," can help you clarify what happened for both of you. Noticing patterns of resistance can clue us in to what our child is thinking, learning, and feeling.

7. *Ask Open-Ended Questions*

As coaches, focusing on asking open-ended questions that encourage longer, freeform answers displays patience and curiosity. Asking close-ended questions with short answers discourages a balanced and engaging conversation. Asking a lot of these questions in a row, however, may lead to the other person feeling cornered or interrogated. Coaches should also be careful of "why" questions (e.g., "Why did you do it that way?"), which have the potential to imply negative judgment.

Here are some examples of open-ended questions, including the three evaluating questions:

- What went well with this goal?
- What didn't go well with this goal?
- What did you learn?
- What would working on this goal look like?
- What are your ideal outcomes for this goal?
- What would have to change to make this goal possible?

Don't worry about memorizing questions or getting it "right." In general, open-ended questions invite your kids to talk. Just being aware of our questions and how they are received will improve them slowly over time. For more ideas about the art of asking questions as a parent, a quick internet search can give you more examples.

8. *Embrace Silence*

We tend to associate stretches of silence in a conversation with awkwardness. Silence can make us worry that our last question or comment was too confusing or prying for the other person to feel comfortable responding. But silence after questions or comments in a coaching space doesn't always indicate a problem.

Silence—especially what we call "comfortable silence"—often comes after a thought-provoking question or comment when people are lost in their own thoughts. When we ask deep or honest questions, we shouldn't be surprised by the time it takes to form carefully thought-out answers.

In a coaching space where we ask thoughtful, open-ended questions, we resist the urge to reword, clarify, or move past our questions unless the other person asks us to. Doing so can interrupt the other person's deep train of thought.

Literally count the seconds in your head after you ask a question to give the other person enough time to respond. Learn what a ten-second silence really feels like—or twenty or thirty seconds—and see how much silence fits easily into our coaching space. It might be more than we think.

We should also be prepared as coaches to receive no answer at all to our questions or to receive answers long after we ask the questions. Sometimes the person we ask needs time to think about the answer on her own outside of the pressure of a conversation, maybe even a few days or weeks. Remember, this is an extended series of conversations. We don't need to press and get answers immediately.

9. Apologize When the Safe Space Is Broken

Knowing when to create a safe space like a coaching space is just as important as knowing how. Since maintaining a safe space takes energy and focus, a time when someone is especially tired, grumpy, stressed, or otherwise preoccupied is not ideal.

We need to know our own limits. If our kid requests a safe space during one of these times, we may need to psych ourselves up for a few minutes to get into the right headspace or simply say, "Now's not a good time for me. Can we try later tonight or tomorrow?"

Sometimes we create safe conversation spaces and then mess up. Sometimes, even if we've just had a whole week of great, safe conversations, we get frustrated, loud, critical, or sarcastic. It happens. Sometimes we break safe spaces.

But they don't have to stay broken.

If we notice something going wrong in the middle of the conversation and we can get it together, we can do it immediately. Then apologize.

If we notice in the middle of the conversation but we can't get it together, we can say we need to take a break and come back later. Then apologize.

If we notice what went wrong after the conversation is over, we can meet up again as soon as possible. Then apologize.

Apologizing for the parts we play in breaking safe spaces will both rebuild the safe space for the future and set an example for our kids to follow when they break safe spaces themselves. No one will be perfect at maintaining a safe space, but we can acknowledge our mistakes and consistently work to keep the conversation flowing.

Coaching through a Goal Loop

Let's imagine what it's like to coach someone through a complete goal loop. For the sake of simplicity in this mental experiment, let's imagine ourselves as professional coaches starting with a new, young client who wants to use the Goals with Kids model. We plan to meet with this kid after school Mondays, Wednesdays, and Fridays for three weeks to have goal conversations.

We'll get to coaching our own kids in greater detail in the next chapter, but seeing the principles in action in this simplified version will help to apply them in a more complex environment later.

Instead of just walking through the seven steps of the loop like we did when we were goal setters, we'll walk through the three conversation stages.

Goal Conversation #1

Introduction

Before the first conversation, we seek to put our young client at ease, explain the pattern of conversations we'll be having, and ask for consent. Here are sample introductions a coach might give a child or a youth.

Child: We are going to have a goals club where we learn how to do goals. Your mom's going to drop you off here Monday, Wednesday, and Friday after school. We are going to brainstorm some things you want and need in your future and choose some goals to get there. You get to pick your own goals. For each goal, we get to ask questions about what went well, what didn't go well, and what you learned. Sound good? We celebrate at the end of each goal loop with a fist bump or high five—you choose. Here's how we get started . . .

Youth: We are going to talk about goals and check in three times a week for a few weeks. Are you okay with that? You are the expert in your life, so you get to choose all the goals. We are just going to ask the same questions about each goal so we can learn something about how it went and about how goals work in general. Here's how the loop goes . . .

For any age, it's helpful to show our client a visual form of the goal loop. This could be a printout of the graphics in this book or even just the words written out on pieces of paper and laid on the floor in a circle. Especially with younger children, having them physically walk around the circle when we are discussing each step can help them learn the loop and participate more fully.

After we've set the stage, we start the first goal conversation, which contains the first two steps of the goal loop: Before a Goal and Choose a Goal.

Coaching Step 1: Before a Goal

Kids need ideas before they can pick goals. As we brainstorm with them, we listen hard to what this kid wants. All the ideas go on the list, and none of them gets laughed at. Asking questions like these might spark new goal ideas:
- What do you want in your life right now?
- What things are you already working on?
- What are your best hopes for your life in the future?
- What roles or responsibilities do you have right now?
- Some main categories for goals are spiritual, social, physical, and intellectual. Can you jot down some ideas in each of these areas?

Let the kid do the talking. We have no agenda or responsibility to make sure this kid picks or avoids certain goals. The kid is in charge.

We can set a timer and brainstorm for two or five minutes, or we can naturally move on to the next step when the kid shows a particular interest in one of the goals mentioned.

Coaching Step 2: Choose a Goal

When we're done brainstorming, we let the kid choose a goal. Remember, we're not personally invested in which goal the kid chooses, so we won't react emotionally to the choice. We're only invested in teaching the kid the goals process. Even if we think the specific goal the kid chose is ill-fated from the start, we aren't dream killers. Reality and the process of goal loops take care of that.

If the kid wants to be the best cartwheeler in the world, run with it and ask questions. What might accomplishing this goal look like? How would you know when you were done? What can you do this week to improve your cartwheels? After a few goal loops, the kid figures out there's not really a worldwide cartwheel competition, so that'll be impossible to win. After a few more goal loops, the kid also figures out that she really wants to be friends with her neighbor who goes to gymnastics and does great cartwheels. Then the goal conversation naturally shifts to how to make friends with someone. And because the shift was discovered and motivated by the kid, there won't be resistance.

Unless the goal is somehow going to cause great and irreversible harm, we let reality do the disillusioning for us. And who knows, maybe the kid will surprise us. You may have more life experience than kids have, but they have way more experience being and understanding themselves.

Just like we anticipated steps 3, 4, and 5 in the choose a goal step as goal setters, we can prep goal setters we are coaching by walking them through the steps they'll be tackling on their own.

To prepare kids to remember, we might need to teach them about how brains react to triggers and the different types of reminders we can use. Ask them what sort of triggers they might want to try for the specific goal they're working on.

To help kids prepare for the effort involved in working on a goal, have them visualize what actually doing the goal will look like. "If you were a character in a movie, what would that character do next to finish this goal?" Don't be afraid to push the goal setter to get specific. "What's the next step you can take?" Ask what obstacles might come up and if they can do things to avoid them or make them easier. "What might get in the way of finishing this goal?"

To prep kids for tracking goals, we might need to teach them about different tracking methods and the danger of setting daily goals. We can also ask them if the goal they're working on needs tracking at all and what kind of tracking they plan to use if it does.

It's critical to set up the next time we're going to check in or meet about this goal. Shorter times between meetings are better at the beginning while the goal setter is getting used to the loop. We already have appointments scheduled for Mondays, Wednesdays, and Fridays after school in this example, so it's time to send them off on their own.

The Grand Pause

During the next three steps of the goal loop—Remembering a Goal, Putting Effort into a Goal, and Tracking a Goal—our coaching task is to not do anything at all. We send the kid out the door to do the goal (or not do the goal, as the case may be). The coach does not give one thought to the kid until the next appointment. If the kid fails or doesn't fail—we'll have no idea until they show up again. (We parents can already tell how this won't be the case for coaching our own kids, but we'll discuss that in the next chapter.)

Because kids are at varying levels of independence and responsibility, they will vary greatly in their efforts and outcomes while remembering, putting effort into, and tracking. Remember that even competent, good-hearted, engaged kids don't necessarily know how to motivate themselves or structure their own learning and goal setting. Failing at any of these steps is natural and expected and does not mean kids are lacking anything they "should" have by now. Hold kids in unconditional, positive regard no matter how these steps go for them.

Goal Conversation #2

The first time we see our young client after The Grand Pause, we build rapport with some small talk, then move on to the Evaluate a Goal and Adjust a Goal steps.

Coaching Step 6: Evaluate a Goal

We start by asking our young client which goal he was working on and then asking the three evaluating questions.

1. What went well and why?
2. What didn't go well?
3. What did you learn?

Help the kid bank any successes or lessons learned. Remember that whatever happened in steps 3, 4, and 5 is no big deal. Take everything in stride and remember the unconditional positive regard we want to maintain by having a calm, positive demeanor. Don't be reactive. Remember that whether the kid failed or succeeded is way less important than what can be learned from the goal loop as a whole because this learning gives the kid traction in adjusting what needs to happen next.

If kids are reluctant to explore things that went badly, we can help them gently "open the envelope," as LeAnn likes to say. The phrase "open the envelope" is somewhere in between "take stock of your situation" and "just rip off the Band-Aid." They're all ways people psych themselves up to face bad news or something that might hurt.

When adults get a credit card bill in the mail, just looking at it can trigger all sorts of negative emotions like stress, depression, shame, and frustration if it demands money we can't spare right then. Sometimes, it's tempting to just bury the unopened envelope under a stack of papers on the counter or even throw it away. After all, another bill will soon be coming. But neither of these options changes the reality of what's in the bill or the negative emotions we will feel when we finally do open it. In fact, ignoring the bill for so long might trigger even more negative emotions once we finally open it.

Opening the envelope means that we take a deep breath and peek inside. We're not pulling out our checkbooks. We're not calling someone up to pay over the phone. We're not moving money around in our bank accounts. We're just opening the envelope, reading the numbers, and allowing the reality of the information there to influence our actions in the future. Opening the envelope is the first step to solving the problem one day. We can't pay the bill until we know how much we owe to whom.

Ignoring the problems that arise in our goal loops doesn't make them go away either. In a goal loop, opening the envelope means we peek inside. We're not pointing the finger of blame. We're not whipping up a new goal to start fixing the problem right away. We're just being curious and seeing what went wrong. As coaches, we can encourage kids to explore the realities of their experiences—including things that didn't go well—by asking specific questions about their efforts and the problems they encountered.

Coaching Step 7: Adjust a Goal

Next, we ask if our young client wants to work on this goal some more. If he does, we help him think of ways he may want to try adjusting the goal. He may want a different or an extra reminder. He may want to change his patterns and types of effort. He may need a better way to track his effort and progress.

If the kid doesn't want to work on the goal anymore, respect his autonomy and be okay with that. Don't try to convince him not to give up. Accept that his reasons for deciding are valid and shouldn't be challenged. The kid will challenge them on his own when he is ready. When we notice a pattern of avoidance or flitting between goals, we ask permission to don our expert hat, tell the kid what we notice, and explore what's going on with the kid.

Introduce the idea of saying goodbye to goals and thanking them for what they taught us, like we covered in the last chapter. Some kids will love this kind of closure. Celebrate completing a goal loop, again using visuals of the wheel graphic or a circle of steps on the floor.

We can take a moment to ourselves to appreciate the things that went well in coaching this goal loop, but remember that the goal, the work, and the reward belong to the kid.

This part of Goal Conversation #2 will naturally lead us back into Goal Conversation #1 and the beginning of a new goal loop. A single fifteen-minute conversation can not only evaluate and adjust an old goal but also brainstorm and choose a new one.

CHAPTER 5
ROLE #3: THE ENGAGED PARENT

WE'VE LEARNED HOW TO BE a goal setter and how to be a goal coach. By far the most common question we get from parents at this point in the Goals with Kids model is this:

"But how do I get my kids to do things they don't want to do?"

How Do I Get My Kid To . . .

This is a parenting question, not a coaching question. This chapter is dedicated to exploring that question: why we ask it, the question we could be asking instead, and how the answers can direct us in our actions.

Let's start by revisiting the country analogy from chapter 1. We parents act as temporary stewards over our kids' countries when they are born, dealing with all the functional minutia necessary to keep the country running. Then, over the course of eighteen years, we teach them how to be monarchs in their own right, and we surrender power and responsibility for the country bit by bit. By the time our kids are eighteen, they are largely responsible for and running their own lives. Our day-to-day frustrations trying to share power and transfer power and get our kids to do things they don't want to do arises from three conflicting needs. Parents need cooperation in the present, they need their kids to prepare for independent futures, and they need to do this while maintaining a good relationship.

Parents Need Cooperation in the Here and Now

We as parents need our kids to act and behave in certain ways just so we can continue to run our day-to-day lives and manage however many countries are inhabiting our households. We can't wait around for them to feel like tackling some goals; we need them to do it now! We need our kids to do things like go to school, manage their anger without hitting, take out the trash, and play fewer video games to meet the needs of the family as a whole. We wield some power in our kids' countries so one country doesn't fall apart and take the other countries nearby down with it. Parents have the right and responsibility to the orderly conduct of their home as they see fit.

Parents Need to Prepare Kids for the Future

As parents, it's not just about how our day or week is turning out. It's not just about making sure the countries we steward are functioning today. We need to be training the new monarchs to take over. We need to teach them things like how to manage laundry, money, time, and emotions. We want them to be prepared for missions, roommates, marriage, college, and jobs. We want to introduce them to activities we think will benefit them or we think they'll like. We all want slightly different things and will teach those things in slightly different ways.

Most parents aren't grooming their kids for a future they hate. We aren't pushing them to be doctors because of a thwarted childhood dream. We are just doing our job, preparing them for a largely unknown, unpredictable future. We are preparing them to be flexible and resilient so they can run their own country without it falling apart once we step back. We are trying to make our job as parents obsolete so our children can parent themselves.

Sometimes, the needs of the here and now can compete with needs for the future. One night, Nichole's kids emptied the linen closet of every blanket they owned, piled them into the crib for a game, and left them scattered around the room when they were done. She immediately saw two needs. First, the need to have a clean house for her own peace of mind and practical functioning. Second, the need to teach her kids how to fold up blankets and clean up messes they make. She felt overwhelmed trying to decide which need was more important in the moment, so the blankets sat in a corner of the room for two weeks, fulfilling neither need. Eventually, Nichole realized that by waiting so long, she'd missed the window for teaching her kids to clean up messes and cleaned them up herself. Choosing either option earlier would have saved her from a cluttered room for two weeks. We don't need to wait around and worry about balancing these needs perfectly. We will have a million choices to make here, and it doesn't matter if we mess up a bunch of them. It's not always easy or possible to decide which need is more important in a given situation.

Parents Want to Maintain a Good Relationship with Their Kids

The real tricky part about getting our kids to do the things we need for the practical present and for the hopeful future is to do it without ruining our relationships with them. We want to get our kids to do things without resorting to yelling or nagging, without always feeling annoyed and powerless when they don't do them, and without feeling bitter or resentful when they don't take responsibility and we do. Sometimes it feels like any parenting solution that gets things done in the short-term comes at the cost of long-term relationships.

Think about arguments that come up again and again with our kids. Is it because they don't do their chores? They fight with their siblings? They won't practice the piano? They're not getting passing grades in school?

Now think of all the things we've tried to fix the problem, both positive and negative. Lecturing? Yelling? Persuading? Nagging? Guilting? Counseling together? Implementing chore charts? Making a plan? Enforcing consequences? Making them think it was their idea to start with? How on earth can we get our kids to do something when all these strategies have failed us at some point in the past? How can we get our kids to do things they don't want to do?

The first step to answering this question is to ask a different question:

Who Owns the Goal?

The owner of the goal is the one who is disappointed if it doesn't get fulfilled. The one who cares about the goal. The one who wants to see it complete. The one who does most of the work and thinking about the goal. The one who is most affected by the outcome.

If a child gets embarrassed by a piano teacher and really wants to practice the piano every week, it's the kid's goal. If a parent gets upset that a kid is wasting piano lessons by only practicing once a month, then getting the kid to practice is the parent's goal, even if the kid is the one who needs to take the action.

The answer to the question, "Who owns the goal?" tells us whether we need to put on our coaching hat or our parenting hat when approaching the goal with our kid.

When our kid owns the goal, it's time to put on our coaching hat and start walking our kid through goal loops to help her figure out what works for her.

When we own the goal, it's time to put on our parenting hat. Then we've got three basic choices:
1. Offer the Goal to Our Kid
2. Stand Strong
3. Let It Go

Offer the Goal to Our Kid

We offer a goal to our kid when we brainstorm possible goals with them. We can ask them directly with language like, "I have an idea for a goal for you. I'm wondering if you'd be willing to give it a try. Can I tell you about it?" Or we might present the goal as a problem we'd like their help in solving. "I've noticed that we've had some contention about this topic lately. Do you have any ideas?"

Elder Dale G. Renlund said, "Now, it would be nice if increased faith were transmitted like the flu or the common cold. Then a simple 'spiritual sneeze' would build faith in others. But it does not work that way. The only way faith grows is for an individual to act in faith. These actions are often prompted by invitations extended by others, but we cannot 'grow' someone else's faith or rely solely on others to bolster our own. For our faith to grow, we must choose faith-building actions, such as praying, studying the scriptures, partaking of the sacrament, keeping the commandments, and serving others."[11] Inviting kids to act or set goals is an important, integral part of growing faith and helping them develop.

Sometimes we need to introduce a goal to our kids several times before they adopt it on their own, so don't view the first option as a one-shot enterprise. Look at offering a goal to kids as a reconnaissance mission where we gain new information about our kids to better understand them the next time we try.

Here are some tips to help introduce kids to a new goal in a way that they might choose it for themselves:

- Explain your reasons. Kids are often quite logical and can be motivated when they understand the reasons behind the goal.
- Plan for short goal experiments with an end date. If kids know they are only going to be doing the goal for a week and not the rest of the summer, they may be more willing to try it out.
- Offer a variety of goals to explore your new idea. Unconventional or novel approaches to a goal may pique your kid's interest. Refer to the types of goals listed in chapter 3 in the treehouse example.
- Ask kids to list reasons they don't want to do the goal. Recognizing both the good reasons and the silly reasons they have for not wanting to do the goal—and realizing that all of them are valid—may reveal obstacles to starting that can be addressed in a separate goal loop or reveal good reasons not to do the goal right now.
- Be prepared to accept "no" calmly and pleasantly and move on in that moment. Don't turn the offer into a debate.
- Have them rate their interest and motivation on a scale from 1–10 with questions like, "How interested are you in this goal?" and "How likely are you to jump in and start tomorrow?" Ask what might move their numbers up a little.

---

11   "Unwavering Commitment to Jesus Christ," *Ensign* or *Liahona*, Nov. 2019.

Parents also have the option to stop offering the goal to their kids at any time and choose to Let It Go or Stand Strong instead.

If we offer the goals to our kids and they accept, our kids now own the goals, and we get to put the coaching hat on and start doing goal loops. We studied what makes an effective goal coach last chapter, but being a goal coach to our own kids is more complicated. Let's take a look at how to wear the coaching hat as a parent, how being a good parent naturally makes us a less effective coach, and what we can do about it, starting with a metaphor.

Coaching vs. Parenting

Think of a goal conversation like radio communication. Radio stations transmit and receive messages through the air. If everything is working right in a channel, the signals are clear and communication is sent and received without problems or confusion. However, interference can distort radio communication, like bad weather creating too much static to hear the music clearly or another radio station nearby making a second song bleed into the first.

One way to solve an interference problem is to isolate your signals—keep them defined and different from other signals in some way. Then the messages won't get mixed anymore. For example, radio stations isolate with time, frequency, and location. If two radio stations are trying to fix an interference problem where both of their stations are being picked up at the same time by listeners, they might agree to broadcast their music at different times, on different frequencies, or in different cities. That way, listeners only hear one song at a time. The communication is sent and received clearly.

The professional coaching model already has built-in ways to isolate signals, making the conversation clean and clear. However, when parents coach their own kids, the coach-my-kid relationship and the parent-my-kid relationship overlap. This overlap can interfere with the safe space of a coaching conversation and distort open communication.

Here are seven types of interference parents need to work around that professional coaching already isolates for:

Goals with Kids

Professional Coach		Parent as Coach
Length and frequency of all coaching sessions are agreed upon ahead of time	**Time**	Length or frequency of coaching interactions varies and is rarely made explicit
All interactions take place in a single, neutral location	**Location**	Interactions may take place in many places, including public or multiuse ones
If a client isn't fitting well with a coach, they are encouraged to seek out other options	**Permanence**	Parents and their kids are bound together for life, regardless of issues of fit
The relationship and conversations always follow a specific pattern of communication	**Complexity**	Parents have multi-faceted relationships with their kids and employ many different communication and parenting patterns
Coaches acknowledge that clients are the ultimate experts in their own lives	**Expertise**	Parents are secondary experts in their kids' lives and are experts in the home
Coaches do not take a client's success or failure personally	**Investment**	Parents can view their kids' successes or failures as evidence of their own success or failure as parents
Coaches have limited legal and moral obligations to their clients	**Obligation**	Parents have extensive legal and moral obligations to their kids

Parents Can't Be Perfect Coaches . . . and That's Okay

Please understand, the things in the right-hand column aren't always bad! Things that interfere with coaching can benefit other aspects of parenting.

For example, a coach spending non-coaching time around clients and watching their goal efforts might negatively pressure clients. But parents spending non-coaching time around their kids is a practical necessity and a way to strengthen relationships and identify and address behavioral problems. Coaches may strive to be as perfectly isolated as possible in all seven ways above, but the goal for a parent isn't to become just a coach to their kids. What is good for coaching communication isn't good for all types of communication.

Many of these types of parenting interference are impossible to eliminate. They are built into the nature of parenting. Parents will always have more legal and moral obligations to their kids than a coach will. Parent-child relationships will always be more complex than a simple coaching relationship. That's okay! Coaching skills, strategies, and mindsets can still help.

We parents won't ever be just coaches to our kids, but we can try to be aware of how the messages we're trying to send and receive might be getting distorted. We can work to avoid adding extra parenting interference where it doesn't need to be, get rid of natural interference where we can, and acknowledge and accept the interference that we can't change. It's okay if our radio channels have a little bit of static in them. We'll still be able to hear the music.

The Seven Parent-as-Coach Interferences

Let's explore some ways we as parents might minimize or learn to work around each of the seven interferences specifically in goal conversations with our kids.

1. Time

Coaching conversations require mutual consent. Both the coach and the client need to be willing to participate, or the conversation can't happen. If one person tries to force the conversation, they are violating the safety of the space.

Making an appointment with a professional coach is a clear way to signal consent from both parties, but parents rarely have such appointment slots for their kids. Even if parents schedule goal conversations, they will still have many hours of unscheduled time spent with their kids doing activities or just hanging out in the same house. Any moment of this time together can potentially be used for goal conversations. This potential can come across as stress or pressure for kids who may feel like a goal conversation can start at any moment.

Imagine you had a piano teacher who wanted you to practice for an hour each day. Now imagine that piano teacher was living in your house. Would you feel an added sense of pressure to practice that might be changing your motivations? Would you feel nervous or embarrassed every time you missed a day because she was right there watching the whole time? Would you avoid starting conversations with her because you weren't ready to talk about why you haven't practiced yet?

How to Deal with Time Interference

There's nothing to be done about living in the same house and spending a lot of time with our kids. Those are good things for a lot of reasons. But kids will inevitably feel more external pressure about their goals if their goal coach is always nearby.

Here are a few strategies we can use to get our kids to trust that we won't take advantage of all the time we spend together to observe, judge, or talk about how they're handling their goals when they're not ready.

Honor The Grand Pause. The Goals with Kids model has some built-in time isolation with its emphasis on radio silence in The Grand Pause, which includes the Remember, Put Effort into, and Track a Goal steps that kids do all on their own.

Radio silence can be hard for parents. We are used to starting lots of conversations with our kids at the drop of a hat. We are also used to throwing out commands or reminders and expecting to be listened to. "Watch your footing climbing that tree," "Don't forget to look both ways before crossing the street," and "Get dressed, we need to leave in ten minutes," are all necessary and caring parts of parenting. But remember, the goal conversation needs to be a safe space, so commands or thoughts about the specific goals our kids are working on are off-limits except in goal conversations.

Having a thought about our kids' goals doesn't mean we're entitled to say it out loud. Even if that thought might be something useful like a reminder or heartfelt advice, volunteering it without permission interferes with the safe space.

When LeAnn and Nichole first began writing *Goal Getters*, LeAnn was an empty nester, Nichole had three kids at home ages five and under, and they lived in different states. LeAnn was writing and creating Goals with Kids full-time, so it would have been easier for her to call Nichole several times a day with questions or topics of discussion. As they set up their work environment, Nichole requested some boundaries. She agreed to a half-hour video meeting every morning before the kids were up to check in, resolve questions, and talk about who was doing what next. If LeAnn thought of something she wanted to ask or talk about during the day concerning *Goal Getters*, she couldn't call Nichole, but rather had to either wait until the next morning or send a text or email so it wouldn't be forgotten and then wait until the next morning to address it.

It was flexible, and of course important calls were sometimes made during the day. But LeAnn was used to calling her adult kids any moment she happened to have a thought. Without the boundary, LeAnn could have been calling Nichole constantly because she thought about Goals with Kids and *Goal Getters* constantly. Nichole could have felt overly pressured every time LeAnn's number flashed on her cell phone, wondering if she had forgotten something or if LeAnn was checking up on her. She also might have felt anxious that she might get interrupted with a call at any moment, drawing her attention away from her kids and interrupting scheduled things in her life.

We need strategies to deal with thoughts or emotions we have about our kids' efforts during The Grand Pause that still allow us to maintain radio silence. Write them in a journal. Tell your concerns to a tree in the backyard. Bite your tongue and remind yourself when your next goal conversation has been scheduled. Remind yourself how awesome it is your kid is experimenting with being independent. Just make sure that whatever strategy you use doesn't affect your kid at all.

Watch Your Body Language. Verbal comments are not the only way we might violate the safe space in a goal conversation or during The Grand Pause. If we hold back our verbal comments but still roll our eyes, sigh in frustration, or keep watching our kids like a hawk, they might still feel judged anyway. A lot of human communication is nonverbal, and it will be useful to pay attention to the things we may be communicating subconsciously that are interfering with our kids' independent efforts on a goal.

Ask Permission to Start Conversations. When it is time for a goal conversation, we need to get consent from our kids. Coaching consent is implied with a professional coach when a client shows up in the office; the client's physical presence in the space is enough to signal that the conversation can start.

But our kids spend a lot of time in our physical presence besides goal conversations. We don't want them to feel threatened by a looming conversation that might start at any moment. Establishing a pattern of always asking permission to start coaching conversations will help put our kids at ease. We might say, "Hey, is now a good time for a Goal Chat?" or "Are you ready to meet at 6:00 like we planned?"

Then we need to respect whatever our kids say. If we've planned it beforehand, they will most likely be ready to talk. But we might get a response like, "I don't know. I kind of had a bad day. Can we meet tomorrow instead?" People cancel appointments with professionals for various and valid reasons, and the same might happen with our goal conversations. If it becomes a pattern, then talk about it with your kid in a future parenting conversation, but remember that productive goal conversations need to have two willing participants.

Set a Time Limit. Professional coaches have a specific time limit that's enforced by the next client in the waiting room. Parents usually have no such restrictions, but we want to avoid making our kids feel trapped in a conversation they can't see the end of.

If our kids don't have a say in when the conversation ends, it's like inviting them into a room with us, locking it, and keeping the key in our pocket. That's enough to make even the most trusting child a little uncomfortable.

Agreeing with our kids beforehand how long we'll be in the conversation room together, and giving them an emergency key to get out early if they need to, helps them feel safe and autonomous. People are more at ease and willing to enter into a conversation if they can see an exit from it. An exit key can be a simple phrase like, "I'm feeling too angry/afraid/judged to talk about this right now."

In general, the briefer the conversation, the better. Most goal conversations can be done in fifteen minutes. Don't be afraid to end early, but don't go overtime. Try to end when both people are still happy to be there. Leave them laughing, as they say.

2. Location

Professional coaches meet in person with their clients in a location that's comfortable for both people. There usually isn't a desk separating them. There is no audience listening in. There aren't distractions or interruptions. The location is always the same and is only used for coaching conversations. When a client walks into a coach's office, they know what to expect. It's easy to focus on the conversation.

Parents meeting with kids in the home often experience interference because of the location and other members of the family who live there. The home is a public place where other people can walk through and see what's going on. The home is a busy place where parents are often in demand, distracted, and interrupted.

Our brains associate certain activities and mindsets with certain places. It's the reason productivity experts tell people not to work where they sleep. If your brain starts to associate your bed with working on your computer, it will be harder to fall asleep there. Since the only thing we ever do in the coach's office is have coaching conversations, merely walking into the room can help put us in the right frame of mind. But we use our homes for a myriad of different tasks. It's harder to get into and stay in the right mindset for a certain activity if we're in rooms or areas that we usually use for other things.

How to Deal with Location Interference

Make Your Meetings Private. Kids need an assurance of privacy to trust the safe space of a goal conversation and be honest and vulnerable. This means that they will trust us to not share their thoughts and goals with others, but it also means that they need to feel that the conversations are not going to be watched or overheard by other family members or people in the home. We need to conduct our goal conversations with kids in a place where we will not be overheard by others to maintain the safe space. This could mean putting a "Do Not Disturb" sign on a room in our homes, or it could mean having our conversations out of the house.

Guard Your Meeting Time. In goal conversations, our kids should feel important and valued. When we allow interruptions and distractions to draw our focus, it sends the message that we'd rather be doing other things than listening to our kids.

There are some things we can do to prevent interruptions and distractions before our conversations even start. We might need to let other people in the house know that we'll be unavailable for a while. We might need to assign an older child to watch a toddler who is still learning about not interrupting. We should definitely mute our cell phones and ask our kids to do the same.

Try New Locations. Having a special place that you use only for goal conversations can help build useful brain associations and help isolate distractions. Avoid particularly negative brain associations like trying to coach your kids in the same spot you send them or their siblings for a time-out.

The Hunt kids started calling LeAnn's minivan her "office" because so many therapeutic conversations happened in the front seat while driving places. Sometimes, conversations would happen in the car just sitting in the driveway. It didn't matter that no one was going anywhere; it just mattered that the car had become a safe space associated with positive goal conversations.

We can experiment with new places to have conversations with our kids. Sitting in the car. Lying on our backs in the grass or on the trampoline. Walking to a certain landmark and back home. Dragging two chairs to a different place in a room and moving them back afterward. Get creative trying to create brain associations and limit distractions.

Be Side by Side. Goal conversations don't need to be formal interviews done face-to-face over a desk. That can be intimidating and replace the partner nature of a coaching relationship with an expert one. Try having casual conversations while you're doing things side by side, like sitting in a car, going for a walk, or sitting on the couch. Sometimes it's easier to talk when we're not facing the other person. It takes away the pressure of maintaining eye contact and answering immediately. If you're going for a walk and someone takes a minute to think, it's less awkward than if you're both just sitting in chairs across from each other fidgeting. Remember that goal conversations are low-key and laid-back.

3. *Permanence*

The relationship between a professional coach and client is an impermanent one. Clients only use coaches during specific periods in their lives. If they don't like meeting with their coach—maybe they're missing a certain specialty or training, their office is too far away, or their personality isn't a good fit—clients are encouraged to seek other or additional coaches. This offers clients an element of control over their lives and who they ask for help. No one coach is qualified to solve every problem in a client's life, and no one coach is going to be a good fit for every client.

Parents, on the other hand, are bound to their children for life, regardless of personality differences or other issues. Clients can go out and get a new coach whenever they want, but kids can't go out and get a new parent. In that respect, they don't get to choose.

Obviously, despite the interference to coaching conversations, this lifelong connection isn't something we want to change. A strong parental relationship offers innumerable positive benefits for kids, but there are still a few permanence-isolation strategies we can use to lessen the interference when we need to.

How to Deal with Permanence Interference

Know Your Parenting and Coaching Limits. If we are having issues connecting with or understanding our kid, we should try not to take it personally and should know our limits. We don't need to be everything to our kid. We can't be. We are our kid's parent, and that is enough. We will likely be one of the most impactful and long-lasting relationships in our kid's life, but we certainly won't be the only one.

If something comes up in conversation that we are unsure of, we can admit it. A simple, "I don't know much about that right now, let me get back to you" or "I'm not sure I'm the right person for that question, but I know someone who is" can build a lot more trust than hemming and hawing over something outside of our area of expertise.

If we feel there is something lacking in our goal conversations, we can set our own goals to improve ourselves, but we can also seek outside help. It's possible that our spouses connect more easily with our kids and could take over some of the coaching conversations or give us some tips.

Ask Your Kid Who Else They Want to Help Them. Being able to find the leadership we need in any given situation is a valuable skill to give our kids. If we come across an area where we won't be a good mentor or source of information for our kids, we can encourage them to seek help from other trustworthy sources, such as from extended family, neighbors, or youth leaders.

We can offer our own suggestions and ask our kids to think of people on their own. Ask them, "Who do you think you could work with on this?" or "Who would you be comfortable talking with about this?" We can even role-play to help our kids practice approaching these people for help or advice.

4. Complexity

Professional coaches have a well-defined, consistent relationship to guide all their interactions with a client. Both parties always know what to expect and have grown used to the unspoken rules and patterns that have developed in the past.

Parents have much more complicated relationships with their kids. As discussed in chapter 4, parents don different parenting hats as situations call for them; coaching is merely one of those hats. There is no default, consistent relationship rhythm parents and kids will fall into. The details of the relationship are always changing. This means that parents can easily accidentally slip into other hats during a goal conversation. Since these other hats have different rules or patterns associated with them, they can disrupt the safe space of a goal conversation.

Because they can wear the coaching hat every time they deal with their clients, coaches can maintain a singular interest and priority for anything to do with that client: do what is best for the client.

Because parents wear different hats throughout their varied interactions with their kids, their priorities change day to day and moment to moment. Sometimes we make decisions involving our child in the best interest of our child, but sometimes we need to make decisions in the interest of taking care of ourselves or another family member, of getting everyone to a doctor's appointment on time, of our career, or of the financial or practical state of our household. Decisions parents make outside of goal conversations often ripple out to affect their kids.

These shifting, interconnected priorities are an inescapable part of parenting. Our relationships are too complicated and our roles too many for our kids' wishes to continuously be the first priority for every decision that involves them. And because our lives are so complicated and interconnected, it can be hard to limit ourselves to the coaching hat when we can see the big picture.

This complexity is a necessary part of a functioning family, but it's still good for us to be aware of the interference this can cause and what we can do about it in a goal conversation.

How to Deal with Complexity Interference

Pick Your Hat. Having a name to refer to goal conversations can help signal to us and our kids that we're wearing the coaching hat. Our kids will know that a family chore meeting is different from a Goal Time meeting. Especially with young kids, we could have a physical prop to help us remember, like a silly hat we wear only during these conversations.

Apologize for Slip-Ups. It's natural to slip up and slip on a different parenting hat in a goal conversation or the coaching hat during The Grand Pause, especially when it's new. The more we learn to be aware of it, the less often it will happen, but we can't expect to eliminate this problem entirely.

If we notice ourselves bringing rules or priorities from different hats into a coaching conversation, we give our kids a simple explanation and apology. This shows them that we know one of the rules was broken and helps to reestablish trust in the safe space.

Acknowledge and Accept Your Rotating Priority. In the first five hundred years of its use, the word *priority* only had a singular form; the word *priorities* didn't exist. You could only have one priority at a time, even if you had several things you cared about deeply. The thing you were putting your energy toward was your priority at the moment, and the other things waited their turn.

Our modern lives are similar, although we may not realize it. Our top priority is constantly shifting. In his conference talk "O Be Wise," Elder M. Russell Ballard phrased it this way:

> As mortals, we simply cannot do everything at once. Therefore we must do all things "in wisdom and order" (Mosiah 4:27). Often that will mean temporarily postponing attention to one priority in order to take care of another. Sometimes family demands will require your full attention. Other times professional responsibilities will come first. And there will be times when Church callings will come first. Good balance comes in doing things in a timely way and in not procrastinating our preparation or waiting to fulfill our responsibilities until the last minute.[12]

We don't need to feel guilty if we don't give our children our full attention or consideration in every decision. Putting effort, care, and consideration into something we value doesn't mean it's the only thing we value.

Of course, a pattern of never putting our children first will negatively impact our relationships, among other things. But a pattern of always putting our children first will cause similar harm.

5. *Expertise*

Coaches believe that their clients are the experts of their own lives. They don't presume to know about the client's history, hopes, strengths, weaknesses, or anything that the client doesn't tell them. They are cautious about donning the expert hat to offer advice, suggestions, or insights, and they never tell a client what to do. They may share what has worked for them or what research has proven works for a certain percentage of people, but they always leave it up to the client to choose. They know that people are all different and that the best person to make decisions for the client is the client herself. The client is the expert in her own life.

---

12 "O Be Wise," *Ensign* or *Liahona*, Nov. 2006.

Conversely, parents are secondary experts in their children's lives. Especially before children can speak and communicate clearly, parents must insert themselves as secondary experts by noticing and communicating things like preferences, personality traits, emotional triggers, strengths, and weaknesses to other caregivers.

However, as kids grow, their thoughts and experiences grow and develop out of the constant, watchful care of their parents, which can often lead to parents thinking they know their kids better than they do. Parents will sometimes assume they know better and second-guess or undermine their kids' statements of belief, thought, emotion, or intended action. They tell their kids what they should do because they think they know better. But this action takes away opportunities for kids to actually learn if their ideas and actions will work the way they think they will. Parents putting themselves forward in goal conversations as the expert in their kids' lives interferes with the safe conversation space by weakening rapport and autonomy.

How to Deal with Expertise Interference

Ask for Permission to Don the Expert Hat. There are times we may wish to give advice or share a teaching story with our children during a goal conversation, especially if they ask us a direct question to which we have an answer. Before throwing on the expert hat in a goal conversation, we ask our kid if she wants to hear advice or suggestions. A simple, "Can I tell you a story about that?" or "Are you ready to hear some advice now?" will signal to our kid that we are momentarily switching hats. It also gives our kid control over the safe space where she can redirect the conversation if she doesn't want advice.

Our kids might not want advice in a particular moment for a number of reasons. Maybe they are feeling extra vulnerable and aren't ready for a comment that may be perceived as critical. Maybe they are feeling particularly confident and want to try something on their own before getting someone else's input. Whatever the reason, we need to respect our kid's wishes. Remember that when acting as a coach, merely having an idea we think will be helpful doesn't entitle us to bring it up whenever or however we want.

Be a Life Expert, Not a Kid Expert. We don't know everything about our kids. When we think we know better about something our kid thinks or believes about themselves, sometimes we're right and sometimes we're wrong. And we never know which it is until after the fact. Contradicting or questioning our kids' beliefs about themselves makes our kids second-guess themselves too. They may feel less confident or capable of understanding themselves.

We may be less likely to directly questions our kids' beliefs about themselves if we imagine ourselves as a life expert instead of a kid expert. Although we don't know more about our kid than they do, we do know more about life than they do. As older, more experienced people, we have knowledge and experiences that can benefit any young, inexperienced person. Our familiarity with our kids even means we might be better able to guess which stories or pieces of advice would benefit them. If our kids are willing to hear stories or advice about what's worked for us in the past, then we can share them. But we shouldn't presume to tell our kids what they should or shouldn't do in a goal conversation.

Practice Asking Questions. Goal conversations already have some questions built into them that apply to every goal loop, but we don't have to stop there. One of the clearest ways to signal to our kids that they are the experts in their own lives is to ask them questions about themselves and their lives. Actively listening to their answers shows that we don't assume we know the answers already.

Asking questions is also a great way to help our kids think through goals they are going to tackle. Remember, asking questions is like walking them through a math problem rather than just telling them the answer. Ask questions about what's working well in the present to empower them. Ask questions about possible future events to help them visualize obstacles and end points. Ask questions to determine how confident and motivated your kids are about specific goals. Ask questions to learn about your kids' worries and concerns. Ask questions that you would ask yourself if you were trying to tackle the same goal they are attempting. Seeking our kids' input whenever we can will increase their feelings of autonomy and build relationships by teaching us more about them.

6. *Investment*

Coaches don't internalize their clients' words and actions. If their clients fail, they don't assume it was a flaw in their coaching that caused it. They may be sad things didn't turn out better, but they don't decide anything about themselves based on how their clients' actions turned out. They don't take credit for their clients' successes, and they avoid guilt or blame for their failures. This helps their clients take maximum responsibility and ownership of their actions, which increases self-efficacy and autonomy.

This also means that clients can focus on their own needs and desires, uninfluenced by the feelings and reactions of their coaches. Clients don't need to worry about making their coaches proud or letting them down since coaches keep their contributions to the conversation as neutral as possible.

We parents, understandably, are not so impersonal when it comes to our own children. We are responsible for teaching our kids certain things, and one of the ways we know we have successfully taught something to our kids is to see them apply it in their lives. We can literally see ourselves influencing our kids in their speech, mannerisms, and actions, so we often take our kids' success as confirmation of good parenting and their failure as confirmation of a parenting failure.

This emotional investment in our kids' actions can cloud their motivation and muddy the waters of a goal conversation. A parent responding with too much positive, congratulatory emotion can shift kids' motivation in the future. They may choose goals that will get them that congratulation and avoid conversations where they feel they haven't earned it. If a parent responds with too much negative emotion, like guilt or shame, it can also shift the kids' motivation and make them feel responsible for their parent's feelings and want to avoid conversations where they feel they are letting their parent down. Strong emotional reactions might come naturally to parents responding to goals in the moment, but it can violate the safe space of a goal conversation, where kids should be able to lead without being burdened by their parents' sentiments.

How to Deal with Investment Interference

Limit Positive and Negative Reactions within the Conversation. In a coaching conversation, parents seek to get their kids' reactions to progress, success, and failure. Our interpretation of their efforts can taint their own interpretation. If a kid is excited to report some progress that we show disappointment in, we are projecting our own emotions instead of honoring our kid's emotions. We can't assume that our emotions will always match. We need to get their view of the matter without superimposing our own over it. When they tell us something tied to a positive emotion, ask them questions to let them retell the story and relive the positive experience.

Maintain a calm, curious, warm interest, but avoid increasing the energy level in your voice and body language too much. Use congratulatory language like, "It sounds like that went really well for you" and "It looks like your effort really paid off." Avoid extreme language that makes what your kid tells you seem more meaningful than it really is like, "It sounds like you had the best day ever" or "That's super disappointing."

If we need a place to share our positive or negative emotions about goal conversations, we can write them in a journal or tell our spouse if it seems appropriate.

Don't Judge Your Parenting by Your Kids. Remember that bad behavior from our kids may be a symptom of bad parenting, but it could just as easily be attributed to the kids' agency or need for new skills. The same goes for good behavior we take as signs of parenting success. We judge our parenting based on the actions we take and can control and not the outcomes we don't. We can pray for revelation on which areas we are doing enough in and which areas we could stand to work on more.

7. *Obligation*

Coaches working in a professional capacity have few legal or moral obligations to their clients. Most are legally obligated to report abuse or an intent to harm oneself or others. The argument could be made that coaches are morally obligated to strive to maintain the safe space surrounding their conversations with their clients. However, these coaches aren't at all obligated to make sure their clients achieve milestones, become happier, or have positive life circumstances. The client-coach relationship is, at its heart, an honest business transaction.

Conversely, parents have extensive legal and moral obligations to their kids. Legal obligations include providing for a child's basic emotional and physical needs such as food, clothing, housing, medical care, protection from abuse, and education. Parents' moral obligations vary based on upbringing and religion, but some common examples are maintaining a supportive, strong relationship with our kids; teaching them rules of civil behavior and manners; teaching them to be good citizens; teaching them basic moral character traits like honesty, integrity, and hard work; and working to build and maintain a lifestyle that will continue to allow us to provide those things for our kids. Most people would agree that once we bring a child into this world or into our family, it's our duty to show up for and do right by that child, however that may look for us.

Tending to all these important obligations as parents contributes to all the types of coaching interference we've previously discussed: time, location, permanence, complexity, expertise, and investment.

As we've mentioned before, a certain level of interference due to these obligations is unavoidable. However, parents sometimes make this interference worse by misinterpreting their obligations or taking them too far. Society, public opinion, fads, or critical comments from family members or neighbors can warp in our minds what is necessary and what is optional. We might see other people following personal promptings and implementing good ideas and feel that we should do the same in our lives or families. We might judge other parents critically and eventually start criticizing ourselves too, holding ourselves and everyone around us to an impossible standard.

The Lord warned his people in Deuteronomy 4:2, "Ye shall not add unto the word which I command you, neither shall ye diminish ought from it." We can't ignore our responsibilities, but we shouldn't blow them out of proportion either.

How to Deal with Obligation Interference

Don't Let Your "Shoulds" Get Out of Hand. Study the shoulds we have hanging over us, the things we feel guilty about not doing or that we are doing out of a sense of obligation. Why do we feel that obligation? Is it worth dedicating ourselves to, or is it an obligation that we or the people around us have blown out of proportion?

These overextensions of obligations are all around us. Parents might assume that their obligation to help their children pursue the education available to them means they need to homeschool full-time or go into massive debt to fund a college degree. They might assume that their responsibility to feed their children is also a responsibility to eat only organic, healthy foods. They might assume that their responsibility to provide an adequate living space means they need to scrub the house from top to bottom every day.

While there's nothing wrong with any of the parenting choices listed above, they aren't universal parenting obligations. Good, moral parenting will look a little different for every family. Many of the core principles will be the same, but the execution of those principles varies based on each family's resources, desires, and circumstances. We can get rid of a lot of guilt if we isolate the principles and the things we really are legally obligated to do. Our obligations are often less than we think.

Keep Calm and Parent On

Now that we understand some of the things that interfere with wearing the coaching hat as a parent, let's put that hat back on the rack for a moment. Let's revisit the three options we have as parents that we discussed earlier: offer the goal to our kids, stand strong, or let it go. We took a break after discussing how and why to offer goals to our kids to discuss how to be effective goal coaches as parents when they accept them. Now let's explore our options when our kids refuse a goal we offer.

Imagine there's a goal you've offered to your kid a half dozen times, in every way you can think of. It could be something that you know they need to do to keep the house functioning, something you know they need to learn for their future, or even just something you think they'll really enjoy. You'd love for them to adopt the goal so you can slip on your coaching hat and help them through it, but it's just not sticking. What's a parent to do?

When we decide to stop offering a goal to our kids, it's time to slip on the parenting hat. The parenting hat is calm, loving, and strong. It differs from the coaching hat in several important ways. While wearing the parenting hat, we can discipline our children or enforce family rules. We can teach and offer advice and counsel. The parenting hat can do a hundred other things besides, and it's up to us and God to determine the lay of the land and decide how to use the parenting hat in any given situation.

One thing we do not control is our kids' actions. We can't *make* anyone do anything. We can create environments that encourage behaviors that we want, but our leverage ends at the feet of our kids. It's a good idea to take a look at our kids' environments and ask, "What am I contributing to the environment that makes this kid think this behavior is okay?" As parents our behavior often feeds into the problem we are trying to solve. When we think about our own behavior, we may discover simple changes we can make to influence the outcome.

When our kids refuse a goal we offer them, we get to decide whether we're going to stand strong or let it go. If we let it go, we decide to drop the goal. If we stand strong, we adopt the goal as our own and work through our own goal loops as a goal setter.

LeAnn was going through a rough parenting time for several months trying to figure out how to gain control of some difficult, rude, sometimes out-of-control teenage behavior. It felt like the teens were in a new stage, had the upper hand, and kept getting the best of her with rude words and entitled demands, and she felt powerless and frustrated. Each time one of the kids would say or do something that normally would provoke an argument, LeAnn would grab her journal, go outside, and lie on the trampoline to ponder, pray, calm down, and try to figure things out. Everyone knew to leave Mom alone if she was on the trampoline because she was angry and didn't want to be bothered. She started writing whatever ideas came to her mind and possible actions she could do next time this situation came up.

By the time LeAnn wrote a few ideas outside the heat of the moment, she had calmed herself. Knowing she had options, that she was the parent, and that this imbalance of power was temporary kept her calm until she could figure it out. She owned the goals that were hers and thought about what actions she could control rather than focus on her kids' behavior that she couldn't. She almost always chose to let it go but spent some time coming up with stand strong strategies she could use later.

Parents don't like to feel trapped. When we feel powerless and anxious, we don't do our best parenting. Our best parenting is done when we are feeling calm, secure, and loving. This doesn't mean weak or passive. It means strong and active but maybe in ways we aren't used to seeing.

We can find comfort in the Serenity Prayer: "God grant me the serenity to accept the things I cannot change, courage to change the things I can, and wisdom to know the difference." Identifying these different categories in our lives can help us stay calm and serene, something we sorely need when wearing the parenting hat. Just because we can change something doesn't mean that we have to, but there is peace in knowing which is which.

Keep Calm and Stand Strong

The number of things we can control might surprise us. We control how the different areas of our home are used and what furniture is in them, who can use the car, where we will drive people, what food is in the fridge, what birthday and Christmas presents people get from us, what cell phones and data plans we pay for, and a thousand other things.

Our kids are *entitled* to none of these things. They are entitled to our love, safety, something to eat, something to wear, and something to shelter them from the elements. Other than that—everything else is a blessing we provide when we decide. Remember when we said earlier that our obligations are fewer than we think? That means that our leverage is more than we think. Our power is more than we think.

Leverage is the power or ability to influence people and their decisions. It's a tool to use in negotiations. It's a way to try and convince people to do what we want or need them to do.

Parents using none of their power might look like providing their kids constant chauffeuring, a personal chef, room-cleaning services, the latest models of cell phones and laptops, and anything else the kids may ask for, regardless of their behavior.

Parents using every bit of power they could might look like only providing their kids a mattress in their bedroom, a PB&J sandwich for every meal, and a change of clothes in the morning until the kid starts following the family policies.

Parents using none of their power become resentful, doormat parents with entitled children. Parents using all of their power with a heart of anger become tyrannical parents, while parents using all of their power with a heart of peace are parents standing strong in an apparently extreme situation.

Neither of these extremes is sustainable. Either the parents or the kids will eventually grow resentful of their ultimate lack of power and lash out.

We don't need to use all our power, but we do need to understand it. We as parents can find an intentional middle ground to handle problems and new seasons in our kids' lives. We want to understand the power we have so we don't misuse it. Using our power as a parent the wrong way—such as out of anger or frustration instead of serenity—can hurt our children and our relationships. When we know what we are capable of, we know what to be cautious of.

We also need to be aware of when our leverage changes. As an example, let's explore the question, "How do I get my kids to wear their seat belts?" On an average afternoon, we might have the leverage to pull the car over and calmly read a book in the front seat until they comply, even if it takes an hour.

But if you're already late for your brother's wedding, you don't have that leverage anymore. You can request that your kids put their seat belts on, but threatening to wait until they do will only make you feel angry and powerless because you're trying to use leverage that you don't have. It's no wonder that parents in situations like this often yell, bribe, threaten, manhandle the seat belt themselves, or drive their kids to the wedding seat beltless. They need what they need now! Long-term, we have a lot of consistent leverage, but noticing when our leverage shifts will help us stay calm and see what we can control and what we can't in specific situations and act accordingly.

Some parents feel uncomfortable using their power. We may be scared of confrontation, of being called or feeling like a tyrant, or of backlash from friends or family who feel judged by our decisions or think we're being unreasonable. We may be scared of ruining our relationships with our kids. One parent working with a counselor to resolve her daughter's drug use worried that if she enforced rules at home, her daughter might run away. "If I enforce rules, I might lose her," she told the counselor. The counselor helped her see that allowing her daughter's entitled behavior was enabling her drug use and her destructive habits in family relationships. In some ways, she'd already lost her.

Some parents hide behind things to avoid standing strong in their parenthood and owning the things they want or need. Some parents only stand strong when they believe morality is on their side and that they are only doing things that everyone should be doing. Some parents don't stand strong because they want their kids to be independent, not realizing that having some boundaries and rules is essential to true independence.

For some parents, if their lives are functioning pretty well, needing to wield power won't even occur to them. But for every parent, there comes a moment where they get frustrated and angry because they can't get their kids to do what they need them to in the here and now or to prepare for their future.

If we choose to Keep Calm and Stand Strong to get our kids to do something they don't want to do, here are some tools and principles to consider.

Find Your "No Matter What" Reason

Now that we know just how much power we have over the environment in our homes and families, let's explore what might push you to use it. What's your "no matter what" reason? What bad behavior or life choices from your kids might push you to use all your power to correct them, even to the point where you may risk the relationship? Metaphorically speaking, what hill are you willing to die on?

Some parents can't easily think of an answer to this question, but one of the strongest "no matter what" reasons is the well-being of the other people in the family. Parents need to consider if their efforts to save one child are jeopardizing the experiences of everyone else in the household. "You're ruining everyone else's lives, and I will not allow that, no matter what" is a statement of power.

Get Clear on What You Need

When communicating with our kids, we need to be crystal clear about what we expect from them. Using techniques like reflective listening and naming emotions can help both parties stay calm, but reiterating our basic need will help our kids eventually realize that they need to pay attention to it.

Here's an example conversation about taking out the garbage that a parent might have with a child. Pay attention to the reflective listening techniques and how many times the parent clearly states what he needs.

> **Parent**: I feel cheated when I do my chores and you don't do your chore of taking out the trash. I need to have a functioning and non-smelling kitchen. Will you please take out the trash?
>
> **Kid**: But it smells and it's too full now!
>
> **Parent**: So you don't like the smell and you're worried about how to handle the job since it's too full?
>
> **Kid**: Yeah.
>
> **Parent**: Well, I feel cheated when I do my chores and you don't find a way to do yours. I need to have a functioning and non-smelling kitchen.
>
> **Kid**: Well, it's not fair. I have to get another bag and touch the gross stuff so it doesn't spill all over.
>
> **Parent**: So you feel unfairly treated?
>
> **Kid**: Yeah. I do.
>
> **Parent**: It's your job to do the trash. When you wait too long, it gets full and then the job is unpleasant.
>
> **Kid**: Yeah, I know.
>
> **Parent**: I need to have a functioning and non-smelling kitchen.
>
> **Kid**: Okay, I'll take out the stupid trash.

In this example, the parent stayed calm and listened to the kid's words but stood firm in what he needed from his kid. In our lives, these needs could be anything from "I need to have a peaceful living room" to "I need to be at church thirty minutes early for a meeting." Owning our own goals and being able to tell our kids exactly what we need from them is a powerful thing.

Get Clear on Your Policies

Policies are clear statements of what behaviors we expect from our children, often tied to privileges we can use as leverage. These are not punishments or threats. They are not created or wielded in anger or frustration. They are the firm ground we need to stand on as parents. These are ways we create the environments that our children navigate. Family rules are part of that environment. A good fill-in-the-blank policy generator to start with is this:

- I provide (leverage) for kids who (do desired behavior).

Here are some examples.

- I provide cell phones for kids who go to school.
- I provide rides to the mall for kids who finish their homework.

Of course, policies don't always have to follow this pattern. Here are a few more examples.

- In this family, kids who don't brush their teeth pay to get their own cavities filled.
- In this house, kids who leave their shoes all over the house only get one pair of shoes.

Policies don't need to have the leverage explicitly in them. A simple reminder to our kids that "In the public areas of this house, we have a dress code" or "After dinner, we each wash our own dishes" might be enough to get them to adapt their behavior to the expectation.

Parents attach leverage to policies that are being tested or rejected by their kids. If kids aren't pushing against the policy, then there's not a need to escalate. We create policies for problems we encounter where talking isn't working. We don't attach a consequence for every little thing we request from our kids. A good relationship with our kids can do a lot of policy work for us.

Policies Aren't Universal

Most of the policies we make will be unique to our families. We can own our stewardship, the personality and preferences of our family members, and our circumstances. If we let our kids do things that drive us crazy, even if they're not objectively bad or sinful things, resentment will build and weaken us as a parent. Just because we choose to do or try something does not imply that we think everyone should do or try it.

There doesn't have to be a moral imperative propping up our policies. We are strong enough to hold them up on our own.

There doesn't need to be an obvious connection between the behavior we want and the leverage we use. We aren't limited to only food-related consequences if we want our kid to finish their dinner. Don't be afraid to get creative.

LeAnn's sister went on a Travel for Youth, EFY-style trip and asked the seventeen-year-old youth there if they had rules and limits on their cell phones and what they were. Seven out of the eight kids there had cell phone policies to follow, and they were all different. Many parents recognize the need to make policies for their kids. We don't need to be paralyzed by making sure our policies match up with other peoples' policies. Our personal and family policies are ours alone to own.

Policies Aren't Personal

When we make policies and communicate them to our kids, we need to make sure we aren't directing them at our kids personally. Be careful of using accusative or threatening "you" language. It's the difference between telling an angry kid, "I don't provide cell phones for kids who don't go to school" and telling them, "If you don't go to school, I'm taking away your phone!"

Using accusative or threatening language triggers the fight-or-flight response and can draw people into arguments—something we want to avoid as parents striving to keep a calm and centered mindset. "You" language is like wielding a sword at your kids instead of explaining to them the laws of the environment around them, like the law of gravity. The law of gravity doesn't pick on specific people; it just is. Personal or family policies don't pick on specific people; they just are. It's not personal at all; it's just policy.

Using Policies in Coaching Conversations

This same "it's not personal; it's just policy" idea also allows us as parents to bring policies into the coaching conversation in a way that still honors autonomy.

Let's say your kid has a goal to be a professional video game player when he grows up. He's done some research and knows that the professionals play games at least fifteen hours a week, so he wants to make that his goal. Most parents would naturally wish that their kids would choose a more productive goal, but with the coaching hat on, we just let him own his goal. However, if you have family policies in place that say kids can play one hour of video games each night if their homework is done by 7:00, then you can bring up that policy. That way it's not you, the coach, arguing with your kid about why he should pick a different goal.

It's you, the coach, helping the kid understand the environment around him and brainstorming ways to navigate it. You're not threatening; you're reminding him of family policy and asking how he plans to deal with it in his goal efforts. You might end that conversation talking about prioritizing homework so he at least gets his one hour in each night or talking about how he could make a proposal in the next family council to get more time on Saturdays.

Don't *create* policies in a goal conversation while you are wearing the coaching hat, but don't shy away from the reality of how your kid needs to navigate around existing ones when pursuing goals. Kids can't change policies just because they have a goal. If you need a new policy, it's okay to take time to develop it. Just say something like, "I don't know my policy on that right now. Let me think about it and get back to you."

Have a Heart of Peace

Standing strong in our parenthood requires a heart of peace, not a heart of war. Good parenting is always rooted in a place of love. Don't make policies, decisions, or ultimatums in the heat of the moment when emotions are clouding your judgment. Take time to find a heart of peace after the situation and brainstorm ways to address the problem the next time. Make and explain policies when you're calm and confident in your decision.

This means that we as parents may need to remove ourselves from situations that are getting out of hand so we don't do or say things we'll regret later. Walking away is not the same as losing an argument. A simple statement like, "I need some time to calm down and think about this on my own" is all you need to say before leaving.

Kids are intuitive. If we make or enforce policies with a heart of war—if we are angry, if we are seeking revenge, if we are feeling bitter and resentful and powerless—our kids will be able to tell, and it will weaken our relationship with them. When our kids get angry and might be trying to pick a fight, we can strive to maintain an unfightable disposition and calmly reiterate our policies, our needs, and our love for our kids. Making policies work for us short-term and long-term requires a calm and loving heart.

Think about the kinds of things we are trying to get our kids to do: pick up their shoes, attend class so they graduate, practice piano, stop regularly hitting their sibling, get off drugs, or take out the trash. The principles are the same regardless of the intensity of the need. It can be helpful to imagine whatever we are struggling with as just one piece of stewardship that will belong to our kids eventually as an adult, and we just want them to start dealing with it now. It makes it easier to explain things to our kids.

We can also ask ourselves if our kids really need this skill as an adult. What would their lives look like if they never learned to pick up their shoes, practice the piano, or get off drugs? There are some things we need to expect from our kids, but because so much distress is caused by unmet expectations, we can resolve other problems by simply changing our expectations and finding new ways to live peacefully with the circumstance.

Build Confidence

Standing strong in situations or around people we usually yield to can feel uncomfortable at first. We may be accused of or feel like we are being unreasonable. When such accusations or feelings arise, here are some strategies that can bolster our confidence.

1. Pray for the Lord's guidance and assurance. He can help us identify ways to improve and ways we're already doing great.
2. Counsel with our spouse or a friend we trust and ask them if they feel we are being too extreme. They may be able to give us insight into the situation, although it's still our prerogative to ignore their advice.
3. Check the balance of power in our lives. We can't get everything we want, but we can't get nothing we want either. Aim for a middle ground.
4. Make the policy a headline and see how it sounds. Would a newspaper headline that read, "Local mom won't provide cell phone to kid who won't go to school" really sound that bad?
5. Practice, practice, practice. When we try things that are new, we often feel awkward and unsure of ourselves. The more we practice standing strong, the more of a feel we'll get for it. We can ask the three evaluating questions after each interaction with our kids and learn how to tweak our approach and notice times we may have gone overboard. Don't expect to know how to stand strong immediately; learning it is a process.

Our Kids Control the Outcome

After seeing the power in standing strong in our parenthood, let's end on a note of reality: all the leverage in the world used by the most caring and loving parent can't make kids do something they don't want to do. Even with strong, loving policies in place, our kids might choose not to comply. The covenant path is filled with loving policies that people may choose not to follow. That's the power of agency.

If our kid chooses to suffer the consequences of our policies, that doesn't mean our parenting or policies are bad. Remember the Serenity Prayer: "God grant me the serenity to accept the things I cannot change, courage to change the things I can, and wisdom to know the difference." We need to create policies that we can find serenity in no matter the outcome. We can come to terms with our kids not performing a behavior we want and decide what we are going to do when that happens. We can change the environment around our kids to encourage certain behaviors, but we cannot control our kids' actions. We can be peaceful and calm in the knowledge that we are being good stewards of what is within our control.

If our children insist on leaving our homes like the Prodigal Son, we need to respect their agency. We can't go search the cities night and day to drag them back, promising we'll change anything they want as long as they stay. But if they choose to come back and abide by the policies that we've put in place to preserve our home environment and relationships, we can welcome them back with compassion and love, like the father of the Prodigal Son.

So You Want Your Kids to Brush Their Teeth . . .

When we choose to stand strong, we adopt the goal and start our own goal loop to figure out a new environment that will encourage the behaviors we want. We don't know at the start which strategies will work, if any, so we probably need to try a lot of different things. We can get hundreds of ideas for nearly any parenting problem from parenting books, blogs, and classes, just to name a few places.

Let's imagine what it might look like to do two months of parenting goal loops trying to get your kids to brush their teeth every night.

- Day 1: I tried introducing the goal to my kids by giving them a chart to fill in every day, but they didn't want to.
- Day 3: I researched things about tooth decay and tried introducing the goal again by showing my kids pictures of rotten teeth. They thought it was interesting, accepted the goal, and brushed their teeth tonight.
- Day 4: I had them pick out a new toothbrush at the store.
- Day 8: My kids haven't brushed their teeth for three days. I demonstrated good tooth brushing form so they'd know exactly how to do it and offered the goal again. They said they'd rather work on their soccer goal.
- Day 14: I'm going to brush my teeth in my kids' bathroom while they're getting ready for bed so they see my example.
- Day 23: We went to the dentist and my kids had a few cavities, so I'm choosing to stand strong. Our family is going to have a zero-sugar policy for people who don't brush their teeth every night.
- Day 26: I realized that I can't control what my kids eat out of the house, but I'm standing strong by putting all the sugary foods really high in the pantry so my kids need my help to get them down.

- Day 29: It's really frustrating for me to have to get all the food down whenever my tooth-brushing kids want it, so I'm standing strong by not buying really sugary cereals until our whole family has good tooth-brushing habits.
- Day 41: I tried not brushing my teeth for a whole day and talking to my kids face-to-face so they'd see my yucky mouth and smell my bad onion breath. We had a conversation about how they didn't like it and how their mouth hygiene might be affecting those around them.
- Day 42: This goal is causing more contention than it's worth, so I'm going to let it go for now.
- Day 52: This issue keeps coming up, and I feel ready to try again. I'm going to try brushing my teeth in their bathroom again because that worked some of the time. This time I'll play the same song every time to try to create a trigger for them in the future.

Standing strong in our parenthood and creating policies are tools we can use in our goal loops; they're not the entire loop. And like goal loops, there's no shame in letting something go. If a policy we set backfires in unexpected ways, we didn't just fail—we learned something. We can choose to back off standing strong whenever we want to or need to. Maybe our leverage changed. Maybe our priorities changed. Ask the three evaluating questions about the policy we tried and work from there. As long as we're clear in communicating with our kids, we can change policies as we see fit without regret.

Keep Calm and Let It Go

Parents who know how to stand strong in their parenthood don't do it all the time. It's only one of the parenting skills we need to create a safe, functioning space to live and create good family relationships.

It's up to the parents to decide when to make a goal to get their kids to do something they don't want to do. It might be worth it for one parent to stand strong about getting the kid to go to church each week, and not worth it for another parent to stand strong on getting the kid to go to seminary. To make decisions like that, look at the likelihood for success. Look at the importance of the behavior. Look at what's at risk. Pray for personal revelation. We decide what we want because our desires and what we have energy for factors into the equation as well.

One of the moms in LeAnn's workshop talked about how she wished her daughter who was leaving for college next week would have learned to pick up after herself so she'd be a better roommate. But as she reflected, she realized she had to let go of that goal because it wasn't worth harming her relationship with her daughter and she wasn't likely to make progress in the one week she had left in the home. Her daughter would work it out with her roommates.

It might be useful to have a place to write down goals we decide to let go and why. It's natural over time to forget why we made certain decisions. If we write down our reasons, when a goal reoccurs, we can look back and see if the situation really has changed or if the reasons we had for letting it go are still valid.

When we are deciding whether to stand strong in our parenting or to let go of something we want our kids to do, we can't make the mistake of thinking we are caving or giving in if we decide to let it go. We can choose to stand strong in our parenting only for things that are truly disrupting our ability to live together as a family in a reasonably peaceful way.

In a speech given at BYU, Wendy Watson Nelson said, "If you are the voice of authority in someone else's life, you are also the ears of authority. You need to listen. . . . There is an extra level of healing that occurs when ears of authority are able to hear the exquisiteness of a loved one's pain and joy. Change is accelerated!"[13] We parents are the ultimate voice of authority in our kids' lives. When we know when to use our ears of authority to truly listen and coach and when to use our voice of authority to stand strong, we can balance our parenting needs of getting cooperation in the present, preparing our kids for independent futures, and maintaining loving relationships.

---

13 "Change: It's Always a Possibility!" (Brigham Young University devotional, Apr. 7, 1998), speeches.byu.edu.

PART II
INTRODUCTION

WE'VE COVERED A LOT OF goal-setting ground. Part I covered the whole Goals with Kids model with its wagon wheel of seven steps, three conversations, and three roles.

Now we move to the principles underlying goals and goal setting. How do goals actually work? What is improvement really like? What works and what doesn't? How do we motivate kids, and how do we manage the emotional roller coaster that comes along with goals?

One thing that makes accomplishing goals hard is the conflicting advice we get about goal setting and the answers to these questions. For example, some researchers recommend choosing small goals while others recommend just the opposite, choosing challenging goals. To sort out which advice to take, we need to learn to understand principles hidden in the advice so we can apply it to our lives and our goal setting.

Elder Richard G. Scott clearly describes what principles are and how we find them. He said, "Principles are concentrated truth, packaged for application to a wide variety of circumstances. A true principle makes decisions clear even under the most confusing and compelling circumstances. It is worth great effort to organize the truth we gather to simple statements of principle." He also said, "As you seek spiritual knowledge, search for principles. Carefully separate them from the detail used to explain them."[14] President Boyd K. Packer also emphasized the importance of principles: "There are principles of the gospel underlying every phase of Church administration. These are not explained in the handbooks. They are found in the scriptures. They are the substance of and the purpose for the revelations. Procedures, programs, the administrative policies, even some patterns of organization are subject to change. . . . But the *principles*, the *doctrines*, *never* change."[15]

---

14 "Acquiring Spiritual Knowledge," *Ensign*, Nov. 1993.
15 "Principles," *Ensign*, Mar. 1985.

In essence, principles are little nuggets of truth that rule how goals operate in our lives. Principles are what allowed LeAnn and Nichole to write this book beginning a year before the Church changes to the children and youth goal programs were fully rolled out. They had no inside information and welcomed the changes and announcements at the same time as everyone else. They spent a lot of time on the childrenandyouth.churchofjesuschrist.org website for the year before the changes were implemented, reading or listening to everything that was posted.

But mostly they studied principles. They pulled goal principles from positive psychology research, from the scriptures, from Church and business leaders, and from experience. They had faith that, whatever the Church changes brought, President Packer was right: the procedures, programs, policies, and patterns of organization of the Church will change, but the principles of effective goal setting, like principles of the gospel, never change.

When we separate out the principles underneath what makes goals work, we have a better idea of how to start goals and more options when we're stuck in the middle of them.

When we learn true principles, we can begin to apply them to our goal-setting lives. As our kids set goals and as we, their parents, coach them, there are seven underlying principles that, when understood, will make us better goal coaches and goal setters. These principles are found in the following seven chapters and are key to successful, agile, engaged, home-centered goal setting with our children and youth.

CHAPTER 6
PRINCIPLE #1—EXPECTATIONS
HOW KNOWING WHERE OUR GOALS COME FROM HELPS US CHOOSE BETTER GOALS

One autumn evening, Nichole was reading the Book of Mormon on the temple grounds. Her three young kids were home with her husband, and she was spending some peaceful moments soaking in the beautiful, flower-filled, weed-free landscaping. She began to feel bad that her yard didn't meet the temple ground's standards. The beautiful nature there brought her such peace; shouldn't her own yard try and do the same? *Why isn't my yard as beautiful as the temple's?* she wondered.

As she sat there, she felt a clear impression in the form of an answer to her question: "I don't ask this of you. I don't ask this of most people. I may ask this of other people, and you may ask this of yourself, but I do not ask it of you." She felt such a sense of relief. She realized that the temple grounds have a crew to maintain them and have a different purpose and layout than a house's yard. She also realized that she doesn't find great joy or accomplishment in yard work and gardening, and she was fine with that. As she recorded the experience later, it taught her that we can admire another person's success at a goal without getting jealous or copying that person's goal over into our lives.

When we think about goals and brainstorming, knowing who, if anyone, is expecting it or asking it of us helps us and our kids decide whether we should discard the goal or choose to own it for ourselves. The expectation that we set certain goals can come from a lot of different places.

Sources of Goals

Some goals we ask of ourselves. These goals are important only if we think they are. We might want to do a triathlon or take a college class. Our kids might want to join the school band, learn how to do hand-lettering, or enter the spelling bee. We ask these goals of ourselves often because we are "anxiously engaged in a good cause" and doing many things of our own free will (D&C 58:27).

Some goals other people ask of us. People give us advice, counsel, suggestions, or opinions on how we should do things. When we brainstorm with our kids, some of these ideas end up on their list. They might get ideas from coaches, teachers, friends, or teammates. Some of their ideas will come from things they know we expect them to do. Even if someone else suggests a goal, we can decide to make it our own by putting our agency behind it and choosing it for ourselves. We can adapt the idea to better fit us and create a goal we are willing and able to do.

We don't have to choose every idea someone else suggests, but it is a good idea to try some of them. It's a balance. Always implementing others' suggestions diminishes our sense of identity and agency. Never implementing others' suggestions robs us of opportunities to try new things or work through blind spots we would not have noticed on our own.

Not every person who suggests a goal has stewardship or interest in our lives. Help your kids consider who might be asking them to do things, why they might be asking, whether they have the right to ask, and if they have their best interest at heart.

Some goals come from groups we belong to. Leaders of our teams, choirs, classrooms, or other groups sometimes set goals for the whole group. To help kids sort through group goals, ask some questions. Who created the goal? Why do you think they created that goal? Do you want to support the goal? Remind them that they don't have to do someone else's goal unless it's something they agreed to when they joined the group. We can help our kids understand that putting their agency behind a group goal makes it their own. Group goals not only increase practice time or build skills, but they can also help a group bond and bring them closer together. Goals can change the culture of a group by adding purpose or influencing how the group behaves.

In 2018, President Nelson challenged youth to join a group experiment goal. He suggested trying a seven-day fast from social media. He then suggested thinking about how the experiment went and paying attention to how you felt. Thousands of youth took that counsel and chose that goal for themselves. He later challenged the girls, young women, and adult women to a big goal. He suggested reading the Book of Mormon before the end of the year, just three months away. Thousands of girls, young women, and adult women chose to make that goal their own. Thousands of others chose not to make that goal their own, and everyone had a different experience with the group goal.

Some goals life asks of us. There are some things we just need to step up and do because life or our circumstances requires it of us. We all have things we don't choose in our lives as a result of living in a mortal world with imperfect bodies and imperfect people. Life will ask us to deal with things that cause us pain, discomfort, and difficulty. Life will ask us to deal with other people's careless or malevolent actions that may have hurt us, personal trials, challenges like the death of a loved one, or loneliness after moving to a new place. We might face health issues out of our control or disabilities that make certain things difficult for us. Every day we rub shoulders with all sorts of people, including those we disagree with. Life throws us surprises we have no way of predicting, and that may drastically affect our goals. Life asks different things of different people. Ask your kids what life may be asking of them right now so they can choose a goal to address it.

Some of our goals come from commandments, things God asks everyone to do. Elder David A. Bednar teaches us that there are two kinds of commandments: public and private. Public, shared commandments are connected to ordinances, while private, individual commandments are connected to revelation.[16] For example, baptism is an ordinance that is connected to public, shared commandments. Missionaries ask every person who is baptized if she is willing to keep public, shared commandments, including the law of chastity, tithing, the Word of Wisdom, weekly sacrament meetings, and a willingness to serve others.

There are also private, individual commandments, which are the promptings we receive personally from God. Elder Larry R. Lawrence talked about these kinds of personal commandments in his talk "What Lack I Yet?" He gave examples of tiny personal commandments like, "clean your room" and "stop complaining."[17] When the Lord gives us a personal commandment, the timing is important. Also, because the Lord won't give us more than we can bear, personal commandments tend to be very specific and doable, though they may stretch us out of our comfort zone. A young mother said, "Goals should not be so rigid and fixed that you do not listen to the whisperings of the Spirit. Keep your hearts and minds open to know the overriding will of the Lord in your lives."[18]

When we think of these private, individual commandments, we sometimes think of stories we've heard of someone being at the right house at 4:00 p.m. on the last day of their mission. We can get the idea that God is grooming and preparing us for that one moment when He needs us and we can step up and shine. In truth, God needs us now, and we are quite capable right at this moment to assist God in His work. He knows who we are and how we can help. He will prompt us right in the middle of our days to do things we are already prepared to do.

---

16 See David A. Bednar, "Heartfelt and Willing Obedience" (Brigham Young University—Idaho devotional, June 27, 2002); byui.edu.
17 "What Lack I Yet?" *Ensign* or *Liahona*, Nov. 2015.
18 Quoted in James E. Faust, "Womanhood: The Highest Place of Honor," *Ensign*, May 2000.

Sister Michelle D. Craig described the individualized nature of these personal commandments God asks us to do:

> Nephi, the brother of Jared, and even Moses all had a large body of water to cross—and each did it differently. Nephi worked "timbers of curious workmanship" [1 Nephi 18:1]. The brother of Jared built barges that were "tight like unto a dish" [Ether 6:5–8]. And Moses "walked upon dry land in the midst of the sea" [Exodus 14:29].
>
> They each received personalized direction, tailored to them, and each trusted and acted. The Lord is mindful of those who obey and, in the words of Nephi, will "prepare a way for [us to] accomplish the thing which he commandeth" [1 Nephi 3:7]. Note that Nephi says, "*a* way"—not "*the* way."
>
> Do we miss or dismiss personal errands from the Lord because He has prepared "a way" different from the one we expect?[19]

As we sit with our kids to brainstorm goals, sorting out who's asking us to do the goal makes the goal and the motivation clearer and allows our kids to put their agency behind it or toss it out.

Hovering Expectations

When we brainstorm goals, it's not always clear who is asking us to do the goal. We can have "hovering expectations" that don't seem tied to any specific source. Hovering expectations are thoughts in our own mind that we should do something. We can't really point to who is telling us to do it; we just feel like we should. We should have an annual Christmas light display. We should read our scriptures every day. We should have top sheets on our beds. We should take a language in high school. We should wear a dress to church. We should celebrate our anniversaries. We should make cakes for birthdays. We should bring homemade rolls to the potluck. The books on our shelves should be organized by color. Our belts should match our shoes. Where do these hovering expectations come from?

Throughout our lives we hear inspiring stories. These stories are memorable and powerful and contain buried treasure of true principles. When we hear the story, the true principle resonates with us, we are inspired by it, and we adopt the principle as an ideal for ourselves and what we want to be like in our lives. Principles enrich our lives as we apply them in our own unique ways.

---

19 "Spiritual Capacity," *Ensign* or *Liahona*, Nov. 2019.

Elder Richard G. Scott said, "As you seek spiritual knowledge, search for principles. Carefully separate them from the detail used to explain them. Principles are concentrated truth, packaged for application to a wide variety of circumstances. A true principle makes decisions clear even under the most confusing and compelling circumstances. It is worth great effort to organize the truth we gather to simple statements of principle."[20]

Principles are not hovering expectations. They are truths we can apply to our lives. However, the other details of the story can creep into our lives as hovering expectations.

When we hear inspiring stories, we risk not separating out the principles from the details. We risk not separating the principles, which are important, from the hovering expectations, which are not. For example, many of us have heard the story of a prophet who had been given the wrong change and returned many miles to the store to return the coins he had been given by mistake. The principle is to be honest, even in small things, even when it's inconvenient and when no one will know the difference. The practice or detail of the story is to go sort out incorrect change from cashiers.

Principles apply in a wide variety of circumstances. Details apply only once. If we absorb the principles, we can apply them in dozens of places in our lives. We can be honest on a quiz even though it's only ten points. We can be honest on our taxes even if no one will know the difference. If we absorb the practice of always sorting out change with cashiers, it complicates our lives and leaves a hovering expectation that has nothing to do with honesty. Accidentally getting an extra quarter in our pockets is not dishonest, just as getting a quarter less is not a crime. It's the daily flow of normal business, not intentional dishonesty.

If it's such a simple thing, then why not just return the quarter? That brings us to a second risk of hovering expectations: they easily pile up. What if our story bank included these expectations: sort out change, be on time, feed the missionaries, don't waste gas, eat together as a family, and don't lose your cool. All quite reasonable. Imagine going to the grocery store to pick up some last-minute items to make dinner for the missionaries tonight. As you return home and pull up into the driveway, you have a sleeping three-year-old in the car seat, you have just enough time to get dinner ready by five, your gas tank is nearly empty, and you notice that the cashier has given you an extra dollar. On a good day, we would just brush it off, put the three-year-old down, and get dinner going. On a bad day, that mixture of expectations could cause a panic attack right there in the driveway. And if we add returning the dollar to our

---

20 "Acquiring Spiritual Knowledge," *Ensign* or *Liahona*, Nov. 1993.

to-do list, we run the risk of piling up expectations so far it becomes difficult to manage our lives. All from one simple grocery store transaction gone awry.

Brené Brown, a researcher who studies shame and vulnerability, calls these hovering expectations a "shame web." She describes the shame web as a set of competing expectations that are impossible to fulfill. She maps out the sources of the shame web, including film, magazines, books, TV, teachers, health professionals, faith communities, friends, and family.[21] Hovering expectations aren't there because these influences have an evil agenda and are pushing all of these expectations on us (with the possible exception of paid advertising); they are there from the normal course of hearing stories, wanting to be good, and adopting the details of the story rather than the underlying principles that resonated with us in the first place. We gain hovering expectations because we want to be good, and we hear stories from other people who are also on a journey to be good.

The risk of hovering expectations is adopting someone else's personal commandments as our own when it doesn't fit us or constantly pressures us to do things we "should." Nicole, a young mom in Tennessee, was sitting in Relief Society enjoying a discussion on the ward mission plan. She had been a missionary in New Zealand and listened to the women suggest ways we can fellowship now. She loved the ideas and soaked them in, putting each idea on her internal goal shelf. At first she felt excited and energized by the discussion, but near the end she raised her hand because she realized she had been getting stressed out as her goal list piled up with ideas that didn't fit her circumstances. She reminded herself and the group that we each need to find our own way of being a missionary. She separated out the principle of acting on missionary work from the practices everyone was suggesting from their personal experiences.

Besides stories we hear, hovering expectations crop up in a few other places. One is our own imaginations. Have you ever listened to a speaker in church for twelve minutes and created an image in your mind of what their life must be like? Then later, when you actually meet the speaker and become friends, you find that his home life is absolutely nothing like you imagined? When he goes home, he is a regular person. Sometimes we create our own stories about other peoples' lives that come with hovering expectations. We hear these imaginations in little phrases like, "I'm sure Roxanne never yells at her kids" or "I'm sure Nephi read his scriptures every single day." We don't actually know that, and making guesses like that is discouraging and turns faithful, interesting, real people into righteous, mythical heroes in our stories.

---

21 See *I Thought It Was Just Me (But It Isn't): Making the Journey from "What Will People Think?" to "I Am Enough"* (New York: Avery, 2008).

Another source of hovering expectations is conventional wisdom. When an assumption seems so completely obvious that it's a given, it's possible that it's a hovering expectation that we've adopted into our lives without thinking about it. For example, let's look at Elder Boyd K. Packer's approach to feeding his kids:

> Soon after our children come home from school, a hot dinner is waiting for them. About four-thirty or five o'clock they eat. They have been in school all day; their blood sugar is low; they are restless and tired; and when they come home they are hungry.
>
> There are two courses that could be followed. Their mother could serve them cookies and milk or bread and jam in order to tide them over until dinner time, in which case their appetite is usually dulled and they don't eat as well as they should at dinner. The other course is to feed them the dinner when they are most hungry. They eat heartily, and then the snack comes a little before bedtime.
>
> It is interesting to see them, after they have had a good meal, go about their chores or settle into studying or peacefully play or take care of any other activities.
>
> The question is immediately raised: Well, doesn't Father eat with the children, then? Father has his dinner when he comes home. Often the children sit around and visit. And with a snack served later, it is like family home evening virtually every night.
>
> This has contributed much to the peace and tranquility of our home because the children are fed when they are ready.[22]

Elder Packer didn't let the hovering expectation and conventional wisdom that families should eat dinner together get in the way of the bigger picture of what his family needed. They created a solution that worked for them. Don't let Elder Packer's solution create a hovering expectation for you. You can separate out the principles in the story from the detail and make choices that fit you well, and you can teach your kids to do the same.

Another source of hovering expectations is our cultures, including Church culture. We are surrounded by Church culture in our worship, in our peer activities, and in our homes. For any activity, there is Church culture and there is doctrine or policy. They are not the same thing. For example, family home evening is important and encouraged. It's policy to not plan Monday night meetings so families can do

---

22 "Ready or Not, You Will Be Taught," *Liahona*, Dec. 1977.

FHE if they wish. An elderly friend of ours raised her kids in the '50s. She tried so hard to make family home evenings match her hovering expectations of what FHE should look like culturally that she ignored her family's needs. She focused on the rotation of lesson, prayer, snacks, sitting still, and cooperating rather than engaging with her kids meaningfully. She feels like it contributed to her children's later inactivity in the Church.

We are so used to the clear image of Monday night family home evening that we may have missed this carefully worded announcement that came with the two-hour church block: "We encourage individuals and families to hold home evening and to study the gospel at home on Sunday—or at other times as individuals and families choose." Did you hear that? FHE is now on Sundays or whenever you want to hold it. The letter adds:

> The adjusted Sunday schedule allows for, and members are encouraged to hold, home evening and to study the gospel at home on Sunday—or at other times as individuals and families choose. A family activity night could be held on Monday or at other times. To this end, leaders should continue to keep Monday evenings free from Church meetings and activities. However, time spent in home evening, gospel study in the home, and activities for families and individuals is scheduled according to individual circumstances.[23]

Even with this official policy, it may still take a few years for this new practice to catch up with the FHE hovering expectations that linger culturally for many people. What a great opportunity for families to ask themselves, "When do we want to hold FHE? When and how do we want to study the gospel? Do we want an activity night on Mondays?"

We can sort out hovering gospel expectations by thinking about where they come from. When we mix up the commandments with someone else's implementation of them, it can feel like we're in a sea of commandments with waves of them swirling about us. When we keep a commandment, instead of feeling joyful, we feel discouraged because of the other commandments we are not fulfilling in the way we imagine. We see mistakes as bad instead of as opportunities to learn, and we can't relax because we are never done. We never feel enough. Sorting out our own expectations and where they come from can help. Go to the source. Rather than absorbing a generalized "they tell us to" for the source of our commandments, we can read what the prophets and apostles

---

23   First Presidency letter, Oct. 6, 2018.

are actually saying. Often when we read the whole talk surrounding a quote, we get a whole new sense of what "they" are asking us to do. The great thing is, once we separate the principle from the story, we can put the principle into practice in our own life.

Many of our hovering expectations come from stories, but that doesn't mean we stop telling stories. The scriptures are filled with stories that house principles. As President Marion G. Romney said, "The scriptures have been written to preserve principles for our benefit."[24] When we read scripture stories and ponder what we learn from them, we are discovering principles. This practice of separating the principle from the details of the story or practice helps us take in the good and let go of the personal details that may not fit our lives right now.

Sorting through these expectations we experience allows us to be more intentional about our discipleship and our goals. That's why it's so important to ask, "Who's asking?" and then go find the answer.

Help kids sort out the difference between real and hovering expectations. Real expectations are things like the commandment to pay an honest tithe. Hovering expectations are things like believing they need to pay in cash with an envelope on the first Sunday of the month.

Help kids understand that it's normal for our brains to adopt these hovering expectations from the stories we hear. We can sort them out by taking a look at their sources. Asking kids who would be happy or sad if they accomplished or failed this goal can sometimes point kids to its source. We can sort goals out by separating the principle from the story. We can also sort them out by trying them to see if they work in our lives. That's why experiment goals are so valuable: We can act on them to test them out for ourselves.

Owning and Decluttering Our Goals

Have you ever noticed a suitcase sitting in your room and suddenly realized that you came home from the trip a month ago? Or casually walked through your house and had every item sitting out remind you of things you needed to be doing? Just like a buildup of physical clutter, we get a buildup of goals in our lives. We might have a stack of scrapbooking paper we wanted to use to finish our kids' baby books, some flashcards we've been meaning to practice with our kids, a bin of fabric for Nativity costumes we wanted to make, or special pens we plan to use to mark our scriptures. These goals (and clutter) can build up in our lives bit by bit over the years.

---

24 "The Message of the Old Testament" (address given at CES Symposium on the Old Testament at Brigham Young University, Aug. 17, 1979), 3.

Sometimes our backlog of goals is tied to physical clutter, but sometimes it's not. Our backlog of goals might include things like writing our life story, creating a family website, rearranging the bedroom downstairs, getting someone to fix the toilet, and going shopping for white shirts that fit and don't show through. This goal clutter accumulates in our brain closets of intentions and dreams for our lives.

Sometimes our goals can accumulate from well-intentioned traditions. For example, say it's Christmastime, and this year we have a tender experience where we feel inspired to focus more on gifts we receive from Christ than on gifts we receive from each other. We choose a wall in the hallway, and each night at dinner we ask family members to write what they are grateful for on a Post-it note and put it on the wall in the hall. It becomes a great way to start dinner, and our families enjoy it. The next year, the Post-it note wall has already become a tradition. The following year, we make a little wooden manger in a Relief Society activity where each family member can put a piece of straw for every kind deed they do for someone else all during December. We bring it home, but our family is small, and after the first three days of good deeds we all forget about it. Our piddly little "bed" for the baby Jesus doll has just a few strands of straw, and every time we look at it we feel stressed about how to make our family more giving. The next year, we see a cute Christmas mailbox on sale and buy it, thinking we could send cute love notes to each other through the holidays. Add that to the Christmas ornaments we keep buying because our mother-in-law bought our firstborn a "Baby's First Christmas" ornament and we felt the need to buy a new ornament every year.

These traditions snowball in our lives. Just because we did it last year doesn't mean we have to do it this year. An inspired goal for one year doesn't have to accumulate. We can let go of old goals.

Marie Kondo, the Japanese decluttering expert we talked about earlier, teaches people how to declutter their belongings. Her method is to gather every shirt, book, art supply, dish, or sports equipment we are decluttering at the moment and put them into a pile. Our task is to pick up every item in a category and ask ourselves, "Does this spark joy?" If it does, it gets a special place in our home. If it doesn't, it leaves for a new home.

We can do the same thing with our goal clutter. We can take each goal on our brainstorm list and ask if it sparks joy. If it does, we keep it. If not, we thank it for its service to us, for inspiring us four years ago, or whatever it is, and say goodbye to it. The important part about this process is we get to decide for ourselves. We can decide to keep our goal of arranging our books on the bookshelves by color because the idea of pretty bookshelves sparks joy in us. We can also decide to discard our goal of creating a recipe book of favorite recipes because it doesn't spark joy and we always just google new recipes anyway.

President Nelson spoke about the need to declutter our lives. He said, "Examine your life meticulously and regularly. As you do so, the Holy Ghost will prompt you about what is no longer needful, what is no longer worthy of your time and energy."[25]

Many kids aren't used to the experience of having goals, let alone examining their lives for which goals belong and which ones don't. One young man shared his testimony and told the story of climbing Mt. Kilimanjaro with his dad. The first day of the climb was difficult, but he made and accomplished a personal goal to carry his own pack all the way up and down. His dad had challenged him to ponder his own life lessons he could gain from the climbing experience. He said he realized that every experience, activity, adventure, or goal in his life, including this one, had been brought to him by someone else—a parent, leader, or friend. He felt passive, like he was just sitting there in his life waiting for opportunities to come to him. He'd never seen something out there he wanted and independently gone after it. He said he'd never had to find a goal for himself. He was excited to start looking for things he wanted to do, deciding for himself, and going after them.

Sometimes kids can think that they don't get to decide, that everything is decided for them. That their job is just to do what everyone else tells them to do. Even when kids are excited to follow Jesus, they look for what they are supposed to do or what people around them are doing and then do that. They don't realize how much autonomy they have in living the gospel.

President Boyd K. Packer gives us an example of autonomy in the gospel:

> It is important to know the gospel, for instance, according to the leaders of the Church. But an even better starting place is to know the gospel according to one's own self; that is, to take a subject such as the Word of Wisdom and really search our own minds as to how we feel about it. We should read what we can find in the scriptures about the subject and then write down our feelings. Then we may compare those feelings against what leaders of the Church have written or said. . . .
>
> If we are searching inside ourselves in the right way, and we have included prayer as part of that search, we are tapping the same source of intelligence that the leaders of the Church are tuned-in upon.
>
> Then we may become independent witnesses of that principle from our own inquiry. Then our obedience is not

---

25 "Spiritual Treasures," *Ensign or Liahona, Nov. 2019.*

blind obedience. Then our agency is protected and we are on the right course. Then we will do things because we know they are right and are the truth. We will know this from our own inquiry, not simply because someone else knows it."[26]

President Packer is inviting us to receive personal revelation.

President Nelson and all the recent, global Church changes are also inviting us to receive personal revelation and use our agency to figure out how to implement the gospel in our lives. We can help kids see that obedience is not compliance with rules; it's applying true principles in a myriad of ways in our lives. President Nelson, like Moses, wants us all to be the prophets of our own lives. He and other prophets want us to decide and seek the Spirit because that process promotes personal revelation. They want us to be spiritually self-reliant.[27]

It is easier to declutter meaningless goals cluttering up our brainstorm list when we feel empowered to make choices for ourselves.

LeAnn has boxes of her kids' T-shirts stacked in her garage, saved over many years from schools, orchestras, sports, EFY, and other activities that pass out shirts. After her kids grew out of or were done wearing them, the shirts went into the T-shirt box. Her intent was to make a T-shirt quilt when they graduated high school as a loving gift. They never got made. Three years after her last kid graduated from high school, all those boxes were still sitting in her garage.

She ran into a lot of hurdles with this goal: keeping track of boxes of T-shirts for seven kids over six years each, planning ahead early enough to finish by graduation, and kids wanting to keep and wear their high school shirts past their graduation. Nichole eventually made her own cool quilt and inspired LeAnn to forge ahead with the task, but over ten years of efforts and attempts, and with some self-compassionate reflection, LeAnn came to several conclusions. She doesn't like T-shirt quilts. She doesn't like how they're not cozy and soft like other blankets. She doesn't like the scratchy lettering. She doesn't like how they look with all the mismatched colors. She doesn't like worrying about them falling apart if you don't line them with interfacing first. She doesn't like how they feel heavy and stiff if you *do* line them. She still admires other people's T-shirt quilts, but she knows she doesn't want one for herself.

Once she figured that out, you would think it would be easy to just toss the boxes of T-shirts. But she still has them, sitting in her garage. For those of you who are saying, "Sweetheart, let me come over and help you get rid of those"—

---

26 *Teach Ye Diligently* (Salt Lake City: Deseret Book Company, 1975), 99.

27 See Russell M. Nelson, "Revelation for the Church, Revelation for Our Lives," *Ensign* or *Liahona*, May 2018.

all you minimalists out there—hooray! You've got an amazing skill. For those of you who relate and think of your own boxes of intentions scattered throughout your closets, under your beds, and in the garage—welcome aboard. It can be hard to let go of goals.

We may have an entire mental garage full of goals. Some got there because we put them there and some because others asked them to be there. Some are from hovering expectations, from a random comment from our second-grade teacher, or from advice we received when we got married.

We have good reasons to hoard goals. They might be treasures! What if our friend's suggestion to wake up half an hour early *changes our lives*? It could, right? We have good enough imaginations to guess how waking up early could cause a chain reaction and create a huge positive effect in our lives. It's possible. It's possible that a new diet, book, or goal could be the answer to all our problems. It's the possibilities of the goal that encourage us to hold on to it and stick it on a to-do list in the back of our minds that we'll get around to one day.

But we have to be careful not to let the possibilities hide the cost. Goal clutter costs brain space we could use for new, more relevant goal ideas. It costs guilt and embarrassment when we notice them sitting there undone. It costs us time and space when we sort through our old goals and sometimes the physical items that accompany them. It costs us confusion and feeling overwhelmed when we try to decide on a daily basis where to put our efforts.

Some people are afraid to declutter physical objects or goals because they worry they won't get them back. Keep an abundance mindset rather than a scarcity mindset when decluttering. If we discard a goal, that doesn't mean it will never come back into our lives. If a goal is important, we'll be able to find it again when we need it.

Now that we can better see where our goals are coming from, we can do a little tidying up. Just because that goal has been sitting around for a few years doesn't mean we need to keep it around. We can open the closet, clean it out, say goodbye to some stale goals, and start working on goals that matter to us. We get to choose what goes and what stays.

The same principle applies whether you are an adult or a child. Kids haven't had a lifetime to gather up and collect goals in their garages, but they still have some. From the occupations they wanted to be when they were little to the athletes that currently inspire them, kids' goals can hang around long after they are useful.

Kids have people asking them to do things as well as hovering expectations they pick up along the way. They need just as much help as we do sorting out who's asking. One thing to be aware of is that we as parents are often the ones setting the expectation for them. We are the ones doing the asking. They might choose to declutter goals that came from us, which is the wonderful power of autonomy at work.

CHAPTER 7
PRINCIPLE #2—TUNERS
HOW ACCEPTING AND USING OUR STRENGTHS AND WEAKNESSES MAKES US BETTER GOAL SETTERS

"Mom, you just want me to be perfect! I'm not perfect!" LeAnn's daughter Julia yelled one day. Feeling an object lesson was in order the next week, LeAnn brought her daughter out to the yard to rake leaves with her. She put a twelve-inch embroidery hoop on the ground and told her daughter she wanted that spot to be perfect, not a single leaf on it. Happy to sit down while LeAnn raked, she worked until she thought she was done. But when LeAnn inspected, she found leaves matted under the blades of grass. Slightly frustrated now, Julia got back to work until she thought she was really done. A second inspection revealed little tiny leaves the size of corn kernels from a nearby tree that had to be picked up one by one. After a third attempt, it was finally perfect. No more leaves!

But the grass inside the hoop had been plucked within an inch of its life. Some of the bare roots were showing where the earth had been disturbed. It was not a pretty sight. LeAnn and Julia talked about what grass needs in order to grow and decided it needed a middle ground. If every single leaf were left on the grass, it wouldn't be able get sun and would die. If every single leaf were removed, the grass's roots wouldn't be as strong and the soil wouldn't be able to use any of the leaves' nutrients once they broke down, so it wouldn't be as healthy. Both doing nothing and trying to be perfect destroyed the grass. We found a new measure for raking—not perfect, but healthy.

We hear the admonition to "be ye therefore perfect" when we study the scriptures (Matthew 5:48). We also know perfectionism can be destructive and debilitating. Just like we saw in the raking-leaves story, seeking perfection in one area of our lives creates a net negative effect. How do we resolve this admonition and the maladaptive perfectionism so widespread in Church culture? How do we prevent it in ourselves and in our kids? Understanding the principle of strengths and weaknesses can help us reduce perfectionism.

There are over seven billion people on earth today, and every one of them is unique. Imagine all of the characteristics that people can have. They can be kind or cruel, patient or antsy, funny or dry, full of zest or serene. It wouldn't be hard to come up with hundreds of different characteristics. We are people outfitted with strengths and weaknesses. We developed some in pre-earth life. We received some strengths and weaknesses as gifts from God and received others in our mortal genes. Some were influenced growing up in our specific families, and we have strengthened or neglected others in our efforts as mortals so far.

Now imagine each characteristic lined up like the dials and sliding tuners of a sound board. Imagine each tuner with numbers from zero to ten. Every single person would have zeros and every single person would have tens. We are all strong and weak in different ways. No one person is good at everything, and no one person is bad at everything. Each combination is unique. That's intentional.

Elder Uchtdorf said, "While the Atonement is meant to help us all become more like Christ, it is not meant to make us all the same. Sometimes we confuse differences in personality with sin. We can even make the mistake of thinking that because someone is different from us, it must mean they are not pleasing to God. This line of thinking leads some to believe that the Church wants to create every member from a single mold—that each one should look, feel, think, and behave like every other. This would contradict the genius of God, who created every man different from his brother, every son different from his father. Even identical twins are not identical in their personalities and spiritual identities."[28]

Noticing how our kids' tuners differ from our own helps us better understand and relate to them.

The genius of God needs all sorts of people on earth. God has one work and seven billion pairs of hands to do it with. He needs people with different strengths and weaknesses, talents, thoughts, experiences, and circumstances. No one else can do things exactly like you can. We each have an "individual premortal, mortal, and eternal identity and purpose."[29] We do not need to be flawless to be good and to do good in the world. People can do good in the world around them exactly as they are now. Our purpose isn't to push all our personal tuners to ten but to use our unique package to uplift and participate in our families, schools, teams, churches, and friends.

Accepting Who We Are

When Nichole's three-year-old daughter protested eating her vegetables one evening, Nichole explained to her that she had to eat healthy foods to grow bigger and stronger. Her daughter nodded, seeming to process it, then announced with a surety, "Oh, because I'm not big enough or strong enough yet." Nichole was

---

28 "Four Titles," *Ensign* or *Liahona*, May 2013.
29 "The Family: A Proclamation to the World," *Ensign* or *Liahona*, Nov. 2010, 129.

speechless for a moment because that didn't seem quite right. Her daughter didn't have to eat vegetables because she was weak or small. She had to eat vegetables to prepare herself for the future.

Eventually, she explained to her that even though she wasn't as big or as strong as Mommy or Daddy yet, she was just as big and strong as a healthy, three-year-old girl should be. She was enough just the way she was. But she wasn't going to stay that way forever, because she wasn't done developing, and healthy foods like vegetables would help her as she did.

Spiritually it's the same. We have to hold two truths in our minds at the same time:

1. We are enough right now.
2. We will continue developing, growing, and putting effort toward change.

As we put on our coaching hats to coach our kids through goals, maintaining that unconditional positive regard for our kids and believing they're okay the way they are is imperative. At the same time we are looking at goals for their futures, we are sending the message that we accept them as people regardless of the outcomes of their current goal loops.

It's hard for many of us to absorb this kind of acceptance of ourselves. Here are five common reasons why:

One, we compare. It's hard to believe we're okay just the way we are when we compare ourselves to others. President Ezra Taft Benson warned that comparing leads to pride and unhappiness.[30] It's something to be aware of in ourselves and in how we talk to our kids. Kids wilt under comparisons even when they come out on top.

Two, we may believe that the only purpose of life is to move all our tuners to ten. We may think that's the definition of being perfect. It's not. President Nelson clearly laid out in his talk "Perfection Pending" that being perfect is about reaching a distant end, not flawless performance.[31] Rather than believing we need to maximize all our tuners in order to be the kind of person God can call upon to use in any setting, Elder Uchtdorf asked us to lift where we stand. He told the story of some men trying to move a piano. After several attempts at getting just the right positions, one man suggested they all just stop and lift where they stood.[32] None of the men lifting the piano in his story said, "Wait, let me go work out and get stronger first so you can then use my strength." They simply lifted where they stood, and the piano was moved. Lifting where we stand takes into consideration our current circumstances, where we find ourselves, as well as our current package

---

30 See "Beware of Pride," *Ensign*, May 1989.
31 See "Perfection Pending," *Ensign*, Nov. 1995.
32 See "Lift Where You Stand," *Ensign* or *Liahona*, Nov. 2008.

of strengths and weaknesses. Striving to maximize all our tuners is a little like going to college and taking every single class offered rather than choosing a major and getting a degree. It's okay to specialize and be different from one another.

Three, we are on a celestial journey in a telestial world. As Elder Neal A. Maxwell put it, "Following celestial road signs while in telestial traffic jams is not easy, especially when we are not just moving next door—or even across town."[33] This gap that we see, the seemingly massive distance we need to leap to become celestial beings after a telestial earth experience, can be disheartening. How can we possibly be okay here when we still have so far to go?[34]

Four, we all have hovering expectations about who we should be and how we should live our lives. These hovering expectations come from our families, from inspirational stories we hear, from role models we want to be like, and from how we imagine our lives will be. They make it hard for us to feel like we are enough or that it's okay to be who we are.

Five, we may look at our past and regret what we could have and should have done. And it may be true. We may have missed opportunities in the past. The hard reality is that the past has brought us here to this moment today, and spending hours thinking about it won't do anything to change it. Some people get stuck moping about things that they wish were different. What if this is as good as it gets? What if our circumstances never change? What if our greatest weakness, like a thorn in our flesh, never goes away?

Accepting the weight and reality of who we are right now doesn't mean not changing or never feeling sad about it. It means facing the reality of who we are right this minute because that's what we have to work with. Michelle D. Craig said, "Each of us, if we are honest, feels a gap between where and who we are and where and who we want to become. We yearn for greater personal capacity. We have these feelings because we are daughters and sons of God, born with the Light of Christ yet living in a fallen world. These feelings are God given and create an urgency to act."[35]

LeAnn's daughter Morgan went to college with the belief that she was a good student since she'd gotten good grades in high school. When she struggled during college, it took her several semesters to accept that she wasn't a good college student. Once she realized that, she started practicing the skills a successful college student needs, like time management and better study habits. Before accepting that she needed to improve, she might have blamed the college system, her roommates,

---

33 "Notwithstanding My Weakness," *Ensign*, Nov. 1976.
34 For those who are interested, this same talk by Elder Maxwell lists fourteen insightful ways we can manage feelings of inadequacy.
35 "Divine Discontent," *Ensign*, Nov. 2018.

or even her mother for her failures. She would have avoided some sadness from realizing that she wasn't who she thought she was. But along with that acceptance came the ability to improve. Accepting that she wasn't a good college student was like being on a trampoline that had accepted all the weight of who she was. It may have felt like the lowest point of the jump, but it's what propelled her into action.

Goals to Correct Our Weaknesses

When we think about goals, we often think about improving ourselves, about correcting our faults or our weaknesses. For example, we might work on how we deal with anger to improve our relationships. We might work on our diligence to improve our performance at school. Those would clearly be worthwhile improvements in our lives.

Sometimes, in an effort to be a good person, we overemphasize our weaknesses. Like a hypochondriac always taking our own temperature, we fixate on fixing our weaknesses. We may be down on ourselves and endlessly discouraged and frustrated. It's not helpful to set goals because we don't like ourselves. This inward focus discourages us, distracts us from more important things, and leaves little time to do positive things in our lives.

Some weaknesses really do need to be improved, but others simply don't matter all that much. Don't go looking for weaknesses to tackle as goals just to have something to do. Instead, pay attention and notice which weaknesses are actually getting in the way of our lives and relationships. Then we can address them. For example, it may be helpful for a mom to be an intense, feisty person at work, but that same quality might strain relationships at home. Choose goals that work to overcome weaknesses carefully and sparingly.

Think back to the soundboard analogy. A soundboard or audio mixer has dozens of tuners that serve different purposes. They work together to adjust the volume, control for audio feedback, blend instrumental and vocal tracks, and apply audio effects. A good sound technician knows how to adjust various tuners and dials to fit the acoustics and size of the room, the style of music, the number of people in the audience, and the equipment being used.

If the drums in a song that is being mixed are so loud that the singer can't be heard, it would make sense to shift the drum tuner down, making the song objectively better. If things are causing problems, we should try adjusting the tuners that are involved. But if the song is already pretty well balanced and the different parts can be heard well enough, trying to shift tuners can introduce more problems.

Sometimes what we perceive as weakness God will put to good use.

President Hinckley struggled with impatience. What did the Lord do with that shortcoming? He turned it into President Hinckley's greatest strength. Consider what he accomplished during his years as president of the Church. At the October 1997 General Conference of the Church, he announced the inspired plan for building small temples. At that time there were fifty-one temples worldwide. Three years later in December 2000, there were 102 dedicated temples. It took from 1836 to 1997 to get our first fifty-one temples and three years to get fifty-one more. That is a miracle. President Gordon B. Hinckley was sent to earth to become the greatest temple builder in world history. The Lord took a weakness and turned it into a strength that blessed the entire world.[36]

President Nelson also told us in conference about one of President Hinckley's strengths. "President Hinckley's love of learning is catalyzed by curiosity. He grasps every opportunity to learn from others. On one occasion, I heard him quiz a local security officer for nearly an hour regarding crime control in a major city. I have heard him converse with building contractors, reporters, and those who specialize in the arts, architecture, business, government, law, medicine, and other disciplines. He knows their vocabularies, their challenges, and their strengths."[37]

Telling our kids stories like these can help them become more accepting of their own strengths and weaknesses.

Goals from a Position of Strength

Martin Seligman, the father of positive psychology, worked with other researchers to identify character strengths that people have. Their research yielded twenty-four strengths. They consider the top five to seven our signature strengths, those strengths we feel comfortable wielding and use often and easily.

A person armed with zest is going to approach goals differently than a person armed with self-regulation. Working from our strengths produces more traction and progress in our lives and our goals. We are more engaged and feel more energized and hopeful. Operating from a position of strength improves not just our progress but also our overall well-being.

We can even work on our selective weakness goals from a basis of strengths. Say we want to work on that anger problem that's burdening our relationships. If our strength is humor, we could watch a funny YouTube video when we get angry. If we have a love-of-learning strength, we could take a class or read some articles about what causes people to have anger problems and learn strategies

---

36 Randal A. Wright, *Achieving Your Life Mission* (Springville, Utah: Cedar Fort, 2009), 44.
37 "Spiritual Capacity," *Ensign*, Nov. 1997.

to control anger. Do what works for you. Use your own package of strengths to approach your goals.

Of course, the twenty-four strengths listed here are not the only strengths available. The scriptures contain many examples of strengths. Doctrine and Covenants 46 lists some specific gifts of the Spirit like the faith to heal, faith to be healed, ability to prophesy, and knowledge. Elder Marvin J. Ashton added other smaller gifts we might not recognize as strengths.

> Let us review some of these less-conspicuous gifts: the gift of asking; the gift of listening; the gift of hearing and using a still, small voice; the gift of being able to weep; the gift of avoiding contention; the gift of being agreeable; the gift of avoiding vain repetition; the gift of seeking that which is righteous; the gift of not passing judgment; the gift of looking to God for guidance; the gift of being a disciple; the gift of caring for others; the gift of being able to ponder; the gift of offering prayer; the gift of bearing a mighty testimony; and the gift of receiving the Holy Ghost.[38]

Take a free survey at viacharacter.org to find your signature strengths. There is a survey for children and youth too.

STRENGTHS:
Love of learning
Perspective
Creativity
Curiosity
Spirituality
Gratitude
Honesty
Hope
Judgment
Love
Zest
Forgiveness
Prudence
Leadership
Social intelligence
Bravery
Fairness
Kindness
Perseverance
Teamwork
Humility
Self-regulation
Appreciation of beauty and excellence
Humor

Help kids see their own strengths in the four areas of personal development: spiritual, social, physical, and intellectual. Have them list their strengths or take the survey to find their current signature strengths. Have a conversation about their strengths or put each person's strengths on a family strength chart

---

38 "'There are Many Gifts,'" *Ensign*, Nov. 1987.

in family home evening. Try posting a sticky note on your computer to remind you of your kids' strengths. When you ask, "What went well and why?" in goal conversations, point out how kids use their strengths to contribute to things going well.

We can also bring our own strengths and personalities to our conversations with our kids as we coach them through goals. If we seek counsel from the Lord, He can help us see strengths and weaknesses in ourselves and in our children.

In an effort to create strengths, some people naturally want to push all their attributes to ten, to be perfectly patient or perfectly healthy or perfectly consistent. But that's like turning every tuner on a soundboard all the way up, which would ruin the sound. Each performance requires some adjustments to the tuners to produce the best overall balance of sound.

For a person, maximizing all the tuner strengths is not only a bad idea, it's simply not possible, and it's not our covenant charge. Rather than trying to maximize all our weaknesses from low numbers to tens, consider the idea of expanding our range for a weakness and for a specific circumstance. We may be naturally impatient people, but we can train ourselves to be patient for periods of time where it's important. Our ability to love, serve, and function in our families, callings, and careers is part of what drives how we select what goals to pursue.

LeAnn's daughter Elena has the strength of being diligent. When she decides to clean the kitchen, she doesn't hesitate; she jumps in and gets it done. In the office, she is known for being completely reliable and getting her work done quickly. When she has a workout goal, she comes home and tells LeAnn about how her workouts energize her. These strengths help Elena accomplish a lot. On the flip side, these strengths make it hard for her to relax. She risks getting burned out and overworking herself. Her go-getter personality would rather achieve, and it can be hard to turn it off sometimes.

Just like a soundboard, we sometimes need less of an attribute for a situation and not more. If diligence and the ability to relax are two ends of the same tuner slide, what if we could wield our diligence when we needed to and wield our ability to relax when we needed to? What if Elena could expand her range of available responses to relax when the situation demanded and be diligent at other times?

We will have strengths and weaknesses our entire lives. But, regardless of our current personal package, our weaknesses are a finite list. We are unlikely to develop new ones. That's why we bump up against the same kind of problems over and over again. Yes, we have weaknesses, but they are limited and countable. We can live with some of our weaknesses. Others are really messing up our lives. We can be selective about which weaknesses we pour our efforts into improving.

When LeAnn's son Jackson was young, he was both in the gifted program at school and a terrible speller. The whole family joked about him being the worst speller in the family, even worse than his sister who didn't learn English until she was fifteen years old. They wondered if he had dyslexia, but it didn't affect his reading or his grades, so they never pursued getting it figured out.

In college he took advantage of a free screening in the disabilities office and took a battery of tests to pinpoint what was going on. The tests came back showing him as an average speller, right at about the fifty percent mark. It was low for a college student, but with his high abilities in other areas, he was able to compensate for his weakness in spelling and pass his classes. He had lived for years believing he was a terrible speller since he was comparing an average skill of his to the strengths of people around him.

What can he do with this weakness? He could set a goal to become a better speller, but at this point in his life, his efforts might be better used pursuing other goals. Does he really have to become a better speller? It's up to him. Jackson is also a strong computer programmer. If he had a hundred hours to spend on a goal, he might want to build his programming skills rather than work on his weakness in spelling. We only have so much wherewithal, and we get to decide where to put our efforts.

A Parent's Love

God loves us right now as we are. At the same time, He expects us to have experiences and grow, change, and improve. Both can be true at the same time. President Monson reminds us, "Your Heavenly Father loves you—each of you. That love never changes. It is not influenced by your appearance, by your possessions, or by the amount of money you have in your bank account. It is not changed by your talents and abilities. It is simply there. It is there for you when you are sad or happy, discouraged or hopeful. God's love is there for you whether or not you feel you deserve love. It is simply always there."[39]

He loves us, and He knows us. He knows us better than we do, including our talents, strengths, weaknesses, and needs. He sees all the good we can do, what we can learn, and ways we can develop. He sees all the ways we mess up and all our private failures. He loves us now and at the same time is excited for us to grow, change, and develop.

We can do this for our kids. Like Nichole's three-year-old daughter who worried she wasn't big enough or strong enough, we can assure our kids that they are big enough and strong enough even though they need to put effort toward

---

39 "We Never Walk Alone," *Ensign* or *Liahona*, Nov. 2013.

personal development. We can love them now and at the same time be excited for them to grow, change, and develop.

When we read of Christ healing, each story holds this moment where the leper, the woman, the centurion, or the daughter is cleansed, made whole, or forgiven. In that moment we can imagine the feeling of wholeness, peace, and being enough that would encompass them. At the same time, the leper was still himself, the woman still herself. Their strengths and weaknesses remained side by side with their increased testimony and desire to follow Christ. In our efforts to improve, the more we seek that connection, sense of peace, being enough, and wholeness that comes through Christ, the more we release the pressures of flawless performance.

Everyone will always have ideas about how to improve to be more intelligent, kind, orderly, diligent, brave, or playful. We will never be completely one hundred percent satisfied with everything about ourselves and our lives. We will always have things we like about ourselves and things we don't; things we're proud of and things we're ashamed of; past successes and past failures. We all have things we are capable of handling right now and things we aren't yet capable of handling.

If we want to start a goal, there's no place to start but where we are, and there's no better time to start than right now. Sounds obvious, but we can spend a lot of time complaining, blaming, whining, and arguing with ourselves about not being where we want to be. We think we are somehow behind if we are not as good as someone else. Radically accepting that we are where we are allows us to turn up the humility a bit, become more teachable, acknowledge our zeros and our tens, and move on with our lives and our goals with added wisdom and awareness.

Understanding the tuners and dials of our strengths and weaknesses helps us avoid perfectionism and helps us choose goals. It also helps us avoid comparing and be happier with our own goals and journeys.

The Savior spent His life turning outward, helping and lifting those whom He encountered one by one. We can do the same, "notwithstanding [our] weakness."[40] We can follow the example of Jesus Christ, who "went about doing good" (Acts 10:38). Elder Bednar defines Christ's character as looking, turning, and reaching outward when the natural, instinctive response of man is to turn inward and be self-absorbed. He called the character of Christ "the consistent capacity to turn outward and minister to others in the midst of affliction."[41] If we wait until we

---

40 Neal A. Maxwell, "Notwithstanding My Weakness," *Ensign*, Nov. 1976.
41 *Act in Doctrine: Spiritual Patterns for Turning from Self to the Savior* (Salt Lake City: Deseret Book, 2012), 10.

are Christlike enough to turn outward, we miss the whole point of what being Christlike means. We have to believe that as we lift where we stand, our weaknesses become either irrelevant or strengthened as we stand up to do the work we are able to do in the here and now.

CHAPTER 8
PRINCIPLE #3 – MOTIVATION
HOW WE CAN SUPPORT CLEAN MOTIVATION IN OUR KIDS

IMAGINE A GIRL SITTING AT a desk doing schoolwork. We can see what's going on with her moving pencil and concentrating face, but we can't see what's going on in her mind. But what's going on in there is critical. No matter how smart she is, her results depend on what else is happening besides the assignment at hand. They depend on her motivation.

Motivation means being moved to do something, and it matters a lot where that initiative to move is coming from. As parents, we sometimes get the mistaken belief that we need to be the ones to motivate our children, that we need to get them to move. We do influence their motivation, but the desire to get kids moving sometimes causes us to behave in ways that actually do just the opposite and make them unmotivated instead.

One key assumption of psychology's foundational Self-Determination Theory is that people are normally action-biased.[42] We are naturally motivated to explore, make sense of, experiment in, and find our place in the world. We bump up against the people in our families, schools, churches, and neighborhoods and learn from those interactions. Our exploration is endless; as we develop through natural stages from infancy to adulthood, our environments regularly change as we move through school grades, make friends, take jobs, and have families of our own. To the extent that we are able to act within our environments and relationships in ways that are self-directed, we continue to be action-biased.

In this natural exploration, kids are motivated to adopt some of the values and rules of their homes and cultures. Our kids already share some of our same mannerisms, tastes for food, and languages. They have adopted some of our clothing preferences and may share the teams we root for. They know how

---

42 See Richard M. Ryan and Edward L. Deci, "Self-Determination Theory and the Facilitation of Intrinsic Motivation, Social Development, and Well-Being," *American Psychologist* (Jan. 2000), 55(1), 68–78.

mealtimes and money works around our house and what's going to happen if they throw their dirty socks on the couch. The truly great thing is that there is no one correct response to the socks. Every family does it differently, and kids absorb these differences.

When we look into how motivation works, it helps us become better motivators as parents. It helps us motivate without meddling. There are two kinds of motivation that we experience: clean and tangled. Clean motivation is self-determined. Tangled motivation is pressured in some way.

Clean Motivation

Clean motivation is self-determined, which means that we feel like we have a say in our lives. There are three different kinds of clean motivation: intrinsic, goal-oriented, and integrated.

Intrinsic motivation is the first clean motivation. These activities are things kids do naturally, like playing, exploring, or climbing a tree just to see if they can do it. Kids do intrinsically motivated things because they are enjoyable, interesting, or invite a challenge. No one makes them do them. Of course, different activities or behaviors will be intrinsically motivating for different kids, but every kid has things he likes to do naturally. When left to their own devices, kids figure stuff out. Deci and Ryan, creators of Self-Determination Theory, assume that humans are active and tend to grow, master, and integrate what's around them.[43] But it doesn't happen in a vacuum. As helpful as natural play and exploring are for learning, we don't plunk kids down on a playground for ten or twenty years and come back to pick them up all grown up. Other kinds of motivation are involved in child and youth development.

The second clean motivation is goal-oriented behavior. Kids will do things they don't enjoy when they want the results they produce. A kid will wait patiently in line to climb a rock wall at the recreation center if she wants to climb the wall and can see that waiting patiently is the only way to get there. A kid will willingly study a driver's manual if he wants to pass the test to get his learner's permit. If the end result is self-determined, kids are more willing to do whatever it takes to get there, even if the task is unpleasant, boring, or difficult. That's why people usually set goals. They see the end result and the effort it takes to get there. Studies with students who were motivated by these personally chosen, goal-oriented activities enjoyed school more and had more positive coping styles when things didn't go well.

---

43 See Edward L. Deci and Richard M. Ryan, "The 'What' and 'Why' of Goal Pursuits: Human Needs and the Self-Determination of Behavior," *Psychological Inquiry* (2000), 11(4), 227–268.

The third clean motivation is integrated behavior. This is when something has become such a part of people that they do it naturally. It almost feels like play again—they do it because they naturally enjoy the experience or the challenge of it. When a kid gets good enough at piano and playing is part of who he is, he will more often just play for the enjoyment of it. The same is true for kids going to church, doing well in school, or participating in sports or a hobby. Even something as simple as daily hygiene becomes integrated when kids are competent at the routines and it has become a part of how they see themselves, a part of their identity. Individuals motivated this way are more interested in the task, enjoy it more, and feel more competent. They also cope positively when things don't go well in a particular situation.

These clean motivations are all self-determined. Kids feel like they are directing, choosing, or driving their own lives. They feel like they have the opportunity to say no without disappointing or upsetting anyone but themselves. It is truly their choice, so the effort doesn't feel like effort.

Tangled Motivation

Tangled motivation is when kids do something that is not self-directed. They are doing the goal or behavior for someone else. They also might be doing it for themselves, but they feel pressure of some kind to do it. There are two different kinds of tangled motivation: extrinsic and "should."

The first tangled motivation is extrinsic motivation, or outside pressure. This is when something outside the kid is prodding, pressuring, or even rewarding him to do something. Outside pressure can also be a deadline, intimidation, or threat; it can be a point chart or treat. Rewards, punishments, or even merely someone's physical presence can serve as outside pressure. The pressure doesn't have to be mean and intimidating. It can be sweet and subtle. Kids feel outside pressure when they want to do a task to please someone, get someone off their back, or avoid getting in trouble. They are often afraid or feel the need to impress someone. Kids perceive the pressure as coming from outside of themselves.

The real problem with extrinsic or outside-pressure motivation is that it complicates or tangles what's going on inside the kid's mind. If someone is practicing a musical instrument or sport with clean motivation, it's just practice. If someone is doing it because Dad or a teacher is forcing him or her to, there's going to be a lot more going on with his or her emotions and thoughts. It's pretty simple. People don't like feeling forced to do things.

Researchers have found that this motivation doesn't work well. In the middle of the task they are performing, kids tend to be less interested, put forth less effort, not persist well, not value it, and blame others when things don't go well. Even if the task gets completed and the homework gets turned in, the real learning doesn't happen. Kids tend to just go through the motions to look busy and accomplished. Even getting good grades can happen without the attendant learning. Other research found that money rewards—a form of outside pressure, even though they are rewards—do work for repetitive manual tasks, but when people have to think, reason, or be creative, rewards actually do the opposite of what we expect, and the person performs worse than having no reward at all.

Things change when we see that outside pressure tangles up what's happening inside. The brain can't focus on the task at hand when it's also focusing on how to meet the requirements of the one applying the pressure. We think more about who's making us do it, why we have to do it, and how to just get it over with. We distract ourselves with other things that feel better than being forced, worry about what the enforcer will think, whether we will get caught, or how we might get in trouble or disappoint the enforcer. We look for the quickest way out without really learning anything.

The second kind of tangled motivation is "should" pressure. This is pressure kids put on themselves. The pressure comes from the inside, but it doesn't feel self-selected, so it's still a tangled motivation. It's as though they have swallowed a goal whole, without digesting it or really deciding for themselves that they want to do it. It feels like there's a hovering "they" out there that is pressuring or expecting them to behave in certain ways or have certain goals. When asked about this motivation, someone might say, "They say doing this makes you healthier, so I should do it." The ubiquitous "they" is always there, but you couldn't give him or her a name. When we really drill down, often these ideas or expectations come from some magazine article we read in a doctor's office waiting room, a comment our third-grade teacher made in class one day, or something our mother said over and over to our brother. We pick up these "shoulds" subtly from our environment. Often we don't even realize we have them. We just think that's the way the world is and that everyone shares these expectations.

Inside-pressure motivation produces effort, but it comes at a cost. We are filled with anxiety, overwork ourselves, and never feel like enough. Even if the discomfort is low-grade, the constant pressure of it often causes long-term stress and even health issues. When people inevitably fail, they don't cope very well with this kind of motivation. When we are motivated by inside pressure, it constantly hovers over us, and we feel like there's no escape. "Should"-motivated people often get a lot done but at great cost to themselves and their health.

Because this pressure is felt from within, we don't always recognize that it is happening. Some clues can help us listen for this inside-pressure motivation.

First, listen for the word "should." Sometimes kids will brainstorm some goals with the word "should." Another way is to see how much they enjoy the thing they are doing. If they don't enjoy orchestra, it may be that they are only doing it because they feel like they should. Anxiety can be another warning sign of hovering expectations in your child's life.

You might be asking yourself if there's such a thing as a lack of motivation—having none at all. There is. There are a lot of reasons people might not be motivated at all for a certain task. They might not feel competent, not care about it, or not believe their efforts will matter. Sometimes kids seem to not want to do anything at all. Often an unmotivated kid is a discouraged kid.

Clean and Tangled Motivations

Clean motivation matters, and tangled motivation either doesn't work well or it works, but with harmful side effects. When kids experience clean motivation, they feel like they have a say in their lives. With tangled motivation, they don't. The same is true for adults. We can experience clean motivation or be motivated in tangled ways by a controlling boss or an internal picture we create for ourselves of how our lives should be.

When we experience clean motivation, we will still do some unpleasant things on our journey to our outcome, but the unpleasantness doesn't bother us, because it's self-imposed. That means we can change it when we want to. It's not the same when we experience tangled motivation. We feel trapped into doing something we don't want to do. We feel like we have no choice.

We can experience a mixture of both clean and tangled motivation. A kid may want to learn piano because she enjoys it and she wants to impress her friends, and at the same time have a nagging parent that makes it hard to practice because she feels forced to do it the parent's way at the parent's time.

Parents' Secret Sauce of Motivation

As parents, we have to require our kids to do some things. We need our households to run in the here and now, and we are preparing our kids to launch into their futures. At the same time, we want to support them in their goals and keep ourselves untangled from their motivation so it stays clean.

There are three secret-sauce ingredients kids need to keep their motivation clean, which we can provide for them. The three ingredients are autonomy, competence, and relationships. When kids have autonomy, a feeling that they have a say in their lives, they are more willing to do the work it takes to have a good life. When kids are competent, they don't shrink back hiding or waiting for someone else. When kids have relationships they can count on, they go about their days experimenting and exploring, knowing they have a safety net to fall back on, someone who cares about them and their lives.

Controlling

Years ago, LeAnn had a family home evening about being slothful. They read the scripture about "being a slothful and not a wise servant" (D&C 58:26). Then they looked at pictures of sloths and talked about what they did all day. When they got to the part about how to change slothful behavior and how to get a sloth to move, one kid suggested picking up the sloth and throwing it to where you want it to be. His sister said, "Yeah, but if you throw a sloth, it's still a sloth." We don't just want our kids to arrive at our desired outcomes; we want them to be able to develop the motivation and self-regulation to get there themselves.

A study compared controlling teachers with teachers who encouraged autonomy by sending in substitute teachers to the first-hour classroom. The kids who were used to a controlling teacher were rowdy and out of control. So much so that the substitutes had to break protocol of the experiment and take measures to regain control. The kids who were used to being given autonomy used their well-developed internal controls and allowed the substitute to lead a productive class.

Excessively using our power, control, or leverage to get kids to do things will work well for now but clearly not in the long run. When kids are pressured to do a task, they don't do as good of a job and they focus more on looking done than on really doing anything. If it's a mental task, like homework, the outside task gets done, but the inner learning doesn't happen. The relationship with the controlling person gets worse, and when the kid gets big enough to not be controlled or the parent or the teacher isn't around, they stop complying with the behavior.

When LeAnn's husband, Daryl, taught early morning seminary in Virginia, he had a student who came only because his dad said he would buy him a drum set if he came to seminary every day. He was faithful in attending but rarely participated. The next semester, he stopped coming. When Daryl asked him about it, he said, "There's nothing I want enough anymore for my dad to get me to go to seminary."

Sometimes when a parent is controlling it's because she needs a kid to comply just to have a functioning family, just like teachers sometimes use control to have a functioning classroom. But we want kids to learn to manage themselves and not just do things when we're watching them. We have immediate needs and long-term hopes for these kids. Control works immediately but not as a pattern. We're looking for a long-run solution here. We're looking for them to develop internal controls and learn to regulate their own behavior. When kids grow up with a long pattern of controlling parents or teachers, they tend to either rebel or shrink into a life they didn't choose.

Autonomy

Kids need autonomy to stay motivated and to regulate their own behavior. Autonomy is the sense that we have a say in our own lives. Our agency is honored and our inner life and opinion matters. We feel some ability to direct or control our own lives.

As parents, we thwart a kid's autonomy when we do anything that makes him feel like we have all the control.

The country analogy from chapter 1 really fits with autonomy. We are truly granting kids the ability to self-govern in ways they are ready for. They have the honor of making more and more choices in their own lives and the responsibility that comes with it. All along the way, they maintain their agency and have a sort of veto power in what they choose to do. As parents share power, their kids slowly learn to govern themselves.

When you support kids' autonomy, it's not permissive. It doesn't mean they get to do whatever they want. It means they have a say in decisions that affect their lives. Honoring autonomy is also not a completely hands-off approach. We don't just back off and detach from their lives and their development. Autonomy is a conversation. It's sharing power. Since a parent starts out with one hundred percent of the power at the beginning and a young adult ends up with one hundred percent of the power when she is fully launched, the balance of power is going to shift over time and be different in different areas of their lives.

Autonomy support is in the middle of the two extremes of being too controlling and being too permissive. It's giving kids a say, figuring out together how to share the power. This middle ground of autonomy support is where growth and development live.

The word *sharing* in *sharing power* is an interesting word. As LeAnn raised her family, she learned we only shared things we could cut into equal-sized pieces. Otherwise, we were taking turns. When the Lord began the united order with everything in common, people did not just equally share every piece of land and furniture and clothing. They were given stewardships. If they joined the order, they would donate everything they owned to the Church. Then they and the bishop would have a conversation about what they needed and, interestingly, what they wanted. They would counsel together, and whatever land, property, home, or business they and the bishop agreed upon was deeded back to them to be their sole ownership and stewardship. Then as they ran their business, any excess profits were given to the whole group to share. The stewardship lines were very clean and clear, and every person had personal ownership and responsibility. A conversation to share power with our developing teens might be similar. We can clearly divide different responsibilities between us, giving them personal responsibility and ownership of greater and greater portions of their lives, belongings, and contributions.

Elder Dale G. Renlund points out that "our Heavenly Father's goal in parenting is not to have His children *do* what is right; it is to have His children *choose* to do what is right and ultimately become like Him. If He simply wanted us to be obedient, He would use immediate rewards and punishments to influence our behaviors. But God is not interested in His children just becoming trained and obedient 'pets' who will not chew on His slippers in the celestial living room. No, God wants His children to grow up spiritually and join Him in the family business."[44]

Our job as parents is to help our children grow up spiritually. That means they need space to exercise their agency. Alma says there was a space granted unto man, a time to prepare to meet God (see Alma 12:24). In that space, God expects us to use our agency to make choices about our own lives and to learn by experience.

How to Support Autonomy

To support autonomy, give kids meaningful choices. The choices need to have options that we are okay with. Kids need to be able to say no and know for sure that we will be fine with either choice and won't get frustrated, angry, or passive aggressive. Until kids know they can truly say no, they don't feel free and autonomous to say yes. For example, as LeAnn was developing Goals with Kids, she worked with a young man who volunteered to experiment with some goal loops. In their first goal conversation he chose two goals: taking a strengths survey to find out what his strengths were and doing an internet search to read about a college he wanted to attend. They decided to follow up with texts, but as LeAnn texted him, he didn't respond. After a while she offered to find another participant, letting him know it was okay if he didn't want to continue. He decided not to continue and not to do the goals. A few hours later she got a text telling her what his top five strengths were from the strengths survey. As soon as he was sure that he could say no, he felt free to say yes and took the survey on his own.

Acknowledge a kid's inner experience to build autonomy. "We are going to the movie you didn't choose. You can be happy about it or frustrated and sad.

---

44 "Choose You This Day," *Ensign* or *Liahona*, Nov. 2018.

That's up to you." Ask your kid's perspective. Ask about your kid's emotions. Explain the why behind things you want your kid to do.

Avoid using control, rewards, threats, judgment, deadlines, and surveillance. And those are just the ones they've done research studies on. We could probably think of other ways to squish autonomy. Parenting sometimes includes some of these tactics, but use them wisely and sparingly. If you use one or more of these occasionally, remember first that it's more about patterns than what happens sometimes.

Try family councils. Family councils are a great place for parents and kids to experiment with sharing power and having a say in things that affect them. Nichole has regular couple and family councils. Each family member can propose changes to the family rules. Sage, their five-year-old, recently proposed that the kids could use their one hour of screen time to watch YouTube videos. They tried it successfully for several months. When the kids started watching YouTube videos with their friends, Nichole realized that having such young kids choosing YouTube videos made her anxious and feel like she had to police their choices constantly. She was worried they would run across inappropriate content accidentally. She talked to her husband, and they had a conversation at the next family council to change the rules so that only Mom and Dad could pick YouTube videos until the girls were older. Even though her decision was eventually overruled, Sage knew that she still had the power to influence family rules in the future and that her suggestions would be taken seriously.

Give kids reasons for your requests. Help them see that they aren't just little robots doing what you ask, but rather help them see a parent who has a household to run and kids to raise and who needs their cooperation.

Let your kids have their way sometimes. Look at the last ten disagreements you've had with your kid. Who got their way each time? If we won every time or if our kid won every time, we need to make some changes. Introduce ways for your kids to influence decisions concerning them. One preteen discovered that the best way to get his parents' attention was to create a PowerPoint describing why he wanted a change in the family rules or chores.

Goal conversations are about change. It's about allowing sloths and cheetahs and whoever you have in your family an opportunity to put effort into something they want for their futures. Then when that effort isn't forthcoming or doesn't get them where they want to go, we unpack change. We get curious and talk about what did and didn't go well that time. And eventually we talk about patterns that show up and brainstorm ways to break those patterns. That's why finishing goal loops is so important. That's why finishing goal loops is progress even when your child doesn't finish the goal. And every time you finish a loop of goal conversations, you learn more about your child, about how change really happens, and about what's getting in the way of progress here.

Competence

The second secret-sauce ingredient is competence. Kids need a sense of competence to maintain motivation. They act on their environment not just to make sense of it but also to master it. They need to feel up to the task and challenged, but able to figure it out. They want to feel like a contributing member of their groups. They need to have some ability to understand, manage, influence, and negotiate their environment.

Kids without competence soon lose interest in doing things because they don't believe they can figure them out or master them. When we feel stupid or incapable, we are less likely to act. Even if we are actually capable of doing something, if we don't believe we can, then we generally won't try. Parents can undermine competence by constantly putting their kids in over-challenging situations, saying things that make them feel stupid and incapable, being over-critical, expecting flawless performance, or doing tasks for them. Learned helplessness can be frustrating for parents, but some patient and persistent microgoal loops can help get kids back on track with feeling more competent and confident in their lives. It snowballs. The more competent they become, the more they are willing to try and risk, which in turn builds more competence. We put effort into what we believe we can accomplish.

How to Support Competence

There is nothing like success to motivate success. When we master a skill, it teaches us that we are capable of not just that particular skill but of learning and mastering new content and abilities. It's motivating to be competent. It feels good to be good at things. Progress and achievement are the best motivators.

Usually it's best to avoid easy goals since goals are meant to produce change in ourselves and the world around us. Easy goals don't give us the struggle necessary to increase strength or produce change. But sometimes it is useful to choose a series of easy goals that can give us small wins. Easy goals can help us understand how goals work throughout their life span. Easy goals can also give us some easy wins and build some self-efficacy. If our kids can't do something, we can break it down until we find something that they can.

Self-efficacy—or our belief in ourselves regardless of our actual competence—also influences motivation. When kids believe in themselves, they're more likely to tackle goals. Self-efficacy influences how kids meet stress and challenges. It determines how much effort they will expend to reach their goal and how long they will continue to pursue it. It helps them own the goal so they blame others less often.

If kids are lacking self-efficacy, research shows four things that can increase it.[45] Mastering any skill helps kids feel more confident in their own power. Watching another person do a goal they want to try helps them realize that it's possible for them too. Positive conversations can convince kids that they are capable of something. A kid's current mental state of being influences self-efficacy. Kids who are in a bad mood, have anxiety, or struggle with depression will generally have less belief in themselves for the moment.

There is a rule of thumb in parenting that we should never do for our kids what they can do for themselves. When we do, it's like robbing them of development, and we become developmental thieves.

The same day that LeAnn was writing this section, her just-turned-four-year-old granddaughter, Claire, pulled a loaf of bread from the counter and opened it to get a slice of bread. LeAnn naturally reached over to get it out for her. With the imagery of a developmental thief fresh in her mind, she handed Claire back the bag of bread and let her granddaughter practice getting her own slice of bread without dumping out the rest of the bag. It's surprising how often we rob our kids of developmental opportunities without even thinking about it.

One of the authors' Goals with Kids workshop participants told a similar story of "helping" her six-year-old daughter slide a piece of paper into a plastic sleeve without wrinkling it or folding the corners—a tiny but surprisingly useful and difficult adult skill to develop. The mom saw the daughter struggling and simply took it and did it for her. The six-year-old said, "Mommy, I was trying to learn how to do that. Don't do it for me."

Sometimes we steal opportunities for development by removing obstacles and snowplowing our kid's path. We may also hang around for too long, helicoptering just to make sure nothing bad happens. For example, we may keep giving advice to our adult children so nothing bad happens on our watch as parents, until we realize too late that our watch has been over for some time now. It's the job of good parents to work themselves out of a job and become obsolete.

Every skill is an art and a science, and every goal can be broken down into steps to reflect both the art and science of learning and living. A goal as simple as learning to drink from a cup is remarkably complex. It's fascinating to watch

---

45 See Albert Bandura, "Self-efficacy: Toward a Unifying Theory of Behavioral Change," *Psychological Review* (1977), 84(2), 191–215.

the number of ways toddlers can mess it up. They have to learn to hold the cup steady with two hands, even while moving it to their mouth. They get the edge of the cup to their mouth, tipping it without getting water up their nose. They have to remember to keep it straight after they drink it and not just forget they're holding it and dump it out. A one-year-old is already accomplished at a skill they will use their whole lives, while a ten-month-old will drink, get distracted, and pull her mouth away while the cup pours water down her dress. By the time kids are eight, they are so competent in daily living we can forget that learning new things still takes time and lots of mistakes. Those mistakes are necessary for kids to become competent, whether the skill is cup-drinking or speaking French.

Parents provide opportunities for kids to learn to drink from a cup. They all do it differently, and children take to it differently. Some parents start early, coaxing all along the way. Some use sippy cups to prevent spills for varying lengths of time. Some parents neglect teaching the skill, and the kid just learns at a friend's house or from discovering random leftover cups on the table and trying them out. Most parents just experiment in natural dinner settings whenever they feel like it or notice the kid is interested.

When LeAnn's kids got their first puppy, they went to a class to learn how to train him to walk without pulling at the leash, pee outside, and sit for a snack. The family joked about parenting being one-part relationship, one-part teaching, and one-part puppy training. Especially with young children, a touch of puppy-training know-how will help settle our kids into routines and behaviors that benefit the whole family. Think about training a nine-month-old to ease down the stairs backwards on his belly for safety or training an independent two-year-old to stop at the end of the sidewalk and wait for you to hold her hand crossing the street. A kid can be "trained" to do those simple things with simple repeated practice. We train kids to do things because we want them to be safe and it allows them to be more independent. Being competent in a few vital skills creates a web of competence, safety, and trust that allows parents to give kids more freedom. We can wait for them to burn themselves on the stove and figure it out for themselves, or we can do a little training to not touch stoves. Of course, our kids are not puppies, and teaching them to learn and think for themselves matters much more than simple training.

Relationships

The third ingredient to the motivation secret sauce is relationships. They can be with parents, grandparents, an aunt, an uncle, a supportive teacher, or someone at church. They are less about specific support to a kid's motivation and more like a backdrop to a kid's well-being. With some good relationships in the backdrop, kids feel safe and encouraged to try things, to continue exploring and bumping up against their environment. Without that relational background, kids get discouraged and don't feel like they have a safety net to help them recover if they fall or fail.

Kids are separate beings built to become independent, autonomous individuals. But independence is not lonely and it's not permissive. Independence isn't about being able to do whatever you want. It's about choosing for yourself, but it's also about being responsible and capable of taking care of yourself. But just because kids are separate and are driven for independence doesn't mean they don't want to have a relationship with you. They are also built for connection.

Connection and relationships are essential to healthy development and functioning. Kids and parents need to stand strong in their own personhood and work together to manage this dual need to be independent and to have close relationships. A solid, caring relationship is a core ingredient for kids to be motivated to keep engaging with their environment and to keep interacting with teachers, friends, grandparents, and schoolwork. In essence, to keep developing in their world.

Kids who have a backdrop of a supporting relationship are more likely to interact with their world and develop in healthy ways. Kids feel more secure to go out and explore when they have that relationship at home to support them. Even young toddlers are more willing to explore a new playground when a parent is safely nearby to check in with them.

Researchers studied at-risk children in Kauai, Hawaii, and followed them from infancy through adulthood.[46] The study found that even though the children grew up in at-risk circumstances, a third of them created successful lives. The resilient third of the participants shared this one characteristic in common: they had at least one competent, emotionally stable person who was sensitive to their needs. That person didn't have to be a parent. It could be an older sibling, aunt, uncle, grandparent, or any caring adult. The kids needed someone who had their back, someone who asked about their homework, and someone who they could wake up in the middle of the night.

Relationships matter that much. One solid, caring relationship can overcome a multitude of at-risk factors for a child. Develop warm, positive relationships with your kids. Be that person who doesn't mind being woken up at two in the morning.

---

46 Emmy E. Werner, "Risk, Resilience, and Recovery: Perspectives from the Kauai Longitudinal Study." *Development and Psychopathology* (fall 1993), 5(4), 503–515.

How to Build Relationships

Unconditional positive regard, which is essentially accepting a person no matter what he brings to you or no matter what he says or does, is a great relationship builder. This does not mean that we like the person, that we agree with what he is doing, or that we need to tolerate his behavior in our home. It means we respect the person's right to make his choices and we assume that each person is doing the best he can at the moment. This regard for people's personhood changes how we show up with them, how we talk to them, and how we respond to their behavior. We set clear boundaries, we don't get upset, we don't allow them in our home, and we respect their right to choose their lifestyle. On a smaller scale, we don't give dessert to kids who don't finish their dinner, but we don't ridicule or shame them for it.

There are a lot of ways to intentionally strengthen a relationship. Spending time together, using a calm, interested voice, listening well, and working through problems without yelling all contribute to relationships. We can also communicate to build relationships without talking. Sometimes a series of texts, tiny handwritten notes, or letters can say things that are difficult to say in person.

All relationships ebb and flow, but anything we can do to build the relationship matters. Try doing simple things together, like taking a walk around the block, going for a drive to get a soda, or lying on the trampoline and watching the stars at night. We know not every day is like that. We're often busy, swamped, and struggling. But we don't have to do these every day for them to count.

One great way to build relationships is to have a strengths conversation. List some strengths each of you has. It's especially helpful to take the free strengths survey at viacharacter.org to get a list of each of your top character strengths. Talk about which strengths turned up on your list and theirs. Ask what resonated with them. What surprised them? Later when you're having goal conversations, point out which strengths may have helped them do their goal or handle a setback or difficulty.

When you see your kids putting forth effort or weathering a failure, tell them you are proud of them. Ignore that occasional church discussion where someone says not to tell your kids you're proud of them because pride is a sin. Yes, pride is a sin when pride is comparing or hating or dismissing people. Saying "I'm proud of you" is not comparing. It's a feeling of excitement for them. It acknowledges their efforts. Remember the growth-mindset mantra of praising effort, not saying a kid is smart, fast, or talented. Notice their efforts and tell them what you see. "I noticed you kept going even after you said your homework was hard." "You seemed brave when you made that phone call even when you were nervous."

Goal conversations can build relationships. When you evaluate a goal with your kid, the three questions are meant to create a curious, open atmosphere that builds your relationship. Being kind and gentle when things go wrong helps your kid feel safe with you. When things go right, we can also respond well. We sometimes meet someone's good news by telling him things that could go wrong or asking if he's thought about something negative. Other times we overreact with our own excitement. Remember, the accomplishment is his and not ours. The most effective way to respond to our kids' good news is to ask open-ended questions that help them relive the experience. "How did you find out? What happened right before that? What happened next? What did you say? What did he say?" Encouraging them to relive the experience with us and tell us all about it allows them to savor it a bit more and lodge it in their memory bank of positive experiences. It builds relationships as well.

Readiness to Change

Now that we know the parents' secret sauce for motivation, let's look at another model of motivation that lets us know when people are ready to change. Even when we're ready to help them, sometimes kids just aren't ready to change. James Prochaska studied patients who refused to change even after being told they would die if they didn't. He found that there are five stages of change. Rather than immediately trying to motivate people by encouraging them to take action, even positively or gently, he found that different strategies applied depending on which stage of change they were in.[47] These strategies can be useful for kids too, especially for things that are good for them but that they don't want to do right now.

The five stages in their simplest forms are, "I won't or I can't," "I may," "I will," "I am," and "I still am." We tend to know how to respond when kids are actively planning or working on a goal, but we don't often know what to do when they refuse or feel unable to do a goal.

The most common stage is "I won't or I can't," also called pre-contemplation, where people have no intentions of changing a behavior anytime soon. Sometimes they don't feel competent enough to make the change. Sometimes they are resisting outside pressure and don't feel any autonomy. Other times they are uninformed and don't see a good reason to change. Sometimes they want to change but have failed before and are afraid to try again. Deep down there may be a part of them that actually wants to choose the goal and make a change, but at the same time

---

47 See James O. Prochaska, "Decision Making in the Transtheoretical Model of Behavior Change," *Medical Decision Making* (2008), 28(6), 845–849.

they aren't ready to. Whatever the underlying reason, Prochaska's research turned up several strategies that help others become more ready to change:
- Recognize that our kids can both want to do something and have no intentions of doing it all at the same time.
- Honor our kids' autonomy by reminding them they don't have to do the goal.
- Ask our kids to list all the good reasons *not* to do the goal. There are real reasons not to do good goals. Get them out in the open.
- Create a pros/cons list of reasons to change and to stay the same.
- Explore what's worked in the past with a similar goal. It can build self-efficacy to remember times when things went well.
- Together, imagine a default future if our kids never make the change.
- Alternatively, imagine that a miracle has happened and the change already occurred without our kids knowing—how would they notice things were different?
- Ask what the source of this goal is. Who wants them to change and why?
- Avoid trying to get them to act when they are not ready to change. It generally just increases resistance.
- Normalize, don't catastrophize. Remind them that a lot of people don't want to do goals like this.
- Take a break from this goal and work on something else.
- Choose tiny experiments or thought goals to see what it would be like, to create confidence or to remove barriers.

Later, if our kids get started on a goal but then have trouble maintaining it, relapse, or get bored, there are a host of other skills we can teach them to avoid slipping back into old patterns, like switching up the goal we're working on to make it more interesting. Remain judgment free. Just because our kids slip up a bit when they've had a goal down doesn't mean they're starting from ground zero. It's no big deal when there's a hiccup in the execution of a new goal. Reframe hiccups and lapses as temporary setbacks. Learn from the failures and begin a new goal loop toward the same goal.

This model is useful when you're having goal conversations and brainstorming goals with kids. It gives specific strategies when your kids seem to be dragging their feet. The strategies help us unpack what's happening and shift motivation when a kid wants to do a goal but isn't ready to start. Rather than pushing kids to take action when they are not ready, see if they are willing to choose microgoals to think about, feel about, or learn about a goal to help them decide if they even want to do it. It's a way of getting them off the fence to either outright reject or accept the goal.

Parenting and the Arena

As we turn our kids' countries more and more completely over to them, we send them out into the world in increasing measures. They grow, develop, and become more independent. How we prepare them for these encounters and for their ultimate independence is one of our greatest tasks. President Theodore Roosevelt said:

> It is not the critic who counts; not the man who points out how the strong man stumbles, or where the doer of deeds could have done them better. The credit belongs to the man who is actually in the arena, whose face is marred by dust and sweat and blood; who strives valiantly; who errs, who comes short again and again, because there is no effort without error and shortcoming; but who does actually strive to do the deeds; who knows great enthusiasms, the great devotions; who spends himself in a worthy cause; who at the best knows in the end the triumph of high achievement, and who at the worst, if he fails, at least fails while daring greatly, so that his place shall never be with those cold and timid souls who neither know victory nor defeat.[48]

When LeAnn's son Jackson was on a mission in Russia, he and his companion were cornered and beaten up by some street thugs. When LeAnn heard about it, she was stunned and felt both helpless and as though she were the one being beaten as she imagined what it would actually be like to be hit repeatedly by someone who intended harm.

Our kids enter arenas where they are alone, where they will struggle, and where we will not be there to protect them. That desire to protect and rescue them doesn't go away even after they are grown and independent. That's one reason transferring the power of kid's countries takes so much preparation. We prepare them not only for their preferred future that they are pursuing but also for the surprises that may come up along the way, so they can handle them on their own. We prepare them to be in the arena with their face marred by dust and sweat and blood and to know who to look to for support, how to ignore the critics, when to keep going despite the struggle, and when to beat it out of there.

---

48 "Citizenship in a Republic" (speech given at the Sorbonne in Paris, France, April 23, 1910).

Our kids face arenas like this every day where they walk into the world on their own. Their arenas might include school, a new friendship, football team tryouts, or even a single geography test. Their arenas might include church, a difficult sibling, or the eternal homework struggle. We stand with them at the doors to their arenas, sending them off with a kiss, a high five, and a "you got this." But we are more than just cheerleaders. We are parents and coaches waiting in the wings for their return.

These coaching moments happen at the crossroads of their lives as they enter and return from their arenas. They happen in our brief goal conversations. "How's it going out there in the arena? How did that goal go? What went well about it? What didn't? What did you learn?" It's more than just cheering them on. It's being a coach and counseling with them, then sending them back out into the arena where they face their lives alone.

But they aren't alone. They walk out into the world physically alone, but they know they have strong relationships at their back. We—their parents, uncles, aunts, church leaders, and teachers—have their backs when they return. Having their backs means we offer clean motivation and support with no strings attached. Our kids know that whether they win or lose, our love for them doesn't change. They feel like they have a say in which arenas they choose and in how they show up in those arenas. They've developed competence and understand the reasons we ask them to do things. They know in their hearts that they will be accepted as a person even when they disagree, say no to us, or fail. Parents matter more in the life of a child than anything that happens to them in the arena.

Imagine the parents of Helaman's stripling warriors, who taught their children so deeply that "if they did not doubt, God would deliver them" (Alma 56:47) that their sons went off to war never having fought, yet not fearing death, their only battle cry, "We do not doubt our mothers knew it" (verse 48). Their inexperienced children returning from the arena of war contained a miracle of "preservation [that] was astonishing to [the] whole army" (Alma 57:26). And the miracle was this: that "there was not one soul of them who did perish; yea, and neither was there one soul among them who had not received many wounds" (verse 25).

Kids with goals are like these stripling warriors. They are kids going into battle wielding faith in the teachings of righteous parents. They are kids who will endure many wounds and be marked by dust, sweat, and blood. They are kids who will once again step into the arena to face their futures. They are kids with parents who stand at the door of the arena, catch their kids as they return, dust them off, patch up their wounds, and send them back into the arena to face their futures.

CHAPTER 9
PRINCIPLE #4—OUTCOMES
HOW WE CAN PURSUE GOALS EVEN THOUGH OUTCOMES AREN'T GUARANTEED

Effort Does Not Guarantee Outcomes

As a senior in high school, Nichole's friends called her the valedictorian long before she finished high school with the highest GPA in the school. In her junior year, she took a look at the valedictorian application and noticed that it was possible to get a higher score if she were an artist rather than a musician because only AP Art was offered as a weighted fine arts credit. She went into the principal's office to ask about the unfair weight that could benefit students who took art over music electives. He assured her that it wouldn't happen and inappropriately joked about art students not having the kind of grades she had. Well, one did. In her friend group of six, one friend took AP Art and became valedictorian, and the other five in the friend group became co-salutatorians, tied for second place, even though Nichole had the highest GPA in her class. Excellent effort does not guarantee expected outcomes.

When we have an expectation that doesn't turn out, it can be really tough to swallow, especially when we put our effort into it and it was reasonable to assume we would earn the results of our hard work. Life's not fair and can be disappointing.

Even faith and righteousness don't guarantee mortal outcomes. When Shadrach, Meshach, and Abednego refused to bow to the idol, the king sentenced them to be burned in a hot furnace. They said their God would save them, but if not, they would choose faith anyway (see Daniel 3:17–18). The key phrase "but if not" separates two truths: we believe the Lord can save us, but we also recognize that He may not, and we have to be okay with both answers. These three were saved from death by fire, but an equally faithful Abinadi was not rescued from the flames (see Mosiah 17:12–15). Alma and Amulek were restrained from saving righteous women and children being consumed by flames (see Alma 14:8–11).

Elder Bednar asked this question of a young man facing cancer: "Do you have the faith not to be healed?"[49] Essentially, he was asking if the young man's faith would allow either outcome and not falter. We don't understand why a miracle is forthcoming in one situation and not in another, but we do know that faith produces spiritual strength regardless of outcome. And that strength is what matters in the eternities.

Similarly, faithful parenting spiritually strengthens us regardless of our kids' outcomes, which are out of our control. Elder Holland said, "Our children take their flight into the future with our thrust and with our aim. And even as we anxiously watch that arrow in flight and know all the evils that can deflect its course after it has left our hand, nevertheless we take courage in remembering that the most important mortal factor in determining that arrow's destination will be the stability, strength, and unwavering certainty of the holder of the bow."[50]

We launch our kids into the future, but we don't get to control where they land. Accepting the uncertainty of our kids' futures calms us and gives us perspective. But the fact that our kids will one day land in places, marriages, habits, and lives we don't desire for them doesn't mean we can't be stable, strong, and unwavering parents now. How do we do that?

Accept Our Separateness

First, it helps to radically or completely accept that our kids are separate beings from us. They have agency. They have their own mortal journeys. And no amount of amazing parenting can guarantee our kids' landings.

When one of LeAnn's friends adopted siblings from Eastern Europe, the kids were older and already mostly the people they were going to become. They had already been taught to work hard and to tell the truth, and they already had their unique personalities. The fifteen-year-old sibling, Nastia, had an infectious smile, a cell phone, and a boyfriend named Artiom. The parents spent a month getting to know the kids, and they mutually agreed to adopt one another as family. Even with the language barrier, they tried talking to Nastia about her relationship with Artiom. They made kissing sounds and asked, "You and Artiom?" Nastia blushed, laughed, and said, "No, no, no!" The parents had to come back to the United States for a ten-day waiting period and were worried about the possibility of Artiom pressuring Nastia to have sex with him before

---

49 "That We Might 'Not . . . Shrink' (D&C 19:18)" (CES Devotional for Young Adults given at the University of Texas Arlington, Mar. 3, 2013).
50 "A Prayer for the Children," *Ensign* or *Liahona*, May 2003.

she left forever. They had talked about it the best they could before they left, but they had to radically accept that they had no control over whether Artiom and Nastia had sex before she came to America or not.

That radical acceptance did something for the parents. First, it calmed them. They knew that whatever happened, including the possibility of a pregnant fifteen-year-old, they would be family and they would figure it out.

Second, they realized that they weren't responsible for the behavior of any of their children—adopted or biological—even though they raised them for all or part of the last eighteen years. They certainly influenced them. They certainly sacrificed the greater part of their lives caring for them. But they didn't get to take credit or blame for who the kids turned out to be. Kids live their lives and make their choices. That radical acceptance helped them become better parents.

Untangle from Kids' Outcomes

We all learn parenting skills that help us to become better parents. It feels great to try a new skill with a tantrum-throwing toddler or a school-aged kid who forgot his lunch and have the strategy work well. Even when we build our parenting repertoire, we don't get to count on them as guarantees. Our behavior does not guarantee their behavior, no matter how skilled a parent we are. Success with a parenting technique today does not guarantee success next Tuesday.

When we radically accept and really see that we can't guarantee any particular outcome or future, then we show up differently as parents. Untying ourselves from our kids' results, whether it's their behavior in class, their execution of chores, or the occupation they choose in adulthood, releases us from internal pressures that can change our relationships with our kids.

Let's look at a baseball metaphor. Say our kid wants to play baseball on a team with his friend. Awesome. We sign him up. We take him to practices. We go to the games and cheer. Say he hits and gets on base the first time. Say this triggers a memory for us from our childhoods. We create a story in our minds about how being a kid who gets on base is a kid who is popular or successful in other areas of life. Something shifts, and we suddenly want this kid to get on base again. The minute we start hoping for a certain outcome, it's like we've tied a string from our wrist in the stands to his ankle out there on the field. It changes everything. It changes the way we cheer, the way we practice with him at home, and what we say on the way to the game. Just adding that simple expectation can create disappointment when he doesn't get on base the next time. And if this kid senses that hovering expectation, he will notice the string and will be more likely to get tripped up in his own performance.

Researchers have found that when our minds are preoccupied with how someone might think of or judge us, our performance suffers.[51] When a kid has a parent whose happiness or sense of worth as a parent is tied to the kid's performance, the performance actually gets worse. It's like the archer in Chuang Tzu's poem "The Need to Win": When he shoots for fun, his shots are more skillful, but "if he shoots for a prize of gold / He goes blind / Or sees two targets. . . . He thinks more of winning / Than of shooting— / And the need to win / drains him of power."[52] The prize divides his effort and concentration and wastes his skill. His performance suffers from the extra target hovering in his head.

Plan for Plans to Fail and Unfold

One way we can be stable, strong, unwavering parents in the face of uncertainty is to plan for plans to fail and unfold at the same time. This includes both our own plans as well as our children's plans for their futures.

A class of eleven-year-olds was discussing their futures and came up with three truths. First, if you don't plan for your future, life just happens to you. Second, planning for your future gets you where you want to go. And third, you can't predict the future, because an earthquake might happen in five minutes. They talked about holding all those truths in their minds at the same time. Their discussion ping-ponged. Planning for the future gets us where we want to go. But we can't predict the future. But planning for the future gets us where we want to go. But we can't be one hundred percent sure something won't happen to get in the way. But if we don't plan, we'll have zero control over what happens to us. They decided that they needed to plan for their plans not going according to plan and to be flexible so that when an earthquake knocks a tree into their path, they can find a way around it.

This mental agility is a hallmark of mature adults and is what the goal loop can teach children on their way to *becoming* adults. The ability to be agile and flexible in our thinking, holding more than one true principle in our minds at the same time, helps us to navigate a covenant path on mortal terrain. And because we are always navigating that terrain, not only will our plans fail and get interrupted, but we will also create new plans on our own as we better learn what we want from life. As we turn corners on the path, we see new terrain that can change our ideas of where we're going and how we're going to get there. Our plans continue to unfold as we execute them.

---

51 See Claude M. Steele, *Whistling Vivaldi: How Stereotypes Affect Us and What We Can Do* (New York: WW Norton & Company, 2011).

52 Quoted in Thomas Merton, "The Need to Win," *The Way of Chuang Tzu* (New York: New Directions, 1965), 107.

Prepare with Process Goals

Our efforts do not guarantee outcomes, but they definitely make them more likely. We control how we prepare. If we have a math test on Friday, we could choose from an abundance of preparation goals. We could do every homework assignment leading up to the test. We could practice math problems at home. We could ask the teacher or a parent to explain math problems we don't understand. We could give up a TV show we like this week to spend time working hard at math. We can even control how we show up for the test. We can eat breakfast in the morning before school. We can pray for Heavenly Father's help. We can take a deep breath and relax before the test to help alleviate stress and concentrate. We can't completely control the outcome of the test, but we can make it more likely that the outcome will be better than if we hadn't made goals and put effort toward it.

Edwin Locke and Gary Latham have studied goal setting for decades. They've discovered a number of variables that affect goal performance. In addition to the difficulty of the goal, it also matters whether we focus on process or outcome. When we face a task, especially a complex one, a focus on process or learning goals like finishing homework or practicing a specific strategy produces better results than focusing on outcome goals like getting an A on the test.[53] These learning goals put our efforts where they will matter most and make the accomplishment of our goals more likely.

Begin

"Begin, just begin in the simplest way." This is how Joy D. Jones invited us to start implementing home-centered goal setting.

When LeAnn and her husband, Daryl, lived in Virginia, they were called to teach Primary in the Dulles Branch, a branch of mostly Southeast-Asian refugees from Laos and Cambodia. He taught the nine-, ten-, and eleven-year-old boys, and she taught the same-aged girls. Only two or three of the many children on the roster showed up to church. The Primary president asked LeAnn and Daryl to call every child on the list. With a great deal of hesitation, they began calling. One boy said he didn't have time to come to church because he was studying to be a doctor. Another wanted to come but never had a ride. Another refused to come to the phone even after repeated attempts. And one father hung up on them because they couldn't pronounce the Asian name properly. This simple beginning of a few phone calls turned into five years of the most amazing

---

53   See Edwin A. Locke and Gary P. Latham, "New Directions in Goal-Setting Theory," *Current Directions in Psychological Science* (2006), 15(5), 265–268.

adventures activating and growing with the children in those classes. The critical step was to begin.

It's almost like before the phone calls, the goal territory of being a Primary teacher was limited to showing up and teaching for an hour each Sunday. After the phone calls, a whole new territory opened up where the names on the page became real people, and goals that didn't exist before unfolded. Now the teachers wanted to know who those kids were, to go to their homes, to meet them, to get to know them, and to invite them back to church and activities. The phone calls broadened the horizons of their Primary-calling goals to include new days of the week, new kids, new parents, new apartment buildings, new activities, new conversations, and new foods. It's difficult to imagine all the memories that would never have happened without that first step of making some phone calls. To begin is to open the door to a whole new world—a whole new goal map. Don't let the uncertainty of non-guaranteed outcomes paralyze us. Begin.

Enter a Beginner Mindset

Beginners naturally try things out and learn by experience. When we learn how to walk, we fall down a thousand times, and that's okay. But by the time we're three or four, falling down feels like a failure. By the time we're eight, we're so used to basic competence that it's hard to enter a beginner mindset. This is even more pronounced with parents, who are older and have people depending on them. But holding our first newborn baby turns us into newborn parents. As beginner parents, we need to have a beginner mindset by letting go of the expectation that this has to turn out a certain way.

New things are uncertain, and there is no guarantee it's going to turn out or that we are going to be any good at it. There are still so many things to learn as an adult, even when we are in the middle of adulthood. We can fight the uncertainty by embracing a beginner's mindset where we have permission to fail, permission to look silly, and permission to not get it at first. We can both model it for our kids and teach it to them directly.

Have an Action Bias

At their core, goals are about action. We sometimes get bogged down in planning and thinking about goals. Instead we need an action bias. We have an action bias when we tend to take action at the earliest opportunity again and again.

When we set a goal, the outcome is not guaranteed. One reason is that as we pursue the outcome and begin moving toward it, the action teaches us things about ourselves and about the goal. We may find new goals to get us to the outcomes we want, or we may find we want a different outcome all together. Either way, it was the action that taught us what needed to change.

For example, when we have a new calling to teach a classroom full of youth, we can learn more in five minutes at the front doorstep of their home taking action to meet them before the year starts than in five months of regular Sunday lessons.

LeAnn's son Jackson worked on some BYU student-animated films when he was a student there. Sometimes a student would be asked to create a model or small animation sample for a film she was working on just to see if it would look right in the film. Both the student and the director knew it might not end up in the film, but they needed to see it in order to decide. Even though it cost a great deal of effort, this prototyping was necessary for the student to create her best work. She had to act and then make decisions based on the results of each experiment.

Many of us are overthinkers. Careful thought can protect us from some mistakes, but it also holds us back from greater progress. We don't have to figure it all out before we act. We act in order to figure it all out. We launch first and fix it later. We take action and learn from the experience. We set goal loops and evaluate the good and the bad. An action bias jump-starts the stalled engine of our overthinking. An action bias blasts through the life plans we have stuck in our heads because theoretical plans generally don't survive contact with reality.

You didn't pick up a book on goals expecting to not do goals. Engaged goal setting requires taking action early and often. It requires an action bias. When we engage like this, goals truly do become the engine of growth and change.

It might seem like we don't have time for these kinds of mistakes, but that's all we do have time for. This is the great plan of happiness. We learn by experience, and we gain experience by taking action.

We proposed at the beginning of the book that engaged parenting is the answer to good-enough parenting. Believing we're entitled to the outcomes we want for our kids because of our parenting efforts will only lead to disappointment. We're not baking a cake; we're raising a kid. Even attempting to follow the same parenting recipe will turn out different results with different kids. We can't guarantee outcomes, but we don't need to. Whatever outcomes we think we need to be good parents are constructs of our own minds. We can, however, engage with what's really going on right in front of us with our kids right now. We can accept our separateness, plan for plans to fail, prepare with process goals, begin, enter a beginner mindset, and have an action bias to parent in the face of uncertainty. That's engaging. That's the covenant path. That's good-enough parenting.

CHAPTER 10
PRINCIPLE #5 — IMPROVEMENT
HOW FAILING FREQUENTLY WITH SMALL GOAL LOOPS FUELS PROGRESS

We often hear the advice, "Just be a little better every day." That's encouraging because it reminds us that small steps are the currency of improvement. It's also discouraging because it paints a picture of a continual line that always goes up, a little better every day, leaving no room for backsliding, plateauing, or messing up. But that incline, even if it's a gentle slope, doesn't reflect reality.

When we put effort into goals, we don't necessarily get better in each twenty-four-hour period. Improvement fluctuates more than that. For example, the Church's website addressing pornography addiction specifically details the many roads to improvement and talks about the backsliding and cycles that normally occur. We backslide, plateau, experiment, make mistakes, get worse sometimes, and try things that don't work during our upward climb. That's the messy reality of progress, and we get discouraged sometimes if we believe the road to improvement is a straightforward stepladder or a predictable rising slope.

Rather than a climb that always goes up, imagine the road to improvement, like the covenant path, laid out on earthly terrain. Imagine a goal laid out as a path through curving mountains, valleys, forests, fields, and deserts. Pursuing a goal gives us direction through the terrain and a way to measure our progress. It forecasts possible pathways to attain the goal. We then follow those pathways until we adjust either the destination or the path to get there. Some goals are accomplished quickly while others wind their way through months and years. Each time we consider our goals, the map we've laid out can change.

From a bird's-eye view, you can see the curves of the path weaving in and out and switchbacking up mountains. You can watch people walking the goal path and see where they're headed and the progress they're making. But down on the path the jungle is hot and sticky, you don't know what's around the bend in the road, you've temporarily lost sight of the destination, and it doesn't feel like you're making any progress at all. Sometimes it even feels like it's getting worse.

Let's look at the nature of improvement and progress. We already know that improvement is gradual. Sister Ann M. Dibb said,

> Thinking back to when I was a young woman, I recognize that I did not understand the magnitude of what was happening in my life. I did not realize that my participation in each and every Church activity was helping me develop a lifelong pattern and commitment to follow the teachings of Jesus Christ. I didn't understand that I was being prepared for my future life as an individual, a wife, a mother, and a leader. I didn't understand that as I tried to choose the right, I was honoring my baptismal covenants, exercising faith, increasing my virtue, and preparing to go to the temple. I couldn't see all of this then, but in very small, incremental steps, I was becoming a believer—and "an example of the believers."[54]

Her progress was so gradual that she didn't even realize it was happening. Some actions make a real difference in the long run but are hardly perceptible in the short term. Drinking eight glasses of water a day will improve our health, but it's just as easy not to drink the extra water. Praying every day looks, at least on the surface, a lot like not praying every day, even though it connects us more closely to God. These kinds of actions are just as easy not to do as they are to do because their results aren't noticeable right away. Goals like eating healthy, exercising a little, or practicing mindfulness make a remarkable difference throughout a lifetime, but because the results are cumulative over a long time, it takes a great deal of faith to execute them regularly.

Improvement is gradual, but it is also piecemeal; it comes sporadically, bit by bit, drop by drop. When we realize that the road to improvement plateaus, dips, and curves, we can be kinder to ourselves when things aren't going well in the moment. But often we don't recognize where we are and mistake the normal terrain of progress for hopeless failure.

For example, in this moment, we, the authors, are in the middle of writing this book. We have made good progress, are confident in our abilities as writers and researchers, and yet yesterday we were both lost on the path. We were stuck writing one part of the book and editing another, and it felt as though we would never get done. We seriously considered calling it quits. We were sure we weren't making any progress and felt deeply discouraged. We felt the progress we were making was taking too long and that there was no possible way we could meet our

---

54 "Be Thou an Example of the Believers," *Ensign* or *Liahona*, May 2009.

deadlines at the pace we were going. Because we were literally writing this chapter, we took our own advice and zoomed up to a bird's-eye view of our goal. We saw that we were making progress—we were just in a temporary valley. There was no way out but through, but instead of continuing to push and push and push, we stopped and discussed our options. We encouraged and supported each other. We didn't know how it would turn out, but we found a way, and you are reading this now.

There is a difference between how a goal feels when we set it, how it feels when we're executing it, and how it feels when we're looking back on it. When we set the goal, we know it's going to be hard, but we're excited about the possibilities. In the middle of the goal, there is no one generalized way it feels, but it always seems to feel different than we expected. Because it feels different than we thought it would, the surprise can derail us from our goal. We can believe that our goal is not working out when, really, it's working out just fine. That's why engagement is so important.

Engaging with a goal is the magic. Engaging means we don't hold one idea of how it is supposed to go too tightly. All the emotional roller coasters, backslides, and experiments are just terrain. Effort and engagement are continual; improvement is not. And what does engagement look like? It looks like goal loops, where we check in regularly to see what's going well, why that's going well for now, what's not going well, what we are learning, and if we still want to pursue this path.

When we feel lost or discouraged, hate our goal, or are ready to quit, that's just a flag reminding us that we are lost for the moment. Remember that "hug a tree" advice we got as kids in case we ever got lost in the forest? That advice helps kids calm down and stay put so they can be found. The minute we find ourselves overwhelmed, quitting, angry, or sad about a goal, we can use that as a signal for us to realize we're lost in the real estate of our goal. It's time to zoom out, take a bird's-eye view, and adjust our goal or our approach to our goal.

Improvement Fatigue

Sometimes in our efforts to improve, we run faster than we have strength (see Mosiah 4:27). We may take on too many goals at once. We may feel the pressure of too many people handing us goal maps that worked for them and let that influence us to choose goals we don't really want to do. We may have the idea that we need to be hustling to improve every single day.

Any of these pressures is a recipe for improvement fatigue. The idea that we are on a never-ending treadmill of improvement is exhausting. When we keep missing the mark in our improvement efforts, we can feel stressed about getting it right or we might give up setting goals entirely.

The better we understand the nature of improvement, the better we can avoid improvement fatigue and use goals selectively to help us get what we want in our lives. The word *selectively* is important. Sometimes we get this overwhelming feeling that we need to be improving every single day. What if today we need to just be executing our day? Simply making breakfast, getting kids off to school, going to work, being kind when we get home, and making it through the day. Goals are important, but they don't always have to permeate our lives.

The Nature of Improvement

There are different kinds of improvement. Recognizing the variety of ways in which we can improve can help us better understand the nature of improvement and navigate the terrain of our goals. There's never just one way to measure our effort, our improvement, or the results of our goals.

When we set a goal to lose weight, is the scale the only measure of improvement? Weight can vary as much as five or six pounds in a single day. Exercise or eating patterns can take weeks to produce results. So measuring results solely by weighing ourselves every day can be counterproductive. To truly engage in the goal of weight loss is to get curious about what really works. Since results often take a couple of weeks, making two-week experiment goals makes a lot of sense. A lot of different diets and exercise regimens work. The question is, which works for us for right now? With a series of experiments on weight loss, the scale would be only one of the data points toward improvement. Other ways to measure the results of our experiments would be to write down how we felt, our energy level, our hunger level, our agitation or frustration with that eating style, a list of foods we ate, and a list of what we learned. Today's number on the scale is less important than figuring out what's going on and how we can maintain our weight loss in the long run.

Nichole, like most young moms, struggles to keep the kitchen clean. It's a never-ending task that would require a ridiculous amount of constant effort to always stay clean with three young kids running in and out, making messes. She recently chose a goal to finish certain kitchen tasks once a day and created a dish routine. The kitchen is rarely model-home clean, but neither does it have huge stacks of dishes hanging around to haunt her or literal beans sprouting in the damp dish rags in the bottom of the sink. When she measured her success by only a clean kitchen, she was constantly disappointed and down on herself as a homemaker. When she created a routine and made executing the routine her goal, she could walk by a mild mess without feeling bad because she knew her routine would address it soon enough.

We need to be intentional with our goals and how we measure the outcomes. There are different kinds of improvement just like there are different kinds of terrain. Awareness of the various ways we can improve will help us set clearer goals and better recognize our progress.

Some improvement is like learning to ride a bike; we never forget. Barring illness or injury, we never forget how to sign our names, type on a keyboard, play a musical instrument, or make Mario jump. This kind of improvement is more than a drop of oil in our lamps that will get burned for light later; these are skills that accumulate in our lives and only get rusty from disuse instead of disappearing entirely. If you practice swimming freestyle with impeccable form, you may be out of shape later, but you'll still have that muscle memory to know how to swim well.

Some improvement has a short shelf life. Like muscles, you can lose it without the continued use. Sharon, a friend of ours, worked out regularly and then had to stop for a few months because of a back injury. When she went back to working out, she had to start with much lighter weights than she'd left off using. Her muscles were weak and hadn't stored up her previous efforts. She was so frustrated that all that working out hadn't amounted to anything. Of course, it had while she was doing it, but it had a short shelf life. President Henry B. Eyring reminds us that even "faith has a short shelf life" and needs to be used regularly rather than stored up like oil that sits on the shelf, unused and slowly turning rancid.[55]

Some improvement, like music and sports, is the result of practice and learning. LeAnn has wanted to be a speaker and inspirational teacher since she went to a youth education week class when she was sixteen. Over years of teaching opportunities in the Church, she learned dozens of specific skills and techniques to become a better teacher. For example, in order to lead better discussions, she learned how to ask open-ended questions and practiced writing out good questions before she taught. She watched how other teachers taught and wrote down phrases they used that she liked. She practiced responding to participants with a "thank you." When she first started asking questions, she didn't like the silences, so she would jump in too quickly. So then she practiced asking a question, then literally watching the clock for up to twenty-five seconds of silence before jumping in. Each skill was a separate burst of improvement that overall changed the quality of her teaching.

Some improvement can be accomplished by improving the shining moment. We might improve a moment with a spontaneous microgoal, we might change our own behavior, reach out to help someone else, or make some changes to our environment. To improve the moment requires us to be aware of what's going on around us and to understand what would actually be helpful in the moment. We don't always need to have a grand plan for improvement to occur.

---

55 "Spiritual Preparedness: Start Early and Be Steady," *Ensign* or *Liahona*, Nov. 2005.

One of LeAnn's ancestors received a free plot of land in the town of Woburn, Massachusetts, in 1640 with the agreement that her ancestor's family could keep it if they improved the land within fifteen months. That meant they had to plant crops. Improvement can mean doing something useful like this that benefits ourselves, our families, and our communities.

LeAnn has a friend who has a five-year-old sticky note on her mirror reminding her of her goals to pray and be more diligent. Sound familiar? There are some goals we never fully arrive at, so we keep them around for a long time. To keep these never-arriving goals fresh and relevant, we need to create specific goal loops around how we want to work on our goal. We need something to look back on that shows our progress.

For example, Brook, a participant in LeAnn's Goals with Kids workshops, wanted to get control of her finances. She is not employed and wanted to contribute to the family finances, so she decided to become a better financial steward. First, she read some blogs about budgeting. Then she chose the envelope method, where you put cash in envelopes for each category. It was eye-opening to see what they were spending, but it was inconvenient to take kids into the gas station to pay for gas and always carry envelopes around. She read more articles and moved to having seven different accounts for different purposes. That was frustrating and confusing because different things were due different times and didn't align with the paychecks, not to mention the required minimums. Last year she set out to create and stick to a budget, but quickly changed her goal to track every penny in a spending log. She stuck with that goal for a year. Then she took the Church's personal finance class.

None of these goals lasted forever. None of them brought her all the way to her goal of being a good financial steward. Many of them contained an element of failure. But they all contributed to her never-arrive goal by giving her new skills, knowledge, and experiences. She knows where the money's going. She knows some methods that don't work for her. She talks to her husband about money and has gained more respect from him. They feel like more of a team because of her interest in the family's finances. She's had enough failures to know what success looks like. It's maintainable and rewarding for her. She realizes that this goal will always be a work in progress.

We never arrive at some goals, like health and relationship goals, because the results need continual attention. Other goals, like financial goals, often change with our circumstances. Even at a basic level, think about how many skills you need to manage your finances in modern life. Tackling some goals, like having your finances completely under control, can feel like we never arrive because they are complex, have a lot of moving parts, and take years of effort to truly master.

It doesn't have to be discouraging to work on never-arriving goals. We can identify and bank progress by our creative efforts to design interesting goal experiments. We can mix it up with a variety of approaches to our goals. We can learn new, underlying skills that support our ongoing efforts to improve in those areas.

Small, sustained efforts over time create real improvement, but there are limits to the promises of daily goals. One mythical example of daily improvement is Milo of Croton. He became strong by picking up a newborn calf and carrying it up the hill every day until it was a bull. It's a great story to teach this principle of gradual improvement, at least until you realize that at some point, human muscles can't lift more weight, and that a bull is going to get extremely awkward to lift with all its bulk. There are human limits to our progression that, when ignored, will cause us to doggedly work at something that is simply not possible to change.

Nichole once had a Relief Society sister help her understand the nature of improvement. The sister gave the example of yelling at our kids and explained a scenario: Say we decide we don't want to yell at our kids anymore, and we make a goal to breathe and walk into the bathroom for a few minutes to calm ourselves instead. The next day, just after we finish yelling at our kids, we remember we weren't going to do that anymore. The next day, we remember just as we yell our last words. The next day, we recognize right in the middle of yelling that this is what we don't want to do, but we can't stop ourselves. The next day, we remember earlier and shift gears in the middle of yelling and stop. The next day, just before we get ready to yell, we remember not to yell at all and take that break instead.

Catching yourself earlier and earlier is a form of improvement. We can remember in the middle of what we are doing wrong, and that is still progress. There is a gradual noticing that happens earlier and earlier. This doesn't mean we will never yell at our kids again; their ages and stages will change. We will change. Our circumstances will change. Then, in six months, we are yelling again for a different reason and can address it again at that time. But for now, it's better.

Another way to we can improve is to build habits to the point that we do them more often than not. Too often, our goals point to flawless performance when they don't need to. If we can exercise or practice a musical instrument more often than not, that may be enough. Goals that require daily commitment, like feeding a pet, are occasionally necessary, but more-often-than-not goals tend to be more useful, encouraging, motivating, and produce the needed growth. There's nothing magic about a daily goal.

We sometimes jump to the conclusion that if something is good, that means it's worth doing every day or as often as possible. Play with different goal cadences. Experiment with what works for you. Bank the days you do it and don't beat yourself up on the days you don't. Think about what you are actually trying to accomplish with a goal that repeats itself.

When LeAnn was actively working out, she started sticking her used gym wristbands on the inside of a kitchen cupboard. After a while, all the bands would flutter when that cabinet was opened. There was no negative consequence when a day was missed, except for missing the workout itself. But the accumulation of bands from working out more often than not was really inspiring to her and to her teenage kids.

In order to survive the onslaught of data our brains receive every second from all of our senses experiencing the world around us, our brains do an incredible amount of things automatically. Not just the truly automatic things like breathing and heartbeats but also that thing that happens when we go on autopilot and drive to a destination and don't even remember how we got there. We were doing a complicated task, driving somewhere safely, but our brain handled much of the work automatically without our awareness.

Sometimes we can use this to our advantage to train our brains to respond in certain ways. For example, people with anxiety can hook up their finger on a probe connected to a computer that shows their heart rate, blood pressure, and body temperature. With just a little practice, they can slow their breathing and thoughts in ways that literally slow their heart rate in just moments and watch it happen live on the screen. With some practice they can train their brain and body to automatically breathe slowly in stressful situations in order to calm everything down.

The improvement comes when we can take things that currently require a great deal of effort to do in our conscious minds and make them automatic. And we do this by simply practicing them, allowing our brain to produce new neural pathways to connect new stimuli to new responses.

Navigating Goals

When we understand the kind of improvement we really seek, we can choose more meaningful goals, take a bird's-eye view to understand our progress, and better adjust our goals.

Understanding the nature of improvement is key to choosing and navigating good goals and not getting lost in the middle of them. There are a few simple steps we can take to get a good start navigating our goals.

Start Where You Are

We can do as Elder Uchtdorf suggested:

> Start where you are.
>
> Sometimes we feel discouraged because we are not "more" of something   more spiritual, respected, intelligent, healthy, rich, friendly, or capable. Naturally, there is nothing wrong with wanting to improve. God created us to grow and progress. But remember, our weaknesses can help us to be humble and turn us to Christ, who will "make weak things become strong." Satan, on the other hand, uses our weaknesses to the point that we are discouraged from even trying.
>
> I learned in my life that we don't need to be "more" of anything to start to become the person God intended us to become.
>
> God will take you as you are at this very moment and begin to work with you. All you need is a willing heart, a desire to believe, and trust in the Lord.[56]

Awkward Beginnings

New goals can be awkward at first. It's like learning to paddle a canoe. The balance feels off, and the river of life keeps bringing us new obstacles. If we paddle for a long time, we use new muscles that get sore. Our first efforts at paddling don't usually bring us where we want to go. It's normal for new goals to be awkward at first, but with some practice, they won't stay that way.

The Idea of a Goal

Realize that the idea of a goal isn't the same as executing it, just like planning a hike through the woods and up a mountain isn't the same as the actual hike. When scrapbooking was a thing, LeAnn's scrapbooks always had comments by the photos. A photo of the family relaxing at the bottom of the Grand Canyon might say, "We had sore legs and couldn't bear to stand." A beautiful forest campsite would be subtitled, "Mosquitoes ate us alive—twenty-three bites on one arm." It's not that she wanted to complain; the photo just didn't capture the whole experience. Things on paper look different.

Planning a goal uses a bird's-eye view where we can see the larger path and destination laid out on the terrain below us, but we can't see details of the path.

---

56 "It Works Wonderfully!" *Ensign* or *Liahona*, Nov. 2015.

Executing a goal is down in the nitty-gritty on the path. We can see the obstacles in our way, but we occasionally lose sight of the larger picture. Goal-getters need to be able to switch between perspectives in the middle of a goal when necessary.

Failure

The most significant misunderstandings we have about navigating our improvement and our goals are about failure. We don't plan for it when we create our goal maps, we don't like how it feels when we're down in the middle of it, and we will go far out of our way, taking the long road if you will, in order to avoid it. It's only when we zoom out to take a bird's-eye view that we get a glimpse of how far failure can move us along the path toward our goals.

Fail-Frequently Principle

LeAnn cleared some wedding invitations from her fridge door the other day and noticed that one invitation had been there for six months. Buried inside that invitation was a goal to send them a gift because she hadn't been able to attend the reception. After six months, the embarrassment of sending a gift so late overcame the regret of not sending a gift at all, and she finally declared the moment a failure and threw the card in the trash. She immediately felt relieved and was astonished that she had carried that silent task on her to-do list for so long.

President Monson said, "Our responsibility is to rise from mediocrity to competence, from failure to achievement. Our task is to become our best selves. One of God's greatest gifts to us is the joy of trying again, for no failure ever need be final."[57] No failure ever need be final because there are always new ways to approach a goal. For failure to be final, we would need to give up completely.

At the same time, when we hold on to hope endlessly for the same goal, it can create a backlog of intentions and desires that aren't being actively worked on simply because we don't want to acknowledge failure. Unfinished goals lounge around our brains and get stuck on our mental bookshelves and stashed in our mental closets to get to someday. Then when we see something that reminds us of our unfinished goals, we feel bad and it causes us undue stress.

LeAnn graduated with honors from BYU. The process involved taking some honors classes, writing a thesis, and having an interview. During the interview she discovered that she hadn't read a lengthy list of books and articles required to graduate with honors. With graduation only weeks away and finals to complete, she knew she would never be able to read all of the books and accepted the fact that she wouldn't get the honors designation. The interviewer felt bad for her and asked if she would promise to read the books after she graduated. LeAnn agreed and graduation commenced.

---

57 "The Will Within," *Ensign*, May 1987.

The interviewer did not do LeAnn any favors. LeAnn ended up reading *Don Quixote* aloud with her husband as they drove cross country to their new job and home rather than enjoying the scenery. But she never got around to reading Karl Marx or the rest of the list. She tucked the list away when she got there and felt bad every time she ran across it, but she could never bring herself to throw it away.

She no longer wanted the goal, but because she had already received the reward or credit for it, she felt like she couldn't discard it. Without an end to the goal, the time extension given by the interviewer kept the goal hovering around forever. She finally lost the list and has chalked the experience up to a life lesson in not granting endless extensions and just calling a fail a fail. We sometimes do this with our kids, endlessly giving them a second chance or more time to complete a commitment when it might be better to simply, calmly call it a fail and then work through the goal loop to see what's next.

Think about our wagon wheel covering the terrain of a goal. Each turn of a goal loop moves us closer to our goal. But wait—what about the failures? When we fail, is it like our wagon wheel gets stuck in the mud? Is failure a wheel just spinning uselessly on slick, wet ground and not going anywhere?

Absolutely not. Every failure is a full turn of the wheel, and at the end of each failure we are in new country. We are further along the trail. Failure is not a wheel stuck in the mud, nor is it a spinning wheel getting no traction. After failure, we know new things we could not have learned without the turn of that goal loop. We see new things from a new vantage point with every loop that we close, whether it was a failure or not.

Think about the popular quote attributed to Thomas Edison, "I have not failed. I've just found 10,000 ways that won't work." If we mapped out his ten thousand goal loops, we wouldn't just draw a single wheel mark on the map and note that it spun there ten thousand times. Failure isn't useless spinning in place. It's progress. We would measure out ten thousand revolutions of the wheel and draw the span of all those revolutions. If we used the scale of a pioneer wheel, the journey of those ten thousand wheel revolutions would cover over twenty-seven miles.

Like Edison, in order to move the wheel forward, we need to close the loop. We need to declare each experiment a failure or a success so we can learn from it and move on. To close the loop, we simply ask the evaluation questions. What went well and why? What didn't go well? What did you learn? Then we try a new approach to the goal based on our previous experiences. Instead of stubbornly attacking the stuck goal in the same way over and over, we see our failed efforts as progress and turns of the goal loop. Once we've failed a dozen times, it dawns on us more easily that we need a new approach, not just more time or willpower.

Not closing the loop leaves us with a wheel stuck in the mud, waiting for the next turn to start. The sooner we end the loop and claim failure, the sooner we can get the wheel rolling again. We need to teach our kids that failing is no big deal. In fact, we should welcome it.

Welcoming failure is against our Western culture. We have been taught since kindergarten to avoid it. But when we procrastinate claiming failure, when we keep asking for more time to finish our goal, when we distract ourselves so we don't feel the pain of not accomplishing our goal, we do ourselves a disservice. Sometimes we avoid facing our incomplete goals because we've realized we really don't want that goal anymore, but we haven't yet learned to face the fail, own what we really want now, and gracefully let the goal go.

The idea that no failure is ever final doesn't mean failure is rare; it means it is common. We fail often; we just don't call it that. Remember thirteen-year-old Jaden, who kept trying to read his scriptures every day but never had a flawless week? He kept trying again and again. He never altered his goal; he just pushed through. He racked up ten successful days through his month of effort but still felt like a failure. What if his efforts had been broken down into ten different goal loops of three days each? What if he learned ten different ways scripture study does and doesn't work for him because he evaluated his efforts and completed each goal loop? Even if he claimed ten failures in a row, we can see how different that experience is than never claiming failure at all and just trying, trying, and trying again. With ten goal loops, he surely would have found new experiments to try, new ways to adjust his goal, and new awareness of what was and wasn't working well.

Sometimes it feels like we are afraid of the word "failure" because, deep down, we believe that if we were doing it right then we wouldn't need to fail. We know with our heads that's not true, but somehow we still believe it. We see failure as negative, and nothing negative feels like it should be a part of improvement or progress, so failure must be for those other folks, not for us.

And if failure is negative, then it's something to be avoided or hidden. We don't get training in what to do when we mess up. We are taught in schools and homes how to succeed, but we're not taught how to fail. The essence of failure is curiosity—it's seeing one experiment that didn't work, and then being curious about it and unpacking it to see what happened. We need to let experience teach us something.

When we fail, we have new data. We know ourselves and the world around us better. There are lots of reasons we fail in a goal loop, and every one of them is an opportunity to learn and adjust. It could be that our expectation was too high. Maybe we didn't put in the work or persist all the way to the end. Maybe we misunderstood what was expected, our goal was vague, or we didn't know which action steps to take. Maybe we didn't get the resources or ask for help. Maybe we couldn't stand the boring parts and quit. Maybe we didn't believe someone our age could do that. Maybe our kids didn't care, so they just pretended to set the goal with us because we're their parents. Maybe the expectation was okay and we tried, but we just need more practice. Maybe the goal will take longer than we planned. Maybe that's not the way college applications work and we didn't realize it. Maybe that wasn't an efficient way to study and now we know. Knowing there's a host of reasons that we fail allows us to be open to failure and curious about which reason caused it. When we know where it came from, we know how to adjust the goal or adjust our efforts to turn it around. Owning failure in a goal loop is like taking a bite of a rotten apple and spitting it out. You made a mistake, but you don't have to chew on it a while. Call it a fail, learn from it, and move on.

We can see that for most of these reasons, the quicker we call it a fail, the quicker we can get on with the next attempt. We can adjust our strategy because we've faced the fact that the last one didn't work. Rather than just trying harder, we try differently.

Why We Avoid Failure

Elder Uchtdorf said, "No one likes to fail. And we particularly don't like it when others—especially those we love—see us fail. We all want to be respected and esteemed. We want to be champions. But we mortals do not become champions without effort and discipline or without making mistakes."[58]

If we want to succeed, we have to be willing to fail. That doesn't mean we're going to like it. Failing feels bad for a few reasons.

First, when we set a goal, we create a gap, an intention or expectation. The gap creates the risk of failure and tension. Then when an expectation is not met because something we planned for didn't happen, it naturally feels disappointing.

It's interesting to note that feeling bad about something is related to our expectations of what we thought would happen. We make our own meaning with failure because expectations differ for everyone. Getting a C grade on an English paper can be a success or a failure depending on what you were expecting or hoping for. It can be a relief or a disappointment depending on how much effort you put into the goal this time.

---

58 "You Can Do It Now!" *Ensign* or *Liahona*, Nov. 2013.

Failure also feels bad because, as Elder Uchtdorf said, we don't want others to see us fail. We are social creatures, and it's perfectly normal to care what other people think. Carrying it to either extreme—not caring at all or caring too much—can be debilitating, but in general, mildly caring what people think is a normal part of living. Elder Uchtdorf normalizes this desire to look good for other people: "It is part of human nature to want to look our best. It is why many of us work so hard on the exterior of our homes and why our young Aaronic Priesthood brethren make sure every hair is in place, just in case they run into that special someone. There is nothing wrong with shining our shoes, smelling our best, or even hiding the dirty dishes before the home teachers arrive. However, when taken to extremes, this desire to impress can shift from useful to deceitful."[59]

Because failing feels bad, we often try to avoid it. We overprepare to the point of perfectionism to get good results or to look good. We choose easy goals we know we can accomplish. We get discouraged and skip doing the goal at all. We hide our mistakes or fix them, spit shining failure before anyone notices. We might go so far as to take shortcuts or cheat in order to meet the goal and avoid the uncomfortable feelings that come with failure. Another extreme result when we avoid failure is experiential avoidance, where we avoid so many experiences that it affects our ability to lead normal lives.

Brené Brown describes a particularly subtle form of failure avoidance:

> Oddly, growth and goal-setting can feel like more work than dreaming of perfection. When we try to be perfect, we fail so often that we almost get used to it. After a while, we trick ourselves into believing that forecasting perfection is nobler than working toward goals. It is much easier to say, "I'll be thin by December," rather than "I'll start eating healthy and exercising today." Or "Things will be great when we get out of debt," rather than "I won't buy anything on the credit card this week."[60]

When we set improvement goals, we can learn and grow from both missed and met objectives. If our goal is perfection, we will inevitably fail, and that failure offers us nothing in terms of learning and change; it only makes us vulnerable to shame.

When we understand the terrain of goals, failure, and improvement, we can take the temporary discomfort of failing in stride and focus on the good feelings

---

59 "On Being Genuine," *Ensign* or *Liahona*, May 2015.
60 *I Thought It Was Just Me (But It Isn't): Making the Journey from "What Will People Think?" to "I Am Enough"* (New York: Avery, 2008), 198.

that also accompany failure. We are grateful for the realistic feedback because we understand more about how the world works or why our efforts didn't work. We are excited to implement another loop when we see what went wrong and have new ideas to reach a goal we still want to move toward. It also feels good to be in the company of someone like Edison who has the perspective to realize that failure is a stepping stone, not a stumbling block. We register the feelings of stretching not as stress but as growth.

Permission to Fail

After ten years of piano lessons and a six-week organ course, Nichole thought being called as the ward organist would be a cinch. Learning the stops that controlled the different sounds and which preset buttons were broken wasn't too difficult. A month into the calling, she accidentally hit one of the preset buttons in the middle of a hymn and turned off almost every stop. No one could hear the organ anymore. She frantically tried to find the volume pedals with her feet while continuing to play, and in the three seconds she had between verses, she manually pulled out whatever stops she could find. She ended up playing the rest of the hymn with really loud trumpets. As soon as the meeting was done, she left church crying because she was so embarrassed.

But she had to get up and play again the next week. When no one commented on it later, she realized that no one cared as much as she did. The congregation had still finished the hymn. No one laughed or pointed fingers. Things had carried on even with her mistake. But facing the organ the following week still seemed insurmountable until she thought it through and wrote herself some permission slips. She told herself that she was going to make at least five mistakes, whether they were wrong stops, wrong pedals, or wrong notes. She gave herself permission to make those mistakes without feeling bad about them. Going into it with that expectation took away the power those small mistakes had held over her. And even the bigger mistakes seemed less important. Her goal was being met as long as people were still singing and she was still trying. That was all she could ask of herself and all that God hoped for her calling. Permission to partially fail is what led her to actually accomplish her goal, even if it wasn't perfect.

When we set out on a goal quest, we get excited about that upward journey of progress. We know it's going to be hard or slow going, but we sometimes don't anticipate or dedicate the resources we need. When we stop to think about what we require to accomplish a goal, it sometimes boils down to giving ourselves permission to do what's necessary to accomplish the goal. And often what's necessary is a series of failures.

We can write ourselves permission slips to do what we need to do: Permission to take the time we need or to do it badly at first. Permission to take a break or have some fun with it. Permission to fail or to not grade ourselves at all. Permission to move resources from one goal to another. What kind of permission do we need before we do our goals? We can ask our kids what kind of permission they need to approach their goals and what permission slip they wish they had from us.

We choose goals because we are not good at them yet, but as we get older, we expect ourselves to be good at things right off the bat. We need to give ourselves and our kids permission to be beginners again.

Better Than a Zero

Pursuing a goal and failing is much better than not pursuing a goal at all. Failure is better than doing nothing.

Say your kid is unprepared for a quiz at school. She doesn't want to go to class because she knows she won't do well. There's no more time to study, and she's scrambling to get ready for the bus. There are times it's a good idea as a parent to just excuse your high schooler and allow her to stay home. But here's another approach to take sometimes: let's say this quiz has no make-up, and other than the quiz, your kid is happy to go to school. If she avoids the quiz by staying home and pretending she is sick, or ditching that class, or whatever, then she will get a zero on the quiz.

But what if she shows up and fails? If she takes the test and only gets half right, she will fail. That's the definition in most schools. Fifty percent is an F. But she will still get fifty points. Failure, fifty points, is better than not trying, zero points. What if you explain that to her ahead of time and help her see that failure is better than zero? Tell her you'll be proud of her for showing up unprepared and giving it a go under these circumstances. It totally changes the nature of facing failure when the alternative is zero. This strategy is particularly helpful for ace students who aren't used to getting poor grades. They'd rather skip the points than fail a quiz. Teaching them to embrace failure in this way makes them more resilient and agile in the future.

Try Again, but Different

Elder Uchtdorf said, "Our destiny is not determined by the number of times we stumble but by the number of times we rise up, dust ourselves off, and move forward."[61] In our rising up, dusting off, and moving forward, we can use the evaluation phase to calmly and curiously ask questions about the experience we

---

61 "You Can Do It Now!" *Ensign* or *Liahona*, Nov. 2013.

just had so we don't just bullheadedly stand up and try again, even though it didn't work last time.

We can know what to do differently by persisting in goal loops, evaluating our efforts often, and adjusting them as we see fit in the moment. Elder Uchtdorf said, "Every person, young and old, has had his own personal experience with falling. Falling is what we mortals do. But as long as we are willing to rise up again and continue on the path toward the spiritual goals God has given us, we can learn something from failure and become better and happier as a result."[62] Rising up again and continuing on the path doesn't necessarily mean repeating the same thing over and over again. It may be time to try something radically different. Goal loops allow you to do that, to experiment and be agile in trying new approaches to our goals.

We can seek the Lord's guidance in directing our goal loops. As Elder Renlund reminded us, we are not alone in our efforts: "Even if we've been a conscious, deliberate sinner or have repeatedly faced failure and disappointment, the moment we decide to try again, the Atonement of Christ can help us."[63]

That's the miracle of the covenant path. Even though we may sin and stray, once we repent and turn to Christ, it's as though the covenant path appears before us right where we are. We don't have to trudge through miles of woods to start finding out how we can improve. As soon as we turn to God and seek His help, He makes the path beneath our feet clear enough to take the next step.

---

62 "You Can Do It Now!"
63 "Latter-day Saints Keep on Trying," *Ensign* or *Liahona*, May 2015.

CHAPTER 11
PRINCIPLE #6 – EMOTIONS
HOW CALMING EMOTIONS AND THOUGHTS KEEPS GOALS AND GOAL CONVERSATIONS ON TRACK

Parenting is hard. It's also joyful, tedious, sweet, intense, and just about every other adjective we can think of. It spans at least eighteen years, so of course we're going to have a wide range of experiences and emotions. The emotions we experience over a lifetime of parenting can also happen with goals.

During the life span of pursuing a single goal, we can experience a roller coaster of emotions. We might feel confused about what we want or afraid to try a new thing. We can be disappointed that our goal didn't work out, frustrated that we forgot again, mad that we broke our streak, or satisfied to see our tallies adding up. We are proud when we accomplish something and confident when we learn a new skill. We feel grateful for our sister's help and stupid for messing up in front of other people. We can be excited to conquer something, clever that we figured out a problem, and curious about how an experiment is going to work out. We feel dread at having to make a phone call, bored with practicing drum music again, lost after a big success, discouraged by our lack of progress, and let down after our first success slows down. We can feel ready to act or burned out. We experience improvement fatigue and decision fatigue. We feel the desire to cheat and interest in what we are learning. We feel worthy, even when we fail, and worthless when our friend mocks our goal. Any goal setter may ride this roller coaster, whether she is a parent or a kid.

Despite this roller coaster, as we set goals with our kids and have goal conversations with them, keeping calm is key. Everyone has emotions bubble up in the normal course of everyday life. You could argue that we are always in one emotional state or another, even if we don't notice it, but letting our emotions spill out onto others isn't always a good idea. Learning to surf those emotions with more skill can help in our relationships with our kids and more specifically in our goal conversations. We usually don't get much training in emotion surfing or regulating our emotions growing up. If we pick up any skills at all, it's usually in a therapist's office, a yoga or meditation studio, or with a parenting or self-help book in our hands.

Keeping calm frees our minds to focus on the tasks at hand. It also allows us to coach our kids in safe goal conversations. How do we keep calm, and how does keeping calm help us carry on? First, we understand emotions and practice simple emotional skills. Second, we understand automatic thoughts and practice simple mental skills.

Emotions and Our Brains

When LeAnn was a young mom, she jotted down an idea for a book she wanted to write. It was called *Mom, Interrupted: Why Being a Mom Is So Hard*. It was going to be about the constant interruptions we experience as moms—interrupted sleep, conversation, thoughts, eating, and even interrupted sex with your husband—and how those interruptions do something to your brain and make your life difficult.

LeAnn's oldest son had a speech issue in kindergarten, and his teacher couldn't understand much of what he said. LeAnn didn't learn this until her first parent-teacher conference nine weeks into school. In their discussions of how he coped and when he could start speech therapy, the teacher said that to get her attention during center time, Richard would stand beside her and gently hold her hand until she noticed it and turned to him. LeAnn wished she had taught her children to interrupt her in that gentle way when they were younger. It's never too late, of course, to teach or learn a new skill, so she taught her teenagers this skill one night as a great way to interrupt her. Even now her adult kids will occasionally come put their hand on her arm if she's deep into a writing session or talking with someone else.

Our emotions interrupt us too, more often than our children ever could.

The anatomy of emotions lies in our bodies. The amygdala, an almond-sized cluster deep inside the brain, can hijack our bodies to prepare to fight, flee, or freeze. The whole reaction happens astonishingly quickly—it takes a quarter of a second to register the trigger, a quarter of a second to produce the electrochemical body signals, and five and a half seconds for the hormones and signals to flow through our bodies. This wave is physical, felt in the body, and can be objectively measured with brain scans, facial microexpressions, and all the signs of adrenaline and other hormonal shifts: heart rate, blood pressure, sweating, muscle tension, etc. We experience all of that as a six-second wave of emotion. The amygdala, however, is more than just a fear alarm that hijacks us. It's really more of a professional interrupter.

At any moment, we are in some sort of emotional state. Even during those moments where we don't notice any emotions, we can call our emotional state relaxed, calm, or tranquil. We can be relaxing, reading a book, or going for a walk, and all the while our amygdala's job is to monitor our sensory input, looking for abnormalities we might want to pay attention to. Then it interrupts us.

The amygdala interrupts us for both positive and negative things, anything that it wants us to pay attention to. The reason this works so well is that the tiny amygdala sits right at the gate between our brain and the rest of our nervous system. It has a front-row seat to what's coming into our brains via our senses, and it can use its interrupt button to send quick messages via a wave of emotion we feel in our bodies. Then, when our brain notices the interruption, it stops relaxing and sits up to see what's going on.

Emotions don't mean anything by themselves. They are simply an interruption, a wave of bodily sensations. An entirely different part of our brain interprets this emotional wave and decides what it means and what to do about it. This means we get to decide what to do with the interruption, and depending on how we react, we can teach our bodies to interrupt us more gently and less frequently.

So how does our brain decide what sort of emotions to produce at these interruptions? It learns from our own experience. A body wave of emotion can mean different things. A flushed face can be embarrassed or excited. As the wave of emotion passes over us physically, our brains try to make sense of what just happened by matching our past experience to what's going on right now around us. Our brain is constantly trying to predict what's going to happen so it can respond appropriately, and the only data it has for prediction is our past experiences, stored as memories and brain pathways.

An infant isn't afraid of a lion. But if Dad comes and sweeps the infant off his feet with a terrified gasp, shouts, and desperately runs away, the infant becomes afraid. The next time he sees a lion, the amygdala alerts him to prepare for another panicked run by flooding him with the appropriate emotion. If, however, the infant was looking at a squirrel when the parent dramatically rescued him, he may develop an unnatural fear of squirrels. It all depends on experience.

In an example from an experimental trial, crawling infants who were placed at the edge of a glass-covered precipice avoided crawling on the glass, and their heart rates went up. Non-crawling infants placed at the same precipice had heart rates that remained steady. The infants who didn't know how to crawl yet weren't afraid of being on the edge of a precipice. A crawling infant has, however, had enough experience with movement to be afraid of falling. Our lives teach us what to fear, what to love, and what to ignore.[64]

---

64 See Eleanor J. Gibson and Richard D. Walk, "The 'Visual Cliff,'" *Scientific American* (Apr. 1960), 202(4).

How does this relate to us in our modern world not infested with lions? The amygdala is always on the lookout for what might be interesting so it can interrupt us. It doesn't have to be a dangerous trigger. Triggers and their responses vary in type and intensity. We can hear a comment that embarrasses us and feel a warm wash of shame. We can sense a pleasant calm when we see a teacher that treats us well or a stab of fear when we see a teacher who yells a lot. We may feel stomach flutters when we sit down to take a test.

It's interesting to note that the physical sensations themselves are neutral. They only take on meaning from each person's experience. One person might interpret the pre-test stomach commotion as dread while another interprets it as gearing up to concentrate on the test. We make our own meaning.

The most important characteristic about the amygdala is that it learns. It only alerts us to what past experience has taught it to alert us to. That means if we respond differently to our emotional moments, the triggering mechanism itself will learn that this is the new normal and will trigger automatic emotions less often and for different circumstances. Stephen R. Covey wrote, "Between stimulus and response, there is a space. In that space lies our freedom and power to choose our response. In our response lies our growth and our freedom."[65]

Psychologist Rollo May said, "Human freedom involves our capacity to pause between stimulus and response and, in that pause, to choose the one response toward which we wish to throw our weight."[66]

That powerful idea, that we can throw the weight of our agency to one side or another in the micromoment between automatic emotion and our choice of response, gives us hope. Each time we act in a new way, it strengthens the new neural pathway and weakens the old one from disuse, making that behavior just that much easier in the future.

Emotional Regulation Strategies

LeAnn was recently walking through the streets of Europe in the rain when a tour guide behind her suddenly shouted and dropped the little pole she was holding to guide her group. She had bumped it up against an awning she didn't see. Her face was terrified, she was hyperventilating, she doubled over a nearby gate, and she was saying, "Oh my, oh my," over and over. The crowd around her looked on, perplexed, as she seemed to be overreacting to dropping her pole. Then she said, "Electrica, electrica," and they all understood that touching her pole to the awning had given her an electric shock that jolted her body and scared her.

---

65 *The 7 Habits of Highly Effective Families* (New York: Golden Books, 1997), 27.
66 Rollo May, *The Courage to Create* (New York: Bantam Books, 1975), 117.

An emotional wave can be like what that tour guide experienced. She was reacting to something significant while everyone around her was confused about her reaction. Her experience was real, even if no one else could see it. For each emotional wave we experience, there's a trigger, a wave of emotion, a moment where our brains make sense of what happened, and a recovery period. There are strategies we can use to increase our emotional intelligence and resiliency throughout this whole process to help us keep calm.

When people are upset, naming the emotion they are experiencing helps them calm that emotion. When kids walk up to their parents while upset, they can't think. The way to help them start thinking again is to name the emotion. It sounds overly simple, but it works: name it to tame it. It's almost like a game to try to figure out what emotion our kids are experiencing when they come to us upset about something. We don't have to guess right the first time. We just keep guessing and hang in the conversation until they calm down, which tells us we guessed the emotion right. It works because it creates meaning for our brains to hold on to.

Matthew Lieberman from UCLA explains what's going on in the brain when naming an emotion quiets it down. It started with an experiment to have people tap a button every time they saw a letter, except for the letter R. The letters showed up every second, and the participants got into a pattern of rhythmically tapping every second. When the letter R showed up and they didn't tap, the self-control region of their brain lit up. Lieberman calls that self-control region "the brain's braking system."

He added an experiment to get participants into a rhythm of identifying emotional faces, tapping the button if the face was male, but not if it was female. As each emotional face was displayed, there was a spike in the brain's emotional amygdala region. Even though participants were focusing on identifying gender, the brain recognized the emotional face and responded to it automatically. What's interesting is that when participants had to use self-control and didn't tap, the amygdala turned off and didn't light up even though there was an emotional face. Somehow the amygdala can't deliver that emotional rush if some sort of self-control is being used.

Here's where it gets really interesting. They asked participants to match the faces with gender-appropriate names. The amygdala still lit up with emotional faces like normal, and the self-control region stayed put. Then they asked them to match emotional faces with the emotion they were seeing. For example, they could choose angry or sad. When they had to identify the emotion, the self-control region lit up and the amygdala shut down. Quite literally, naming the emotion calmed the emotion.[67]

---

67 See Matthew D. Lieberman, "The Brain's Braking System (and how to 'use your words' to tap into it)," *Neuroleadership* (2009), 2; 9–14.

Every time we see an angry face, we automatically react with some emotion of our own. If we label that emotion, giving it a word, our brains' self-control regions light up while our emotion regions calm down. So, when we tell our preschooler to "use their words," that's really good advice. We can use this when we talk to our kids. If we don't know the emotion they are feeling, we just guess. We stay in the conversation until they have words for the emotion they are experiencing. Giving kids an emotion vocabulary will help them gain some self-control over their emotional life.

This means we need a broader vocabulary for emotion words for ourselves and our children. Are we confused, overwhelmed, backed into a corner, tired, bored, unmotivated, or lost? We could feel worried, pressured, ambivalent, excited, energetic, or motivated. There are plenty of emotion-word lists on the internet, including some for specific relationships like marriage, work colleagues, and parenting.

We can use this in our own lives, naming our own emotions, and also in our conversations with our kids.

There are other strategies for keeping our emotions not only identified but also calmer in general. Keeping calm matters because when people are upset, they can't focus on the task at hand. Teach kids the following strategies to help them understand and ride out their emotional moments.

1. Make room for it. An emotion that is allowed to exist is usually less intense and goes away quicker. Be sad for a moment. Make room for the fear instead of fighting it.
2. Breathe. Bring your attention to your breath. No matter what the emotion is, take slow, deep breaths and pay close attention to them to help calm emotions. Breathe in through your nose and out through your mouth like you're blowing through a straw.
3. Make the feeling an object. Ask yourself where you feel it in your body, what size it is, what shape it is, if it's moving, or what color it is. Imagining your emotion as an object helps you separate from it a bit and allows you to tolerate it.
4. Ride the wave. When we experience a wave of emotion, we can imagine surfing and ride the wave of emotion until it passes.
5. Have the attitude that "this too shall pass." It came to pass, not to stay.
6. Take a meta moment. Step back and watch yourself experience the emotion as though you were another person. What do you see and hear?
7. Write. Document what you see and hear. Record what's happening with just the facts, like a reporter.

8. Try a mood-meter chart or app. Throughout the day, record the current emotion you are experiencing. It's fascinating to see the range of our experiences in a single day. Creating more awareness of our moment-to-moment emotions helps us realize they will pass and change.
9. Practice mindfulness. Mindfulness is simply focusing your attention on your breath and body. When your mind wanders, gently bring your attention back to your body. Focus on the feeling of your body against the chair or floor, your breath going in and out. Being mindful calms down the gateway by consciously directing your brain to pay attention to these new sensory inputs. Whatever it was freaked out by before isn't there anymore. We are just sitting here. Perfectly fine.

Have you ever had a friend who is a bucketful of drama? Everything that happens to him seems like an emergency. A good friend with good boundaries will eventually learn to say, "Your emergency is not my emergency." Your amygdala is that bucketful-of-drama friend. When a rush of emotion signals a potential emergency, we can take a moment in the pause to say, "Your emergency may not be my emergency," and act on how we want to show up in this moment, rather than react to an automatic emergency button.

None of these strategies makes it pleasant to experience a negative emotion, but the strategies do make it more manageable when it inevitably happens.

Expectations

In our efforts to stay calm as parents, we need to tune in to our expectations. Most of the time when we get angry, yell, lash out, or are rude and impatient with our kids, it's because of our expectations. Think about the times we usually yell at our kids. It's usually when they don't do what we ask them to do; when they are being annoying or noisy; or when they whine, complain, dawdle, or make a mess. For all those things, we expect something different to be happening right now. If we want to stay calm, we need to get underneath the expectations.

If our kids are not meeting our expectations, there are a few different things that could be going on. Maybe they aren't capable. They might be developmentally unable to do what we imagine they should be able to do. They might just be a typical four-year-old.

They might be missing a skill. It's amazing when we break down behaviors how many little skills there are in each one. In a single grocery shopping trip, there are more than a dozen skills kids need to have to make it through without making a scene. Try imagining the behavior we want and breaking it down into teachable skills.

Sometimes we aren't clear on the behavior we actually want. Or we simply expect people to respond in a certain way, and when they don't, it's frustrating and upsetting. The behavior itself may not be rude, disrespectful, or damaging; it's just not what we expected.

Sometimes we expect more of our kids than we do of adults. If our husband's coworker came by our home and walked in the front door with unnoticed mud on his shoes, how would we respond? How do we respond when our kids do the same thing?

To manage our own emotions, we need to manage our expectations.

Baseline of Happiness

Sometimes we set goals because we want to experience an emotion like happiness. We want to be happy, and we want to believe that removing a problem in our lives or reaching a new goal is just the thing to get us there. But there is a difference between happiness and well-being. Happiness is an emotion, and like all emotions, it comes and goes. Well-being is more general, with a definition that expands beyond emotions, including life satisfaction, engagement, relationships, meaning, and health.

Researchers have found that each of us has a baseline of happiness. Tal Ben-Shahar, a Harvard professor of positive psychology, was a national champion squash player. After winning the championship and celebrating with his team, he went home and found that three hours later, the high-riding feeling was over. Even though his elation lasted only three hours, he still benefited from the goal, of course. He was physically fit and had athletic skill, a sense of purpose, camaraderie with his teammates, and a national championship title for his resume. It was the happiness that didn't last long. Even the emotional high of lottery winners and the emotional low of new paraplegics are generally back to their baseline of happiness after just a few months. We all return to our baseline of happiness.

Can we change our baseline? Yes, gradually. As we increase our general well-being and health, our baseline of happiness can go up as well, but it's a very gradual change and is still a baseline around which our normal ups and downs will never stop revolving.

Elder Uchtdorf warns us about believing we will be happy when that "golden ticket" arrives in our lives: when we get married, or move, or finish school, or finish treatments, or reach whatever nebulous thing it is we are hoping to attain.[68] Even when we arrive, we think we will be happier when we meet this goal, and we think it will last longer—but it never does.

---

68 See "Forget Me Not," *Ensign* or *Liahona*, Nov. 2011.

Understanding our baseline means we don't set goals to make ourselves happy. We set goals to change our circumstances, improve skills, lift where we stand, and create things that didn't exist before. Happiness is often a temporary byproduct. We work on our emotional regulation in the here and now as the emotions come up. When we fail, we take a moment to feel sad or embarrassed. Then we take another look at what we want and choose a new step to move toward it.

Thoughts

Emotional episodes brought on by the amygdala don't have to be big. They can be very small and subtle. When our amygdala taps us on the shoulder to get our attention, our brain tries to make sense of what's happening. It predicts what we will be interested in, and then our brain begins to make guesses about what it means. You know that negative self-chatter we all get sometimes? "You're not good enough." "That was such a stupid thing to say." "Why can't you get your life together?" Often these negative thoughts are in response to a tiny emotional hijack. Besides making us feel bad, negative thoughts can derail us from our goals.

In our efforts to keep calm and carry on, sometimes it's our own thoughts that cause us the most distress. We have thoughts that we aren't even aware of that influence our behavior. Sometimes we notice thoughts first, and other times we notice the emotional wave first. Either way, they are an indication that something noteworthy (at least to your amygdala) has just happened. We've looked at things we can do to ride the emotional wave, but there are also things we can do to manage our thoughts.

Automatic negative thoughts are part of the experience of living and pursuing goals. We don't need to be surprised, swamped, or overwhelmed by them or let them distract us from our goals. Understanding and managing automatic negative thoughts is a powerful tool. Automatic negative thoughts are just like automatic emotions—they don't mean anything by themselves; they're just sentences in your brain. Often, they aren't even true, and just knowing that can help. We have the ability to watch ourselves think. And we can play with the thoughts that cross our minds randomly. The point of the thought experiments below is to separate our true selves from the random thoughts crossing our minds so they have less sway over us.

1. Imagine putting each thought on a train car and watching it go by. Or you could try a passing boat or leaves floating down the stream.
2. Say, "I'm having the thought that . . ." and then say the thought. For example, "I'm having the thought that someone will laugh at me." Saying it out loud and labeling it as a thought dissipates its power over you.

3. Thank your brain for that thought.
4. Remember that thoughts are sentences in our brains.
5. Imagine your favorite cartoon or movie character saying the thought. Say the sentence over and over quickly until the sounds of the words become just sounds and don't mean anything anymore.
6. Finish this sentence: "The story I'm telling myself is . . ." For example, "The story I'm telling myself is that they think my text was weird, and that's why they are not replying."
7. Play with new stories or ways to make sense of what's happening. Make up fantastic stories for fun. Notice which stories make you feel better.
8. If the thought is an image, try expanding it, shrinking it, twisting it, or making it black-and-white. If it's a moving image, try putting it on a TV screen and fast-forwarding it, rewinding it, or changing the color.
9. Challenge your thought. Ask yourself if you can one hundred percent know that thought is true. Can you absolutely know for a fact that someone doesn't like you, or that you will never find a job?
10. Try a think-aloud. Simply saying what you're thinking out loud can quickly make it obvious where your thoughts are getting exaggerated or unhelpful.

There are dozens of other ways to observe our own thoughts. We can do what works for us and create our own strategies. Observing our own thoughts helps us sort them out, use what's useful, and let the others drift by.

This whole process is organic, not a math equation; it's more like the rules of gardening than the rules of physics. Our thoughts and emotions interplay with each other. Automatic negative thoughts can both be the result of an emotional wave and trigger a new wave. The amygdala doesn't just see threats in the outside world; it sees threats in the things we imagine, in our thoughts. We can think ourselves into feeling scared, calm, angry, or sad. When LeAnn was a kid, she used to have races in PE at school. To run faster, she would imagine being chased by a lion or tiger. She would feel her heart pumping, and she believed then and now that it made her run faster. She didn't do it often, because it was scary even though she knew she was just imagining it.

We're not implying that we can control our thoughts. It's not about control. It's about awareness, watching ourselves think and emote, having more skills and tools, and being more agile and flexible in our thinking.

Most therapies contain some sort of emotional regulation training. They propose different ways to ride out emotions and manage our thoughts. Some rely on challenging our thoughts, some on looking for other explanations, some on creating new thoughts to practice, and some on ignoring the thoughts altogether as we walk right by them and act on what we value instead. The most important thing is that we develop the ability to notice our thoughts and not get swept away by them.

When we notice a wave, we can ride it. When we notice a negative thought, we can thank our brain and let it pass. When we notice a pattern, we can practice creating new triggers and associated responses. We can experience unpleasant emotions or thoughts and still go on our way doing what we value, moving toward our goals.

Stress

Automatic emotions and thoughts don't just happen when we see a lion. They happen throughout the day, and are so common that often we don't notice them. We may sense a bit of sadness that's been hanging around and realize it's from something that happened yesterday that we've been brooding about without even being aware of it. Or we may notice a generalized feeling of discomfort and link it back to when we yelled at our daughter this morning on the way out the door to school.

Our amygdalas create automatic emotions, and our brains create automatic thoughts without our consent. They can be powerful or subtle. They can be important or meaningless. We don't have to believe the thoughts or be moved to act by the emotions in order for them to have an effect on us.

In our modern world, people often live with daily stressors, and this low-grade, constant stress takes its toll.

LeAnn's stake president is an eye doctor. In stake conference he said that people would often come to him in his profession and tell him about an eye twitch they have, wondering if something was wrong and what they could do about it. What's wrong was stress. Nothing he could treat. Their bodies were accumulating the result of constant stress, in this case in the form of lactic acid that had no way to release itself and ended up manifesting as an eye twitch. He told them to find ways to decrease the stress in their lives. He also told them to get out there and exercise to process and release all the buildup of chemicals that happens when we experience chronic stress.

For kids in an abusive or stress-filled home, it's even worse. The amygdala just keeps pumping warning signals to alert the brain that something's not right, and the kids stay on high alert. The chemicals in their bodies don't get a chance to recover, and it can cause long-term physical and psychological health problems. If we grew up in a home like that, it's not guaranteed that our mental and physical health would suffer. But it is more likely, so if our homes are like that right now, it's critical to find outside support to make the changes we need. If we are overwhelmed with significant issues, we shouldn't hesitate to work with counselors, therapists, or other helping professionals.

The most important takeaway is that none of this is set in stone. We are both influenced by our past and we create it. We use our minds to think on purpose. We study, learn, and solve problems all the time. As we step back from our emotionally reactive habits and realize we have some agency in that moment between stimulus and response, we can begin to create new patterns of behavior that will become automatic over time.

Gap

Every time we set a goal it creates a gap between where we are now and where we want to be. That gap triggers both positive and negative emotions. There can be excitement to rise to the challenge, determination to see it through, and anticipation of accomplishing the goal. There can also be fear of the unknown, worry about not being up to the task, and uncertainty about how to start. We like to imagine goal setting as a positive, peaceful moment with our children. But the moment we set a goal, we create tension. That tension is evidence of our desire to become a better person in some way.

Now that we're familiar with emotions and how they work, it will be no surprise when emotions bubble up for our kids and for us in goal conversations and we'll be better equipped to regulate them.

CHAPTER 12
PRINCIPLE #7—BECOMING
HOW ENGAGING IN GOALS HELPS US BECOME WHAT WE ARE STRIVING FOR

As our kids are figuring out what kind of people they want to become, there will be a lot of ways to describe their options. LeAnn once had a family home evening discussion about healthy foods. Together they made a list of all the different ways they could measure or label foods as healthy or unhealthy. Calories, complex or simple carbs, protein, sugar, low-fat, trans-fats, sodium, heart-healthy, anti-inflammatory, vegetarian, vegan, organic, weight-loss, allergies, soy-based, GMO, free-range, whole-grain, zero-calorie, caffeine, preservatives, good for the skin/heart/eyes/joints, artificial sweeteners, diabetes, insulin, Glycemic Index, fiber, fresh, whole, and the list goes on. A food that's tagged "healthy" could really mean anything on that overwhelming list.

There are also innumerable ways to describe a person. We are infinitely complex and diverse. Just one way to describe someone can never really get at who he or she is as a person. All labels we use for people, even the good ones, can be detrimental because they don't honor the complexity of one individual and our ability to change over time.

Some of the things that define us might be our physical features, likes and dislikes, our emotional reactions to things, our personality flavor, the way we carry ourselves, our habits, our strengths and weaknesses, the things we value, the things that make us angry, or the people we love. Even personality tests or math tests are just a snapshot of one part of who we are on that given day. Like a snapshot on a bad hair day or when we are particularly photogenic, every label captures just a piece of who we are in one moment. We can teach our kids that no one way of describing them will describe them perfectly. We are too complex for simple description. We are a mixture of a lot of different identities all at once.

Many of these identities are naturally created in families from a very young age. Family cultures can cover anything from how we spend money and what physical activities we love to how we deal with confrontation and how we cook a hamburger. These identities that we share with those close to us offer us a sense of belonging, of being similar to those that we love. We create these identities and find places we belong in our families, communities, schools, and churches. To the degree that we can be ourselves and contribute in those communities, we will become participating members. When we have no way to be successful in a community, it's natural to want to rebel or leave. It's also natural to seek out new identities as we see fit.

Speaking of this sense of belonging, Elder Gerrit W. Gong said, "Covenant belonging gives us place, narrative, capacity to become."[69] In our efforts to stay on the covenant path and become, what might it mean to embrace our covenant identity?

It doesn't look like seventeen million Church members who are all carbon copies of each other. There are millions of ways to be righteous. Elder Uchtdorf reminds us, "We are diverse in our cultural, social, and political preferences. The Church thrives when we take advantage of this diversity."[70] This diversity comes as a result of our births and of our choices.

God needs a variety of people to further His work. He doesn't always need the bravest person, the most spiritual person, or the best speaker. The Lord used both Moses and Aaron to further His work even though only Aaron was a good public speaker. If everyone on earth was very diligent in his or her work but nobody was very patient, things would be out of balance. To do the most good in the world, God needs people with a sense of humor and people without, people with intensity and people more relaxed. Not only does He need people with different personal traits, but He also needs each of us to develop a wider spectrum of personal traits and skills to have available to use when we need to.

Our covenant identity will be an important part of our lives—one we will share in common with millions of people around the world—but it's only a part of the group of identities that make up our lives. We get to use our agency to decide how to develop both our covenant identity and our other identities. Agency isn't just the ability to choose between right and wrong; it's the ability to choose who we will become. Elder David A. Bednar said,

> We should not expect the Church as an organization to teach or tell us all of the things we need to know and do to become devoted disciples and endure valiantly to the end (see Doctrine and Covenants 121:29). The moral agency afforded to all of Father's children through the plan of salvation and the

---

69 "Covenant Belonging," *Ensign* or *Liahona*, Nov. 2019.
70 "Four Titles," *Ensign* or *Liahona*, May 2013.

Atonement of Jesus Christ is divinely designed to facilitate our individual and independent learning, acting, and, ultimately, becoming.[71]

Choose Your Own Adventure

God will offer us promptings that point us toward specific tasks or goals he wants us to do, but many things he leaves up to us. Just like there is no one "right" mold for a follower of the covenant path, there is no one "right" path that your specific life is supposed to follow. There is no one right way that God expects us to turn out. Our agency gets a say.

One example of this is the prophetic teachings on the concept of soul mates. Elder Dieter F. Uchtdorf said, "I don't believe there is only one right person for you. I think I fell in love with my wife, Harriet, from the first moment I saw her. Nevertheless . . . I don't believe she was my one chance at happiness in this life, nor was I hers."[72] President Boyd K. Packer put the same idea this way: "*You must do the choosing*, rather than to seek for some one-and-only so-called soul mate, chosen for you by someone else and waiting for you. You are to do the choosing."[73]

If something as important as our eternal companion is left up to our agency, is it so hard to believe that many smaller choices might be too? We get to choose our jobs, our spouses, where we live and go to school, what goals we want to set, how we serve, what hobbies we have, and all the other choices that make up our lifestyles and individual discipleship. The things we choose are important merely because we choose them.

Ruth Chang, a researcher who studies hard decisions, came to the conclusion that some decisions are difficult because there is no one right choice. Hard decisions require us to put our agency behind a choice, to throw our weight one direction or the other, and to declare what it is we want in our life and what we will stand for. That's what makes hard choices so wonderful. It is in the space of hard decisions that we get to use our choosing power to create reasons for ourselves and to create our own lives. Do we want to be a sandal-wearing, Brussel-sprout-eating aerospace engineer in Florida, or a tie-wearing, pizza-eating bank manager in North Dakota? We get to choose.

---

71 *Increase in Learning: Spiritual Patterns for Obtaining Your Own Answers* (Salt Lake City: Deseret Book, 2011), 1.
72 "The Reflection in the Water," (Brigham Young University, CES Fireside, Nov. 1, 2009).
73 "Eternal Love" (Brigham Young University devotional, Nov. 3, 1963), speeches.byu.edu; emphasis added.

Our kids will inevitably have a hard time making choices like these and deciding the future they want. One of the magical things about kids is their potential. They could be anything! But as we grow, we necessarily narrow our lives and our focuses. We sacrifice the endless potential of childhood to pursue the things we really want. What adults lack in options, they make up for in the depth of the options they have already chosen.

Our lives are like one of those choose-your-own-adventure books, where each choice takes us to a different page in the story, and each series of choices takes us to a different end. Part of our narrative will be influenced by the shared covenant belonging Elder Gong mentioned, but much of it will be of our own making. No two stories are the same. We won't write the same story as anyone else did, because life is not a math problem with a correct and incorrect answer. We get to choose who we will become.

How Do We Choose?

With all of these millions of choices before us, we would think we need to know a lot about ourselves to make an effective choice. We don't. People often don't really know what they want. They're busy living their lives. Goals with Kids is like a laboratory that lets us explore what we want in the future and then ask questions to evaluate how it went for us. It's not until we start taking action toward our goals and evaluate that action in a goal loop that we can really decide if we like something or not.

As we put our agency behind our choices, we learn more about ourselves. Elder Ballard said, "All of us must come to an honest, open self-examination, an awareness within as to who and what we want to be."[74] Brainstorming goals helps us understand more of who we are and who we want to be. Kids may not have much self-awareness at first or know right away who they want to be. That's okay. This process of goal loops will help them figure it out by giving them a safe place to experiment.

In all this choosing, remember that we will learn more about a new thing by trying it for one day than by thinking and reading about it for weeks. We try choices on for size by making experimental goals and then evaluating how they went. When we discover what it is we really want, we then adjust our goals to meet what it is. Rather than letting life happen to us like we're objects, we act upon our world and circumstances.

When we brainstorm goals with our kids, the intention is to produce a list of things our kids actually want to do. Sometimes kids don't know what they want to do. That's okay. They can try out things that interest them or explore opportunities around them. Becoming isn't focusing on a single distant end

---

74 "Keeping Life's Demands in Balance," *Ensign* or *Liahona*, May 1987.

that we need to have sight of from the beginning. Becoming involves some exploring.

Sometimes kids don't have a realistic picture of what that goal looks like in real life. We all develop a picture in our heads of what our hypothetical life will be like. Goals can help us test out the reality of our picture and figure out what it feels like to do a certain job. For example, a teenager interested in being a crime detective could schedule a tour of a crime lab to get a feel for what they really do all day. Goals that move us in the direction of what we want can help us decide if that *is* what we really want, if it fits us, and if it plays to our strengths. Acting on a goal tells us if we are capable of it and shows us what the gap is. It helps us learn if we enjoy it or not.

When LeAnn's kids were between seven and sixteen years old, their family applied to be cast members in the Hill Cumorah Pageant for three weeks. After being cast in their roles, each family member followed a complex schedule of rehearsals. When they weren't in rehearsals, they were in different cast teams made up of age-group peers and two adult couples who supervised each age group. The kids spent all day rehearsing and doing activities with their new friends and then all evening with the family. It became a perfect time for the kids to try out new identities.

For example, ten-year-old Jackson told everyone in his group that his name was Andrew. It wasn't until two weeks later that they discovered it, when his cast team leaders were telling his parents how much they enjoyed having Andrew on their team. "Um—we don't have an Andrew," they said.

Fourteen-year-old Jeremy decided he wanted to be cool. He bought new sunglasses and dressed cool and acted cool. He was completely cool. He came to the family dinner after the second day with his cast team exultant. He had done it! Everyone on the cast team thought he was cool! The next day he came back frustrated and discouraged. He realized that everyone thought he was so cool they were afraid to talk to him because they might not fit in or measure up. The next day he reverted to his normal, outgoing, funny self and had a great time making friends.

Each new identity we try on teaches us something. We gain experience. And when we're given the space to try these new things out and see what fits, some of them end up being a major part of who we are. Trying new things helps us become.

Becoming Requires Change

Becoming is hard. It requires us to change intentionally, which takes effort and can be uncomfortable. It can be hard to change our beliefs about ourselves.

Trying to change an identity may make us feel like a fraud. We may worry people will find out we're faking it, something commonly called imposter syndrome. We may worry that our new identity is a passing fad that won't stick. We may try on an identity that we end up not liking and feel stupid for trying it. We may worry that we've changed too much to fit into our lives and relationships the same way we did before. This discomfort is a necessary part of change and becoming.

Not only is change uncomfortable, but positive change is also hard to recognize, both in ourselves and in others. Noticing the change we make in our own lives can be difficult because some of us naturally explain it away. Different people have different explanatory styles. An optimistic explanatory style might look at a failed test as a one-time fluke, not a predictor of their future. They might also look at an A grade as evidence of their hard work, something that will likely repeat itself, and an indication of their overall competence. Pessimistic explanatory styles do just the opposite. They see negative events as evidence of their own lack, generalized to their whole lives, and likely to repeat themselves. They may explain positive events as a one-time fluke, not a predictor of their future. The way we explain our performance has nothing to do with our actual performance, and our explanatory styles can be changed with some practice.

Noticing change can be difficult because it happens in small increments and fluctuates a lot. It's hard to know what is a meaningful setback and what is a normal part of learning and growing. Studies show that most people tend to have a negative bias in how they notice change. We are more likely to judge a positive event as a fluke and judge a negative event of the same size as evidence of real change. It's hard to tell the difference because our progress naturally fluctuates. Research shows, "for example, a handful of poor grades, bad games, and gained pounds led participants to diagnose intellect, athleticism, and health as 'officially' changed; yet corresponding positive signs were dismissed as fickle flukes."[75] Smaller fluctuations in our everyday experience create ambiguity about when there is substantive change and when there is simply a passing trend, especially when some goals are long-lasting and permanent change never seems to arrive.

We can become more optimistic by noticing and savoring any positive movement toward our goals. If we're more likely to assume a single day making it to the gym is a fluke while a single day of missing the gym is showing our true colors, then sticking our disposable gym wristbands to the back of our kitchen cabinet can tip the scales of our opinion of commitment and change. That's why

---

75 Ed O'Brien and Nadav Klein, "The Tipping Point of Perceived Change: Asymmetric Thresholds in Diagnosing Improvement Versus Decline," *Journal of Personality and Social Psychology* (Feb. 2017), 112(2), 161.

banking progress is so important. Any forward progress we make, however tiny or seemingly unimportant, is a drop in our lamps. We bank it to honor it. We don't chalk it up to a temporary fluke. We honor ourselves and our kids by giving the benefit of the doubt, calling a win a win however small it is, and moving forward to the next goal loop to discover what's new about the goal we are currently working on. We can tip the scale toward noticing positive change as real and significant through supporting those changes in others as soon as they become apparent.

How We Get in the Way of Change

Elder Holland gave a talk at BYU while Nichole was a student there. His talk, "Remember Lot's Wife," was the most powerful talk she remembers from her time there; you could hear a pin drop as he chastised those who refused to see the best in people and accept their change and repentance. He told a story about a troubled youth from a small town who was "more or less the brunt of every joke in his school." He eventually found success in the army, where he gained an education, became active in the Church, and distanced himself from his past. When he returned to the small town he grew up in, people only thought of his past self and wouldn't let him forget it. In that town, he came full circle and ended up where he began: "inactive and unhappy and the brunt of a new generation of jokes."[76] It brought home to Nichole the importance of letting other people rewrite their story and us accepting the new version instead of clinging to the old one.

There are many reasons we might be uncomfortable when the people around us change. Perhaps the townsfolk in Elder Holland's story were motivated by some of these reasons, whether consciously or subconsciously. We may see people change and feel left behind or jealous that they seem to have things figured out. We may be suspicious of their motivations, wondering if they're only changing to manipulate us. We may decide that their change is just a passing whim that will fade with time. We may feel threatened or judged by other people improving or changing without us by assuming that they wish we'd change in the same way, even if they've said no such thing. We may think they are getting "too big for their britches," a who-do-you-think-you-are attitude that often comes up when someone is tackling a particularly meaningful or impressive goal. We may have laughed at the new identity they've taken on before—maybe even with them— and aren't sure how to approach them now. We may feel unsure of how to interact with new identities or relationships that we were comfortable in before. Often a person's identity influences—subtly or not so subtly—the people close to them. We may start to resent this influence that we didn't choose.

---

76 "'Remember Lot's Wife': Faith Is for the Future" (Brigham Young University devotional, Jan. 13, 2009), speeches.byu.edu.

These thoughts and emotions are natural, but if we let them run wild and dictate our actions, they can negatively influence the people around us who are trying to change, most notably our kids.

We are going to have a lot of goal conversations with our kids as they develop. Having a curious, open attitude allows them to change and try new things on for size as they develop their identities. We need to let people change. LeAnn heard a story in a parenting class about an eleven-year-old boy who rarely helped his two younger sisters with housework. They nagged him about not cleaning dishes and would make statements such as, "Him? Do the dishes? He wouldn't be caught dead doing the dishes!" One day, the urgency for doing dishes became so great that he helped his younger sister wash them without being asked. When the family noticed, they made comments like, "What got into him? I could never imagine him doing the dishes." The boy's feelings were so hurt by their comments that he stopped helping and vowed to himself he would never help again.

In this story, the boy's family didn't allow him to change. He felt trapped in a lose-lose situation. If he didn't help, he was the boy who didn't like doing the dishes; if he did help, he was teased for actually doing them. His family refused to let him escape from a role that they criticized him in. Had they given credit where credit was due and thanked the boy for stepping in, they might have better supported him in his change.

We can support change by recognizing we are a voice of authority for our kids, and what we say is important to them. The way we respond to them may be the difference between supporting them in their progress and getting in the way of their ability to change. We want our kids to grow and develop in healthy ways, but as parents we must remember the role of agency. Kids get to choose a lot of their identities, and the identities are important because they are *theirs*.

How We Support Change

There are many other ways we can support our kids in their journey to become as they change and try on new identities for size.

We can support change by assuming our kids have good intentions. They aren't judging us, manipulating us, trying to make us change, or trying to make us mad. They are honestly trying to figure out what to do with their life, which is a hard and confusing thing!

We can support change by choosing not to remind our kids of past mistakes they are trying to leave behind them. Elder Holland reminds us that

> when something is over and done with, when it has been repented of as fully as it can be repented of, when life has

moved on as it should and a lot of other wonderfully good things have happened since then, it is *not* right to go back and open up some ancient wound that the Son of God Himself died trying to heal.

Let people repent. Let people grow. Believe that people can change and improve. Is that faith? Yes! Is that hope? Yes! Is it charity? Yes! Above all, it is charity, the pure love of Christ. If something is buried in the past, leave it buried. Don't keep going back with your little sand pail and beach shovel to dig it up, wave it around, and then throw it at someone, saying, "Hey! Do you remember *this*?" Splat!

Well, guess what? That is probably going to result in some ugly morsel being dug up out of *your* landfill with the reply, "Yeah, I remember it. Do you remember *this*?" Splat.

And soon enough everyone comes out of that exchange dirty and muddy and unhappy and hurt, when what God, our Father in Heaven, pleads for is cleanliness and kindness and happiness and healing.

Such dwelling on past lives, including past mistakes, is just not right! It is not the gospel of Jesus Christ. . . . In some ways [it is] worse than Lot's wife, because at least there he and she were only destroying themselves. In these cases of marriage and family and wards and apartments and neighborhoods, we can end up destroying so many, many others.[77]

We can support change by being willing to learn more about our kids' new identities and engaging with them even in small ways. We can show an interest in things that interest them, even though we may not pursue that identity for ourselves. Caring about what our kids care about strengthens relationships.

We can support change by joining in it. If our kids' efforts inspire us or their interests intrigue us, we can make similar changes in our own lives and identities.

We can support change by helping our kids see what goes into an identity they want to try on. Elder Rex D. Pinegar told this story about studying role models:

A friend of mine helped his son set goals in this manner. Don asked his son what he wanted to be, whom he would want

---

[77] "Remember Lot's Wife" (Brigham Young University devotional, Jan. 13, 2009), speeches.byu.edu.

to be like. His son named a member of the ward who lived nearby, a man he had admired for some time. Don drove his son to where the man lived.

As they sat in their automobile in front of his home, they observed the man's possessions and his way of life. They also discussed his kindness and generosity, his good name and integrity. They discussed the price their neighbor had paid to become what he was: the years of hard work, the schooling and training required, the sacrifices made, the challenges encountered. The affluence and seeming ease with which he now lived had come about as the result of diligent toil toward his righteous goals and the blessings of the Lord.

The son selected other men whom he deemed models of successful and righteous living and learned from a wise father the stories of their lives. Thereupon at an early age he set his own goal of what he wanted to become. And with his goal before him as a guide by which to make other decisions along the way, he was prepared to stay on his chosen course.[78]

Talking with our kids about their role models can help them brainstorm goals that focus on the skills beneath their role model's success. Ask what it is they like about the person they admire. If they choose someone famous, we can help them understand that fame is outside their control, but the skills the person developed aren't. Reading a biography about the person often takes them off the fame pedestal and returns the focus to the work that got them there. If one of our kids' role models is a famous YouTube violinist, they can try on the identities of being someone who makes videos on YouTube or someone who plays the violin, but they can't try on the identity of being famous.

We can support change by encouraging our kids through goals. We can start by acknowledging even the tiniest of efforts toward positive change in our kids. "Faking it 'til we're making it" is a valid effort toward change. People won't be perfectly consistent when they're learning a new behavior, so don't point out small setbacks or negative fluctuations as meaningful evidence toward failure. Instead, focus on small fluctuations toward positive change, even if it goes against our natural tendencies.

Elder Uchtdorf reminds us,

> We have all seen a toddler learn to walk. He takes a small step and totters. He falls. Do we scold such an attempt? Of course

---

78 "Decide to Decide," *Ensign*, Nov. 1980.

not. What father would punish a toddler for stumbling? We encourage, we applaud, and we praise because with every small step, the child is becoming more like his parents. Now, brethren, compared to the perfection of God, we mortals are scarcely more than awkward, faltering toddlers. But our loving Heavenly Father wants us to become more like Him, and . . . that should be our eternal goal too. God understands that we get there not in an instant but by taking one step at a time.[79]

We can support change by listening to the good we hear about our kids from themselves and other people in their lives. Don't dismiss reports that your kids are progressing. Try listening in a way that helps kids relive and reconstruct the high points of their day. Let them savor successes. Ask them questions to bring them back to the moment, and have them tell you every detail to support the positive moment in their mind and yours.

We can support change by looking for evidence of positive change. Even if it seems like our kids are failing at a specific change they are trying to make, remember that change is complex and they are probably having small wins too. Try making a list of evidences for a specific change they are trying to make. What could convince us that they've really changed? What would convince us that it was just a phase? Compare the lists. Do they seem fair? What would we notice if things were actually changing? Sometimes our expectations are so narrow that we don't recognize actual change because it doesn't look like what we expected.

We can support change by helping our kids see that they are already making progress toward their goals. Elder Quentin L. Cook tells a story about helping his family see their progress toward their goals.

> When our children were small, my wife, Mary, and I decided to follow a tradition which my father taught when I was a child. He would meet with us individually to help us set goals in various aspects of our lives and then teach us how Church, school, and extracurricular activities would help us achieve those goals. He had three rules:
> 1. We needed to have worthwhile goals.
> 2. We could change our goals at any time.
> 3. Whatever goal we chose, we had to diligently work towards it.
>
> Having been the beneficiary of this tradition, I had the desire to engage in this practice with my children. When our

---
79 "Four Titles," *Ensign* or *Liahona*, May 2013.

son, Larry, was five years old, I asked him what he wanted to be when he grew up. He said he wanted to be a doctor like his Uncle Joe. Larry had experienced a serious operation and had acquired great respect for doctors, especially his Uncle Joe. I proceeded to tell Larry how all the worthwhile things he was doing would help prepare him to be a doctor.

Several months later, I asked him again what he would like to be. This time he said he wanted to be an airline pilot. Changing the goal was fine, so I proceeded to explain how his various activities would help him achieve this goal. Almost as an afterthought I said, "Larry, last time we talked you wanted to be a doctor. What has changed your mind?" He answered, "I still like the idea of being a doctor, but I have noticed that Uncle Joe works on Saturday mornings, and I wouldn't want to miss Saturday Morning Cartoons."[80]

He goes on to talk about other things that distract us from goals, like Larry's Saturday Morning Cartoons, but the point here is that he was taught and then taught his son to actively pursue goals and to see how their daily activities were preparing them for their futures.

We can also support change and notice the progress our kids are already making by using a coaching tool called the miracle question. We can ask our kids something like this: "What if a miracle happens in the middle of the night tonight and you arrive at your goal while you are sleeping. When you wake up, you don't know the miracle has happened. What's the first thing you would notice in your day that things are different now? What else would you notice?" For example, if a kid is tired of her messy room and has a goal to get it organized, she might say the first things she would notice is that she doesn't trip on things in the dark, can find her hair stuff, doesn't keep losing her earphones, and would have a clear desk to do her homework. She's just discovered her pain points that she can begin to work on. Keeping her room clean is going to take a good deal of effort and practice, but now she has some clear places to start.

The purpose of this miracle question is to help kids see the details in what they want to be different. It gives them clues on where to start. When they realize they can start taking action now, we can ask, "What has worked for you in similar situations before?" Together we dig for clues that show how they already know how to take action because they've done it before.

We can support change by not hypercorrecting, which is pointing out everything we see that is wrong. Like an overzealous English teacher, we sometimes

---

80 "Rejoice!" *Ensign*, Nov. 1996.

go around editing each mistake we encounter. Think about the common habit of someone correcting their spouse's story at a dinner party. "It was four ducks, not three. We got there at 5:30 a.m., not 6:30. We were driving through Montana, not Wyoming." The corrections don't matter and they ruin the story. We can see our kids' mistakes without saying anything. Our criticism, no matter how constructive, is often not necessary. This practice of selective neglect allows us to observe lots of technically incorrect or even bad behavior without responding to it. Not responding to every mishap shows trust in our kids. They will make mistakes, but we can trust that they are good and that they will figure it out. When we give in to hypercorrecting, it's not only destructive to the relationship, but it also kills motivation. We don't need to go to the other extreme and trust them in a vacuum, just looking on from afar and allowing them to learn everything from the school of hard knocks with zero input. But somewhere in the middle is a place where we watch kids make mistakes without freaking out, while still coaching them along toward their next goal.

Sometimes we think we're doing our kids a favor by pointing out all the little things they need to change. Author Toni Morrison said that when her kids would walk in the room, she would look them over to make sure they were buttoned up or that their hair was combed or their socks pulled up. She was showing her love and care for them, but they only saw a critical face and wondered, "What's wrong now?" Kids get messages about who they are in these little, seemingly meaningless interactions. She asked parents to ponder whether their eyes lit up when their kid walked into the room. That's what kids are looking for. They just want to know we are glad to see them. We can be better at letting our faces speak what's in our hearts.[81]

As we support and coach our kids through their goals, remember that part of the purpose is for them to explore who they want to be. It's less important to have a run of successfully accomplished goals than it is to have a run of conversations that allows them to be who they want to be.

Our kids are going to become people we never expected. Their futures are, to some degree, outside of our control. Their becoming is certainly influenced by our parenting, as well as by their dedication to the covenant path, but their own agency plays the leading role in deciding their identity. As we send our kids off to their first apartments, college dorms, or mission flats, we can await their return to us, excited to meet the adults they are becoming.

---

81 Quoted in Brené Brown, "What Toni Morrison Taught Me About Parenting," *Brené Brown* (blog), Aug. 7, 2019; http://brenebrown.com/blog/2019/08/07/.

CHAPTER 13
TRACTION AND A LIFETIME OF GOALS

Traction

CAROL DWECK PIONEERED RESEARCH ON growth mindset, the idea that our intelligence is not fixed and that our results depend on our efforts. She conducted a famous study of fifth graders who were given a non-verbal IQ test. They were divided into three groups and, regardless of their actual score, they were all told, "Wow, you got eight out of ten. That's a good score." Then one group was told, "You must be smart." The second group was told, "You must have tried hard." And the third group, which acted as the control group, was told nothing besides the original comment. The results were fascinating. That one sentence of feedback put kids in a fixed or growth mindset.

After the comment, kids were asked if they'd rather work on easier problems or more challenging problems where they would make mistakes but learn important things. Kids who were told they were smart chose easier problems to work on. They wanted to look smart. They gave up quicker and blamed themselves when they didn't do well. They enjoyed the process less, were less motivated, and were less likely to take similar problems home to practice. What's really telling is that, when asked to write about the experience anonymously, a good number of the students who had been told they were smart lied about their scores, and their scores on future similar tests actually went down.

Kids who had been told that they must have tried hard tended to choose more challenging problems to work on. They persisted longer, tried more strategies, and said they needed to practice more or try new strategies when they didn't do well. They enjoyed the process more, were more motivated, were excited to take home puzzles to practice when offered, and their test scores generally went up over time.

The children were randomly assigned to the groups, and the only difference between them was one spoken sentence, yet the differences were visible and pronounced. [82]

Dweck had good reason to start this research. As a child, she was in a classroom where seating was ordered by IQ, and she spent most of her school day avoiding risks and trying to look smart. Since then, many experiments have been done around growth mindset, and it's become quite popular. Schools and businesses everywhere have implemented growth mindset training to teach teachers and managers to praise the effort, not the person or the outcome.

This popularity has actually led to its misuse. Dweck and her colleagues noticed that people were praising effort even when repeated effort was getting no traction. The so-called efforts weren't leading to real learning or results.

When we work toward goals with our kids, it's good to have a coaching presence and be calm and nonjudgmental with them. But we can't lose sight of the fact that someday they actually have to learn the skills they're seeking. The mental effort and practice has to produce an outcome. If we ignore outcomes, no real growth and progress occur, and we are stuck with underdeveloped children, youth, and—eventually—adults.

When King Limhi and his people were in bondage to the Lamanites, trying to free themselves, King Limhi told his people, "Notwithstanding our many strugglings, which have been in vain; yet I trust there remaineth an effectual struggle to be made" (Mosiah 7:18). King Limhi and his people had a goal to be free, and their attempts had failed many times. They trusted that with God and Ammon's help, their many attempts to get free would eventually lead to a successful outcome.

How do we make our struggles effectual? How do we make sure our efforts are a wagon wheel moving us along and not a hamster wheel spinning in place? How do we get traction with our goals? Let's look at a few ways to get traction.

Put in More Effort Than We Are Used To

Elder Bednar taught us the importance of having a challenging goal and a burden to get traction. He told a story about a father who went into the forest to get wood but got stuck in the snow. Once he loaded the truck with cut firewood, the truck was able to get unstuck.

> It was the load. It was the load of wood that provided the traction necessary for him to get out of the snow, to get back on

---

[82] See Carol S. Dweck, *Mindset: The New Psychology of Success* (New York: Random House, 2006).

the road, and to move forward. It was the load that enabled him to return to his family and his home.

Each of us also carries a load. Our individual load is comprised of demands and opportunities, obligations and privileges, afflictions and blessings, and options and constraints. Two guiding questions can be helpful as we periodically and prayerfully assess our load: 'Is the load I am carrying producing the spiritual traction that will enable me to press forward with faith in Christ on the strait and narrow path and avoid getting stuck? Is the load I am carrying creating sufficient spiritual traction so I ultimately can return home to Heavenly Father?'

Sometimes we mistakenly may believe that happiness is the absence of a load. But bearing a load is a necessary and essential part of the plan of happiness. Because our individual load needs to generate spiritual traction, we should be careful to not haul around in our lives so many nice but unnecessary things that we are distracted and diverted from the things that truly matter most.[83]

It's not pleasant having a load. It's a lot of work. But that work, which is more effort than we are used to, may be just the thing to get us the traction we need toward our goal. Like all goal loops, we don't need to commit to an insane amount of effort for the rest of our lives. We can, however, test out putting forth an insane amount of effort for an hour, day, or week, and then evaluate what went well with the extra effort, what didn't go well, and what we learned.

Take Risks and Fail More Often

It feels good to succeed, and that sometimes leads us to choose goals we know we'll be successful at. It's clear that goals have a desired outcome, but it's also clear that the microgoal loops we use to move toward the outcome build character, capacity, skills, and learning. Growth still happens when we fail. We can learn a lot when we fail. It's okay to fail. It's actually more than that—it's necessary to fail. If we're not failing often, we are managing our outcomes too much, avoiding risk, and trying to look smart or busy or righteous rather than actually learning, being productive, and turning outward to lift others.

If outcomes were the only important things about goals, then to fail would be tragic. But failure is not tragic; it is simply a learning experience. Remember that every failure is a real turn of the wheel of progress because it gets you to new

---

83 "Bear Up Their Burdens with Ease," *Ensign* or *Liahona*, May 2014.

territory. If you really want traction on a goal, jump in, act, take bigger risks than you're taking right now, and fail frequently.

Persisting to Gain Traction

Persisting means continuing even when you don't feel like it, even when something or someone else is getting in the way, even when it's boring or hot outside or you're tired, and even when you fail.

There are a lot of ways to persist besides just muscling on, toughing it out, manning up, or pushing through. We persist better when we remember why we set the goal in the first place. It reenergizes us and supports motivation. We can also cycle our efforts. Some effective weight-loss plans, for example, cycle different models of eating to provide variety and motivation. In a similar vein, we can change it up when our efforts plateau or get dull. We can take a break. It sounds counterintuitive, but often taking a break gives us needed rest and perspective.

In writing this book, Nichole and LeAnn often took scheduled brain breaks during writing sessions to walk around the block and even took entire days or a week off as needed. Of course, there are times we just need to push through. Some people do twenty-minute sprints or set timers for other blocks of time to persist in difficult things. It can be helpful to establish a mindset before you tackle your goal to better concentrate or persist in the face of negativity.

Another form of persisting is to return to a goal again and again. Many of us have set New Year's resolutions that look similar year after year. While the life span of a single goal may not produce the results you want, persisting in coming back to a core goal or long-term purpose makes a difference.

For example, persisting in choosing goals related to controlling your anger doesn't mean you keep failing over and over; it means you are committed to doing something about your anger in your life and are willing to try any way you can to make it happen.

Combine Process and Outcome Goals

A process goal, like not skipping any track practices, is much different from an outcome goal, like winning a race. Traditional research has always promoted process goals and a focus on what we can control, but recent research suggests that using a combination of process goals and outcome goals gets better results. Keeping our eye on the outcome we desire while working on what we can control within the process increases our commitment and motivation to do the work necessary to prepare. We train harder and attend more practices if we imagine ourselves crossing the finish line first. That's how a combination of outcome and process goals really gets us traction.

Find Your "No Matter What" Reason

When we really want traction on a goal, it helps to find our "no matter what" reason. Finish this sentence: "I'm going to accomplish this goal no matter what because . . ." Why do we want to do this goal? What is making it worth the effort to us? Some people lose weight not because they care about how they look, but because they want to be able to get on the floor and play with their grandkids. Find our own "no matter what" reason and post it where we can see it to remind us why we want traction on this goal.

Listen to the Experts

LeAnn's son Jackson had a friend that wanted to learn to draw as well as him, so the friend asked for some advice. Jackson took one look at a landscape picture with a bridge the friend had drawn and then the conversation went something like this:

> **Jackson**: I didn't know that was a bridge. Instead of drawing from your head, try drawing from a picture of a bridge.
>
> **Friend**: I don't want to draw from pictures. I want to be original.
>
> **Jackson**: If you really want to learn to draw, use a picture, go to a real bridge, or watch a YouTube video and follow their steps and listen to what the guy is saying as he draws.
>
> **Friend**: I don't have the patience for that.
>
> **Jackson**: There are actual skills for drawing. For example, ancient art didn't have good perspective, but Renaissance art does. The students learned perspective from watching the experts.
>
> **Friend**: I just want to draw.
>
> **Jackson**: Okay, then draw.

If we really want to get traction on a goal, we might need to find an expert and listen to her advice. Experts know how to learn a language, play an instrument well, and create an emotional character arc in a novel. Find an expert, then ask for and take her advice.

Helping Our Kids Gain Traction

When our kids want to gain traction toward a goal but are stumped at what keeps getting in the way, we can be a good goals coach and help them work through it.

Find the Skills behind the Skills

There is a science and specific set of skills behind drawing well. If a kid wants to improve her drawing, she'll need to learn some of those skills. LeAnn doesn't draw much, but she's drawn a little from how-to books she got for her kids. One book specifically taught kids how to draw faces. She was surprised to learn that to draw a face, you draw an oval and then put the eyes at the halfway mark between the top and bottom. That didn't seem right. Eyes are at the top of the face. So she started looking at human faces. Sure enough, although eyes are at the top of the face, they are usually right in the middle of the whole head, which includes everything from the chin to the hair. Knowing that one fact has improved her ability to sketch normal-looking faces by quite a bit.

Last Christmas, LeAnn wanted to learn to draw those cool sidewalk-chalk images that look 3D if you stand at a certain place on the sidewalk. She looked up a YouTube tutorial but still couldn't figure it out by herself, so she asked her son to teach her how for Christmas. Together they made a 3D Rubik's Cube drawing on their driveway, and if you took a picture from just the right angle, it looked like you were standing on a real giant cube. Mission accomplished.

When she was teaching institute, LeAnn wanted to be able to draw a walking figure to show that faith is a principle of action. She watched animated walking sequences online and searched for clip art of people walking. She found one she liked and practiced drawing it. If you ever attend a class where she talks about faith, you'll see her draw the most basic stick figure taking a step of faith. But even though it's a stick figure, it's leaning a little forward, the arms are swinging, and it looks like the figure is taking a step—all because she practiced that specific drawing.

The purpose of these three drawing stories is to show that everything can be broken down into small steps. A drawing journey of a thousand steps doesn't need to traverse every step. Out of the thousand things LeAnn could have learned about drawing, she chose three. If that's all she'll ever learn to draw in her life, she's fine with that.

When we're helping our kids with goals that seem straightforward but really have hundreds of skills underneath the goal, help them narrow down what they want to learn next. Do they want the three skills to learn to make their rocket look 3D? Or do they want the five skills that will make their Mario look more like the video game figure? What is their next drawing goal?

Speak Up and Kindly Say What Needs to Be Said

To help our kids gain traction in their goals, we sometimes need to speak up and say the hard truths that need to be said while still wearing the calm and nonjudgmental coaching hat. Maybe we need to point out that only setting video-game goals won't lead to a balanced life. Maybe we need to tell them that their attempts to be funny to get friends are off-putting. Maybe we need to point out that they aren't improving at their recital song because they don't pause to work on trouble spots.

Real feedback is a part of real traction. First, observe behavior. When you notice patterns or behaviors that get in the way of goals, write them down. It's like being a detective or reporter: just write what you see or hear.

In a goal conversation, bring up what you noticed. Describe what you saw without telling what it means. Ask questions. Get curious together about what's blocking the progress and brainstorm together new goal-loop experiments. We can sometimes expect an emotional reaction when we give feedback. If that happens, we just hear it out and name the emotion to calm it before we proceed.

Use Growth Mindset Encouragement

A growth mindset is the idea that we learn by practicing and exercising our brain. Encourage kids to have a growth mindset with phrases like this:
- When you learn something, it grows your brain.
- I can't do this yet, but I can learn.
- That feeling of writing being hard is the feeling of your brain growing.
- What can you try next?

Ask Questions to Focus on What's Effective

A system of goal loops can be a system of figuring out what the effectual struggle is to reach our goal. Part of the struggle is knowing exactly what we are wanting, knowing how to get there, and knowing how to manage ourselves when it's tricky or hard. We can help our kids focus on an effectual struggle with good questions.
- How will you know you have reached your goal?
- What are you clear about and what are you unclear about?
- Is what you are doing actually making progress toward what you want?
- What is the next smallest step to get you closer to where you need to be?
- What needs to be true to get unstuck and make progress today?
- What is the low-hanging fruit or the easiest step to check off?
- Where can you put the smallest amount of effort that will get you the biggest results?
- What has been working so far?
- What are you avoiding?
- How are our goal conversations going? What's working and what's not?

Explore Competing Goals

This is a bit of an advanced skill, but professional coaches often realize that their clients have competing secret goals. To uncover these hidden goals, ask a series of questions.[84] All behavior makes sense, and uncovering these competing goals helps us understand why we sometimes don't get traction on the goals we set.

First, we identify our goal. Then we list the actions we do instead of our goal. For each action we do instead, we ask what our competing goal or commitment is. Behind that goal is an assumption that we identify and question. For example

- What is your goal?
    - Be kinder to my sister.
- What do you do instead?
    - Yell at her to get out of my room when I'm on the phone.
    - Don't let her come shopping along with my friends.
    - Shush her when my friends are over.
- For each thing you do instead, what is your competing goal or commitment?
    - I am committed to not having my friends think I have to take care of my little sister.
    - I am committed to not being embarrassed in front of my friends.
    - I am committed to not being embarrassed if my sister says something that's not cool.
- What's the big assumption underneath all those commitments?
    - If my friends hang out with my family and my sister is just her normal self, they will see some of the goofy family things we do and they will think my whole family, including me, is weird.

The behavior makes so much sense now. The whole process of these conversations takes a good deal of gentle honesty and openness. Once we figure out our assumptions, we don't bulldoze ahead trying to change them. We pay more attention to them and look for evidence that it's not true that our friends would think our normal family things are weird. Maybe we've been to their house and their family members didn't seem embarrassing. The awareness of our competing goals gives us an opportunity to choose new microgoals to test our assumptions and begin to look at the world in a new way.

Goal Maps and Terrains

Let's look at the terrain of a goal for a minute. At its simplest, a goal gets you from point A to point B. Point B is in the future, so we can't guarantee the outcome, but aiming at point B sets our direction. It makes accomplishing point

---

84 See Robert Kegan and Lisa Laskow Lahey, "The Real Reason People Won't Change," in *HBR's 10 Must Reads on Change* (Nov. 2001), 85–92.

B more likely. And whether or not we actually get to point B, engaging in goals builds character, capacity, resilience, and skills.

Even a straightforward, step-by-step goal is laid out on the mortal terrain of our lives. Not only do our lives have twists and turns, lows and highs, roadblocks and setbacks, but so do our goals. Understanding the geography of our lives and of goals lets us navigate them both without getting unduly frustrated and lost.

In college, LeAnn once hitched a ride with a geology field trip driving from Utah to Mexico. She traveled with them as far as Phoenix as they made many stops at interesting geologic formations along the way and talked about how the earth had come to be shaped as it was. The backdrop of pretty red cliffs became a story to her that day. The rocks were created over time with layers of sediment forming different-colored stripes. When the earth would bend and fold, you could see the resulting movement in the stripes. Some stripes gently curved to make a hill, others jutted up at steep angles out of the ground. You could see where pieces of earth buckled and split apart in some ancient earthquake. She learned to read rocks and understand the Utah mountain and cliff terrain on that trip.

We can similarly learn to read and navigate the terrain of our goals.

Elizabeth, an eight-year-old in our Goals with Kids Club, was in her first week of learning the goal loop process when her mom told LeAnn the following story. Elizabeth was negotiating with her older brother for a gum trade. He was trying to convince her that his gum was better than hers and wanted to trade twelve of her pieces for one of his. Frustrated with the unfair trade, she started to get upset and complain. Mom said, "Elizabeth, you just finished a goal loop that didn't go well. Do you want to keep working on this goal?" Elizabeth paused a minute and said yes. She proposed another trade. The brother wouldn't budge on the twelve-piece trade. She paused and decided to try again. After a third goal loop, she decided she didn't want to work on this goal anymore and walked away from the situation calmly. Mom was surprised that the situation ended without an argument. Later in the afternoon, Elizabeth decided she did want to work on the goal some more and happily negotiated a trade with her brother for half a piece of his gum for three pieces of hers. She'd only been working with the process of goal loops for three days, but it was enough for her to start internalizing them and applying them in her life.

In the course of one year, LeAnn created a business called Life Changing Principles LLC, started a master's degree, researched and created the Goals with Kids model, launched a website, created and taught a six-week workshop, and wrote this book. It was a dizzying pace to be sure, like drinking water out of a fire hose. One of the things that kept her moving and not crashing and burning was an immersion in goals, how they really work, and the simple Goals with Kids model.

She asked the three questions dozens of times of herself and everyone she was working with. She made microgoals to write a single paragraph when she didn't feel like writing another word and macrogoals to guide her writing and workshop launches.

The Goals with Kids model is flexible enough for an eight-year-old to apply to three goal loops in three minutes and an entrepreneur to apply to hundreds of goal loops over a year to create an entire business. Holding this simple model in our heads allows us a great deal of agility and flexibility in our thinking. It's a tool we can pull out whether our goal terrain is a short walk around the block or climbing Mount Everest.

Choosing a goal is like making a map of how to get to something we want. No matter which goal terrain we're traversing, the map is going to change in unexpected ways. We may encounter an obstacle we didn't predict, it may take longer than we thought, or the many pathways we choose to get there may wind and double back. That's the nature of goals.

Our lives may also take an unexpected twist with a new calling or a change in health. Even small things like volunteering to be the room mom at school changes the landscape of our lives. Those unexpected changes in our lives will affect the terrain of our goals. That's the nature of life. We are moving toward what we want in the future, and the map is always unfolding to match the reality we encounter.

As parents, our goal loops are not an extra thing to do. They are a way of talking about what's already happening. Kids naturally want things and are going after what they want. These are their goals. Parents naturally want things for themselves and for their kids and are going after what they want. These are the parents' goals. These goals are already happening in our lives every day.

We are always in the middle of goal loops, and Goals with Kids gives us a powerful way to think about them and talk about them. As we navigate the terrain of our lives and our goal loops, we don't always need formal goals. The same pioneer who marked the spoke on the wagon wheel to track their progress penned these lines: "Come, come, ye Saints, no toil nor labor fear; But with joy, wend your way."[85] To wend our way means to go in a specific direction but in a typically slow or indirect route, making our way there. It doesn't matter that the route is slow or indirect; that is the nature of some routes.

Rick Snyder's Hope Theory says that motivation to move forward comes from two things: agency and pathways. Agency is the energy we are willing to put into a goal, and pathways are the different routes we can use to meet a goal. If people are willing to put in the effort and can see more than one way to get there, then they

---

85 "Come, Come, Ye Saints," *Hymns*, no. 30.

have hope. Even if problems come up, the going gets hard, or we get sideswiped, we have hope if we are willing to act and we can still see other pathways.

As we navigate the unfolding map of our goals and our lives, how we handle the difficult or unexpected terrain is more important than reaching the destination. It's like an Olympic diver being judged on what happens between the diving board and the water rather than on the destination at the bottom of the pool after the dive.

When an obstacle arises in a goal, how freaked out should we be? We don't know at first. That's what makes goal setting vulnerable. I failed a test. Does that mean I'm not college material or that I need a new study strategy? We don't know because we're new at this. It's going to take a while to figure out how this works. Scheduling her first live, online Goals with Kids workshop, LeAnn made three mistakes in a row telling people the wrong time for the course. She didn't know how freaked out to be, and she got pretty upset and worried imagining how angry her new students would be at the mix-ups. Once the class started and she got some feedback, she realized she should have been mildly annoyed. The inconvenience didn't affect anyone's ability to take the class, but some greater effort to get the time announced right in the future would be appreciated. Knowing that our maps and the terrain itself will be in flux helps us be calm in the face of surprise.

We change day by day, year by year, whether we mean to or not. Life keeps coming at us, and we do whatever is in front of us that needs to be done. Without goals, our lives happen by chance. We may change in ways we don't like and didn't want. We may look back and wonder why our lives turned out the way they did and what was directing our choices. We may slowly become someone we don't want to be.

We set some goals because we want to be intentional about our lives. Goals help us take control of ourselves and our futures. President Hinckley said, "Limitless is your potential. Magnificent is your future, if you will take control of it. Do not let your lives drift in a fruitless and worthless manner."[86] Elder Uchtdorf said, "God loves you no less when you struggle than when you triumph. Like a loving parent, He merely wants you to keep intentionally trying."[87] Rather than drift or let our circumstances direct our lives, we can be intentional and choose goals to direct our lives where we want them to go.

Goal Notebook

With a lifetime of goals, we're going to have a bunch of sticky notes, tracking sheets, reminders, brainstorm lists, and goals coming through our lives. We

---

86 "How Can I Become the Woman of Whom I Dream?" *Ensign* or *Liahona*, May 2001.
87 "Your Great Adventure," *Ensign* or *Liahona*, Nov. 2019.

may toss them when they're done being useful or keep them corralled in a goal notebook of some sort.

Recording the events of our lives honors what's happened and helps us better remember the positive things that might generally get swept up in daily living and taken for granted.

When LeAnn was a young teenager, she started a series of journals, each with only two or three pages in them. Every time she wanted to start a journal, it felt like she needed a fresh, clean start so she could really write every day this time. Later as a young mom, she took the journals, cut out the first pages, compiled them into one binder, and threw the rest of the blank books away. Seeing all her journal entries in one place helped her appreciate that she didn't need a completely fresh start every time she set a goal to start a journal. She could build on what she already had, even if it was only three journal entries a year.

She was recently looking back on one of her journals that she had committed to use until it was full rather than starting a new one every year. One entry read, "Jan 8, 1997. Start writing in my journal every day." The next entry read, "Jan 8, 1998. Well, I guess that didn't go well." We can laugh, be kind to ourselves, and trust the process. We can gather years of occasional journal entries, stories, goals, and whatever we decide to put in our binders. LeAnn has about twenty filled books now, but almost never does she have even a week of consistent journaling. She just writes when she feels like it.

With a lifetime of goals, it could be fun, interesting, and useful to keep your goal lists in a goal binder. Even if you take a break for several months from goal setting, the binder will still be there waiting for you when you're ready to return to goals. We could record just a list of goals we choose in our goal loops. We could track a really big goal with all the goal experiments we choose to get closer and closer to mastering the goal.

We could keep a list of our answers to the three questions, "What went well and why?" "What didn't go well?" and "What did you learn?" Wouldn't it be fascinating to have a whole list of things that have gone well in your life? Or a separate list of why those things went well? Such a list might contain things like, "Because I prepared, because I was brave and made the call, and because I took a deep breath before I reacted."

We could also keep a list of what we learned from our goals. LeAnn has a list of two hundred life stories and what she learned from them. It includes things like, "Just because you have a college degree doesn't mean you have common sense," "Big life moments are never what you expected," and "The role of the father in protecting his family extends to spiders in this house."

Engage with Goals

Engaging with goals builds character. Character is your distinctive combination of strengths. You use your signature strengths throughout your life to tackle hard problems, make daily decisions, and help other people. Whether or not you finish a particular goal, engaging in goal loops to move toward it and then adjusting your course strengthens you.

Engaging with goals builds capacity, which is the power to do, experience, or understand something. Like physical goals build our physical muscles, other kinds of goals build our spiritual, social, and intellectual muscles and capacities. President Nelson taught us about the different capacities we can develop: "An infant's body is tiny, and its spiritual capacities are undeveloped. While the body may reach the peak of its maturation in a few years, the development of the spirit may never reach the limit of its capacity, because there is no end to progression." He added that "the capacity to understand increases as one learns and then teaches with diligence."[88]

Engaging with goals builds resilience. Everyone has surprises and setbacks throughout life. Resilience is the ability to bounce back from those setbacks. Without resilience we might get stuck, quit, stop trying, feel bad, become fearful of new experiences, and avoid similar experiences in the future. A youth who has practiced hundreds of microgoal loops in going after a variety of goals in her life will have resilience in facing whatever is placed in front of her.

Engaging in goals builds self-reliance. A kid with goals soon figures out that there are things he wants to learn so that he can take care of himself when he grows up. Goals can help us figure out how to earn our own money, cook our own food, resolve arguments with roommates, and wake up on our own and go to church.

Engaging in goals builds skills. LeAnn's three sons' Eagle Scout projects were building a llama shelter; purchasing and spreading gravel at an elementary school; and building permanent, block wall garden boxes with automatic watering systems for the same elementary school. Within two years, the gravel needed to be redone, the garden box got bulldozed for a parking lot, and as far as we know, the llama shelter is still in use.

The real purpose of the Eagle Scout projects was not to accomplish the goal. The purpose was to show leadership, to learn how to make phone calls to adults, to make a detailed plan, to call the cement company when they don't show up and you have twenty people waiting, to learn to calculate how many tons of rock you need to cover an area, to learn to lay block, to learn how to call the school for permission to connect to the water line, to learn how to calculate how much

---

88 "Spiritual Capacity," *Ensign*, Nov. 1997.

wood you need for a wall, to learn how to call all your friends when they don't show up to your project, and to learn how to formulate a coherent question.

Engaging in goals builds integrity. Over many, many microgoal loops we get a feel for what we are willing and able to do in moving toward a goal. We build trust with ourselves that we will do what we set out to do. Joy D. Jones said, "A succession of small, successfully kept promises leads to integrity."[89] A series of goal loops provides those small promises.

Engaging in goals builds awareness. When we engage with goals, we encounter reality and become more aware of how the world really works and what kind of effort we really need to get us to our goals. Elder Ballard suggests that "it is good, on occasion, for everyone to face adversity, especially if it causes introspection that enables us to openly and honestly assess our lives."[90] That kind of open, honest assessment of our actions happens in every goal loop as we evaluate our efforts and decide if we want to work on the goal some more.

A Garden of Goals: A Parable

A lot can happen in the life span of a single goal. Even more can happen in a life full of them. Let's imagine our lives as gardens where we are the gardeners and the plants are the goals. The goals in our gardens can produce many useful and beautiful things if we put in the work. We each get to design our own garden. We get to experiment with new goals we want and try them out. We decide which plants go where, when we plant them, and when we remove them.

The design of our garden will be different from every other garden we might see over the fence. There are a million types of seeds and a million gardeners, so no two gardens will look exactly the same.

We can change our garden whenever we want. We don't have to keep perennials that we planted years ago that keep cropping up. We don't have to keep planting the same old tried-and-true seeds we usually do. We can pull out a dying goal once it stops bringing us joy. We can pull out a living goal if we decide we want to grow something else in that spot or if it's taking up too much time and energy. Any goal we pull out can be composted and eventually used to nurture other goals. At any point, we can change what's growing in our garden just because we want to.

Our ecosystem and gardening style may prefer certain goal types. The environment around us might make growing some goals easier or harder to grow than other goals. It's important to know which ones will be more difficult and require more preparation or work on our part. It won't work to try to copy someone else's garden goal-for-goal because his or her ecosystem and gardening style is different than ours.

---

89 "A Sin-Resistant Generation," *Ensign* or *Liahona*, May 2017.
90 "Keeping Life's Demands in Balance," *Ensign*, May 1987.

Our garden is uniquely ours, but there are some rules that apply to every garden that we need to know. A garden has limited space. Our patch of dirt is only so big. We can't plant every fruit, vegetable, and flower listed in the goal catalog. We don't have room for all of them. We have to choose.

We as gardeners have limited time and energy. We can only do so much work in a day. Every goal we add to our garden takes time and energy to tend. If we add more goals to our garden than we have time and energy to care for, we will feel overworked and our garden will suffer.

A garden needs a variety of healthy goals and a variety of sweet or beautiful goals. Our gardens shouldn't be just carrots or just corn or just roses. Gardens need a variety of goals to provide for a good, balanced life. Healthy goals like vegetables and roots provide nutrition. Sweet or beautiful goals like fruits or flowers keep our spirits up and remind us of the beauty of the world all around us.

A garden takes a lot of work. Gardens require digging and watering and pruning and harvesting and pest-controlling. We can't plant a seed and expect it to grow all by itself. If we aren't helping it in some way most every day, our goal won't reach its full potential. If we decide not to work and plant our garden, we'll end up sitting on a vacant lot.

A lot of work doesn't guarantee a good crop every single time. There are things outside of our control when we garden. Maybe there's an early frost. Maybe a deer leaps the fence and eats our berries. Maybe there's a drought and there's not enough water. Maybe a goal withers and dies even though we tried everything we could think of and we never know what was wrong. Usually hard work in a garden produces a bountiful harvest, but sometimes the circumstances around us thwart our efforts.

Weeds need to be dealt with. Weeds may be goals that are sometimes useful or beautiful, but if they grow where we didn't intend them, they can take away garden space, time, and energy from more intentional goals. We can either pull the weeds out if we don't want them or incorporate them into our current garden design if there's something about them we like.

Other gardeners around us can help us. We can learn from them and see some of the goals in their gardens. We can talk to the other gardeners and get their advice. If we have a catastrophic event that destroys a lot of our garden, they can even give us food to help tide us over until we can plant a new one. But other gardeners can't come into our gardens and plant our goals for us.

A Lifetime of Goals

When we reach a goal, it's great. It really is. It's important to be able to accomplish what we set out to accomplish. We've created something new in the world that didn't exist before or changed something about ourselves or our environments. We've helped someone or improved something. Setting and achieving goals holds purpose and meaning.

When we arrive at a goal, however, we don't arrive to stay. When Nichole was about nine, she finished a level in her piano lessons, so she and her family went to celebrate. They got some ice cream, and she excitedly opened the present waiting for her. It was the next level of piano books, probably the biggest disappointment of her life to that point. Granted there was ice cream and a fun Pocahontas story and music book in there too, but the reality is there will always be another level to master.

What's it all for if we never arrive, always chasing the horizon?

It's for the love of living and learning. It's for enjoying the process. It's for learning the process of goal loops and getting what we want. It's for learning underlying skills, building connections with people, and creating memories and life stories.

We never arrive, but we also never get tired of the journey. Spending a lifetime engaged in goals, which are simply things we want that we are willing to put effort toward, engages us with our families and creates better overall well-being than living a life without pursuing goals.

Jamie, a participant in our Goals with Kids workshops, invited missionaries to her home for dinner and accepted their challenge to find a family to have them teach. The challenge was issued in May, and the deadline was August 31. In reviewing her goal just three days before the deadline, she felt anxious because she had failed and the deadline was approaching. As she learned to evaluate her goal and answered what went well, she described her desire and her efforts: she said she had prayed often, but not every day like she should. She had invited two different friends to two ward activities and they came, but she didn't invite someone to the last Relief Society weeknight activity. She also said she had made a new friend. The class was surprised to hear her describe her wonderful accomplishments of caring, praying, inviting, and making new friends amidst her discouragement of not meeting her goal and feeling like she "should" have done more.

She was so singularly focused on her large, initial goal that she overlooked the many small successes she'd had along the way. Using smaller goal loops allows us to be more aware of and grateful for our real progress, even if we don't finish the goal.

Using smaller goal loops and evaluating our efforts more often grounds us in the terrain of our lives and allows us to be more grateful and aware of our real progress.

GOAL GETTERS

There are some goals in our lives that never change. If we wrote our current New Year's resolutions on a sticky note and put it on our mirror, it might include "read scriptures every day," "be a little kinder to my family," "be more patient," and "walk or exercise three times a week." If that note could stay taped to our mirror for ten years, we would likely have the same goals. We would also, like Jamie, have some experiences that moved us forward in each of those goals, but it is easy to feel like a failure because we will never arrive.

We never arrive at reading our scriptures every day because there is always a new day when we wake up in the morning, and it needs to be done again. We will never arrive at being a little bit kinder to our families because we always have new situations to live through and new opportunities to remember or forget to be kind. We will backslide and have unkind moments and recommit to our goal. We will never arrive at being more patient because once we practice and become more patient, we will see other areas where we can be more patient still. There are always new arenas where we can practice patience. These New Year's resolutions aren't bad because we never keep them. They are good because we are always acknowledging the good things we want for our lives. We always have a goal. And we are always making progress toward that goal with goal loops and experiences.

It doesn't matter that we never arrive. We are alive and engaged. We are growing and learning. We are living and lifting others. And we are enjoying moments we will never forget. Jenkins Lloyd Jones said,

> There seems to be a superstition among many thousands of our young [men and women] who hold hands and smooch in the drive-ins that marriage is a cottage surrounded by perpetual hollyhocks to which a perpetually young and handsome husband comes home to a perpetually young and [beautiful] wife. When the hollyhocks wither and boredom and bills appear the divorce courts are jammed. . . .
>
> Anyone who imagines that bliss [in marriage] is normal is going to waste a lot of time running around shouting that he has been robbed.
>
> [The fact is] most putts don't drop. Most beef is tough. Most children grow up to be just people. Most successful marriages require a high degree of mutual toleration. Most jobs are more often dull than otherwise. . . .
>
> Life is like an old-time rail journey—delays, sidetracks, smoke, dust, cinders and jolts, interspersed only occasionally by beautiful vistas and thrilling bursts of speed.

The trick is to thank the Lord for letting you have the ride.[91]

We can help our kids learn to enjoy their ride along the covenant path. We can sit with our little countries, side-by-side on the couch, and start showing them the details we've been managing that will soon fall to them. The pieces of stewardship and responsibility we've been carrying for them for years. The things they will soon pick up and start carrying into their adult lives.

We can hand responsibilities over one by one, watching our kids learn how to hold them on their own and coaching them through goal loops that will equip them with the character, capacity, skills, and resilience they need to engage with the futures they want.

---

91 Quoted in Gordon B. Hinckley, "A Conversation with Single Adults," *Ensign*, Mar. 1997.

ABOUT THE AUTHORS

LeAnn and Nichole

Goal Getters is LeAnn and Nichole's first co-writing project. Their writing routine includes daily early-morning calls via computer video conferencing with an occasional kid popping up in the background or crawling up on Nichole's lap. They follow the Goals with Kids model when they remember to, having goal conversations to guide their progress. Nichole writes early in the morning on weekdays, on Saturday afternoons while her husband takes the kids, and in snippets in between the demands of three young children, homeschooling, writing group, and the distraction of 137 tabs open on her computer. LeAnn writes and creates curriculum full time and recently squeezed in some writing time on a trip to Europe with her husband, including an afternoon writing at the Louvre.

LeAnn Hunt

LeAnn is an entrepreneur, a family life coach, and mom of seven adult kids. She has a degree in computer science and a master's degree in secondary education. She is pursuing a master's in psychology from Harvard Extension School. She is the creator of Goals with Kids, which is patterned after her favorite teaching stint of twenty-four semesters teaching and discussing Life-Changing Principles with thirty to ninety women each semester.
lifechangingprinciples.com

Nichole Eck

Nichole Eck is an author and editor. After graduating from Brigham Young University in 2012 with degrees in English and linguistics and minors in editing and Russian, she worked for the *New Era* and *Liahona* magazines and helped proofread the 2013 edition of the scriptures. Nichole lives in Spanish Fork, Utah, with her husband and their three girls, writing science fiction and fantasy novels in between homeschooling, playing the piano, and overcoming her irrational fear of butterflies and grasshoppers. The first chapters of three of Nichole's novels have won awards at the Storymakers Writing Conference (where she also taught a class about emotional regulation and Acceptance and Commitment Therapy). When she finishes her first novel, she's excited to jump into the world of fiction publishing.
nicholeeck.com

GOALS WITH KIDS WORKSHOPS

LeAnn teaches the principles found in this book in workshops and online courses. In engaging, down-to-earth classes with worksheets, homework assignments, and lots of practice and discussion, LeAnn teaches parents how to talk to their kids about goals and how goals and progress really work in our lives.

To register for a workshop, go to lifechangingprinciples.com/goalgetters.